AF477674

Democracy
as public deliberation

MANCHESTER
UNIVERSITY PRESS

Democracy as public deliberation
New perspectives

MAURIZIO PASSERIN D'ENTRÈVES editor

MANCHESTER UNIVERSITY PRESS
Manchester and New York

distributed exclusively in the USA by Palgrave

Copyright © Manchester University Press 2002

Published by Manchester University Press
Oxford Road, Manchester M13 9NR, UK
and Room 400, 175 Fifth Avenue, New York, NY 10010, USA
www.manchesteruniversitypress.co.UK

Distributed exclusively in the USA by
Palgrave, 175 Fifth Avenue, New York,
NY 10010, USA

Distributed exclusively in Canada by
UBC Press, University of British Columbia, 2029 West Mall,
Vancouver, BC, Canada V6T 1Z2

British Library Cataloguing-in-Publication Data
A catalogue record for this book is available from the British Library

Library of Congress Cataloging-in-Publication Data applied for

ISBN 0 7190 6101 6 *hardback*

First published 2002

10 09 08 07 06 05 04 03 02   10 9 8 7 6 5 4 3 2 1

Typeset in Trump Medieval
by Servis Filmsetting Ltd, Manchester
Printed in Great Britain
by Bookcraft (Bath) Ltd, Midsomer Norton

Contents

Contributors

Maeve Cooke is Statutory Lecturer in German at University College, Dublin. She has published extensively in the areas of contemporary political and social philosophy and is the author of *Language and Reason: A Study of Habermas's Pragmatics* (1994) and editor and translator of a collection of Habermas's writings on language entitled *On the Pragmatics of Communication* (1998).

Maurizio Passerin d'Entrèves is Professor and Chair of Philosophy at the University of Cape Town. He has published extensively in the fields of contemporary social and political philosophy and is the author of *Modernity, Justice and Community* (1990), *The Political Philosophy of Hannah Arendt* (1994) and is co-editor of *Habermas and the Unfinished Project of Modernity* (1996) and *Public and Private: Legal, Political and Philosophical Perspectives* (2000).

Matthew Festenstein is Lecturer in Politics at the University of Sheffield. He has written several articles on contemporary political theory and is the author of *Pragmatism and Political Theory* (1997) and co-editor of *Richard Rorty* (2001).

David Miller is Official Fellow in Social and Political Theory at Nuffield College, Oxford. He is the author of many books, including, most recently, *On Nationality* (1995), *Principles of Social Justice* (1999) and *Citizenship and National Identity* (2000), and is co-editor of *Pluralism, Justice and Equality* (1995) and *Boundaries and Justice* (2001).

Shane O'Neill is Reader in Politics at the Queen's University of Belfast. He has published a number of articles in the fields of political and social theory and is the author of *Impartiality in Context: Grounding Justice in a Pluralist World* (1997), co-author of *Contemporary Social and Political Theory: An Introduction* (1998) and co-editor of *Reconstituting Social Criticism* (1999).

Michael Saward is Professor of Politics at the Open University. He has published many articles in the field of democratic theory and is the author of *The Terms of Democracy* (1998) and editor of *Democratic Innovation* (2000).

Graham Smith is Lecturer in Politics at the University of Southampton. He has written a number of essays on contemporary democratic theory and is co-author of *Politics and the Environment: From Theory to Practice* (1999).

Judith Squires is Senior Lecturer in Politics at the University of Bristol. She has published a number of articles in the fields of political and feminist theory and is the author of *Gender in Political Theory* (1999), editor of *Principled Positions* (1993) and co-editor of *Feminisms* (1997).

Corinne Wales is Research Fellow at the University of Leeds. She is involved in a project funded by the Food Standards Agency which aims to increase understanding of effective communication strategies about risk. Her main research interests are the theory and practice of deliberative democracy and the development of participatory models to facilitate democratic dialogue between different stakeholders and publics.

1

Introduction: democracy as public deliberation

MAURIZIO PASSERIN D'ENTRÈVES

One of the most remarkable developments in the last twenty years has been the revival of the idea of deliberative democracy. Set against the previous dominance of aggregative models of democracy derived from economics and the theory of rational choice, the idea of deliberative democracy, or decision making based on public deliberation among free and equal citizens, represents a highly significant development in democratic theory.[1] This development, as a number of commentators have noted, is best viewed as a revival of earlier conceptions of democratic citizenship, rather than as a modern innovation. 'The idea of deliberative democracy and its practical implementation,' Elster notes, 'are as old as democracy itself. Both came into being in Athens in the fifth century B.C.'[2] A crucial statement supporting this view may be found in Pericles' Funeral Oration, where he praises the Athenians for the high value they placed on political deliberation: 'instead of looking on discussion as a stumbling-block in the way of action, we think it an indispensable preliminary to any wise action at all'.[3]

With the re-emergence of democratic government at the time of the American and French revolutions, the nature and function of political deliberation, now located in representative assemblies, became a crucial element of democratic legitimacy. Edmund Burke, in his speech to the electors of Bristol, argued that: 'Parliament is not a *congress* of ambassadors from different and hostile interests . . . but . . . a *deliberative* assembly of one nation, with one interest, that of the whole; where, not local purposes, not local prejudices, ought to guide, but the general good, resulting from the general reason of the whole.'[4] In the nineteenth century John Stuart Mill was one of the most well known advocates of 'government by discussion,' chiefly on the grounds that it would correct false judgments and thereby reduce cognitive deficits.[5] Among contemporary thinkers, both Rawls and Habermas have defended a deliberative or discursive model of politics, the former by specifying the criteria of public reason that citizens and public officials ought to observe in dealing with constitutional issues or matters of basic justice, the latter by developing a procedural conception of democracy based on formal and informal processes of public deliberation.[6]

The idea of deliberative democracy can thus be seen to emerge from a long and rich history of debates about the best way to secure democratic self-governance. But what are the main features of a deliberative model of politics? There are some variations among the leading defenders of this model. Elster conceives deliberative democracy as decision making by discussion among free and equal citizens. For him 'political choice, to be legitimate, must be the outcome of deliberation about ends among free, equal, and rational agents.'[7] Bohman and Rehg claim that 'deliberative democracy refers to the idea that legitimate lawmaking issues from the public deliberation of citizens . . . it presents an ideal of political autonomy based on the practical reasoning of citizens'.[8] Joshua Cohen maintains that deliberative democracy is 'an association whose affairs are governed by the public deliberation of its members', and where 'the justification of the terms and conditions of association proceeds through public argument and reasoning among citizens'.[9] Democratic politics, according to Cohen, involves 'public deliberation focused on the common good, requires some form of manifest equality among citizens, and shapes the identity and interests of citizens in ways that contribute to the formation of a public conception of the common good'.[10]

But is the idea of deliberative democracy feasible or even desirable under current conditions, characterized by a high level of social complexity and a high degree of cultural pluralism? As Bohman and Rehg note:

> given the complex issues that confront contemporary societies, is an intelligent, broad-based participation possible? In societies as culturally diverse as our own, is it reasonable to expect deliberating citizens to converge on rational solutions to political problems? Does deliberation actually overcome or only exacerbate the more undesirable features of majority rule?[11]

The essays collected in this volume, the majority of which were presented at a conference held at Manchester University in

March 1999 under the auspices of the Manchester Centre for Political Thought, seek to provide an answer to these questions. They are arranged in two parts, the first focusing on the normative aspects of public deliberation, the second on the institutional mechanisms required to realize the normative ideals of deliberative democracy. They range from detailed assessments of the key normative arguments for deliberative democracy (Chapters 2–5) to an empirical investigation of the relation between deliberation and decision making (Chapter 6), an analysis of the institutions of deliberative democracy (Chapter 7), a case study of the role of public deliberation in the adjudication of deep religious and cultural conflicts (Chapter 8) and a defence of deliberative politics as the best institutional framework for rectifying social disadvantages (Chapter 9). Taken together, they offer a series of powerful arguments in support of deliberative democracy as a normatively robust and institutionally feasible model of politics for societies characterized by deep inequalities, growing cultural pluralism and increasing social complexity.

Normative perspectives

In Chapter 2 Maurizio Passerin d'Entrèves offers an overview of the main justificatory strategies employed by contemporary philosophers to ground the legitimacy of political institutions. He argues that the justice and legitimacy of democratic institutions are best defended on the basis of a normative theory of public deliberation. Such a theory, he maintains, is superior to the two main normative models of justification that appeal to the ideal of neutrality (Rawls, Larmore, Nagel) or to the ideal of perfectionism (Raz, Galston, Kymlicka).

The question of legitimacy has become particularly acute in societies characterized by the fact of pluralism. Pluralism refers to the existence of a variety of competing and often irreconcilable conceptions of the good life held by individuals and groups in contemporary Western societies. Although pluralism is not a uniquely modern phenomenon, it has assumed greater political salience in societies composed of a number of distinct cultural groups claiming recognition of their collective identities. The type of recognition claimed by such groups, based on their ethnic, religious, gender or linguistic identity, represents a challenge to the standard liberal model of justification, which restricts itself to the recognition of the equal worth of individuals considered independently of their group affiliations. D'Entrèves examines three responses to this challenge: the first centred on the value of neutrality, the second on the value of autonomy or diversity, the third on the value of dialogue or deliberation.

Rawls is the best-known advocate of the model of neutrality, along with Charles Larmore and Thomas Nagel. Given the fact of reasonable pluralism, the aim is to find a basis of agreement that is neutral with respect to competing conceptions of the good life, whether individual or collective. This aim is achieved by the creation of an overlapping consensus among the variety of reasonable comprehensive doctrines embodying different conceptions of the good. The strength of this model lies in the acknowledgement of the fact of pluralism, seen as both inevitable and ineliminable, and in the effort to find a basis of agreement that is least controversial, since it is restricted to constitutional essentials and basic questions of justice. The weakness of this model lies in the strong distinction between public and non-public aspects of identity and the difficulty of defining a non-contestable notion of the 'reasonable'. The model assumes that individuals, in order to achieve an overlapping consensus on constitutional essentials, are able to set aside their personal or non-public conception of the good from the public conception of justice. For many individuals whose personal conception of the good is inextricably tied to the collective conception of the good of their group, this separation of private and public aspects of their identity is difficult to sustain. In effect, the only individuals likely to achieve an overlapping consensus are those for whom the separation of public and private aspects of identity is least troublesome, namely liberal individuals. Secondly, the very notion of what is 'reasonable' remains controversial, since the meaning of the word varies in accordance with the different conceptions of the good held by various individuals and groups living in contemporary multicultural societies. Thus, contrary to Rawls's hope, reasonableness remains a contested and contestable notion.

Faced with these shortcomings of the neutrality model, some political philosophers have opted for a different model of justification, one based on perfectionist ideals, such as autonomy or diversity. They start by acknowledging the controversial, that is, non-neutral character of liberal principles of justice and of the conception of the self that underlies them, and go on to defend liberal principles by arguing for their superiority with respect to available alternatives. This strategy has been advocated, among others, by Joseph Raz, William Galston and Will Kymlicka. Joseph Raz, for example, has argued that a liberal state should protect and foster all those forms of life that encourage autonomy. He believes that autonomy is a precondition of human well-being, since the value of an individual's life is enhanced if it is freely chosen from a range of available options. He also thinks that membership of a community is conducive to human well-being, because it determines the horizon of one's opportunities and helps to shape one's identity. The liberal state is to be particularly valued because, by securing certain rights to individuals and groups, it makes available a range of valuable options that will permit every person or group to pursue their conception of the good, and thus secures the condition for human well-being. A similar argument has been put forward by Kymlicka in his liberal defence of group rights, which stresses the value of cultural membership and a secure cultural context for individual well-being. Other authors, such as Galston, have advocated the superiority of liberal principles by an appeal to the value of diversity, rather than autonomy. The liberal state accommodates diversity better than its rivals, since in its public principles, institutions and practices it affords maximum feasible space for individual and group differences to flourish, constrained only by the requirements of liberal social unity. The strength of this perfectionist model of justification is that it engages in a substantive debate with the critics of liberalism and argues for the superiority of the liberal conception of the good *vis-à-vis* its possible competitors. The weakness of the model, on the other hand, stems partly from its strength: it may allow for greater debate about competing conceptions of the good life in the public–political domain, but it will ultimately favour those individuals and groups whose conceptions of the good or of well-being are predisposed towards the value of autonomy or diversity. The perfectionist model may be a better way of defending liberal principles and institutions but is no less controversial or contestable than the model of neutrality. The aim of inclusiveness, of being able to accommodate the largest feasible range of competing and irreconcilable conceptions of the good, seems, in the end, unattainable on either model. But is this aim actually attainable? D'Entrèves argues that the model of public deliberation is more inclusive than either the model of neutrality or that of perfectionism, but points out that such inclusiveness is a matter of degree. No model can achieve complete inclusiveness. There will always be tragic conflicts and tragic choices. But that should not stop us in our search for models of greater inclusiveness that will lessen the scope for tragic conflicts. The deliberative or dialogic model, he suggests, may provide a greater degree of inclusion than either the neutrality or the perfectionist model.

D'Entrèves explores some of the main arguments in defence of the deliberative model of justification. Among the arguments examined are those advanced by Charles Taylor, Amy Gutmann and Dennis Thompson, Joshua Cohen, Jürgen Habermas and James Fishkin. Taylor has defended a dialogic model of justification based on the recognition of the uniqueness of collective identities. He calls this model the 'politics of difference' to distinguish it from the standard liberal model, which he terms the 'politics of equal dignity'. The example Taylor cites in defence of the politics of difference is that of the French-speaking community of Quebec. They should be granted special rights and immunities so as to be able to preserve their unique collective identity, and to maintain their cherished cultural distinctness from the majority of English-speaking Canada. Taylor's model of the politics of recognition is neither neutral nor perfectionist: it rests on the presumption of equal worth of cultures, and is dialogic, in so far as it promotes cross-cultural exchange among different groups and collectivities.

A similar stress on dialogue and deliberation characterizes the position of Gutmann and Thompson. They argue that controversial moral issues should not be excluded from public debate but should become the topic of collective deliberation. Public deliberation must satisfy certain procedural standards (such as reciprocity, publicity and accountability) and be based on the idea of mutual respect.

An even stronger defence of deliberative democracy as the best institutional mechanism for the adjudication of conflicting moral and political perspectives is provided by Joshua Cohen. By deliberative democracy he means an association whose affairs are governed by the public deliberation of its members and where political debate is organized around alternative conceptions of the public good. The idea is not to suppress difference but to allow differences about competing conceptions of the public good to be debated in common deliberative fora that ensure the greatest degree of fairness to all participants. To this end Cohen sketches an ideal deliberative procedure that captures the notion of justification through public argument among equal citizens, and serves in turn as a model for deliberative institutions. The relevance of such a normative theory of deliberation is that it articulates the conditions under which a fair debate among competing collective identities and conflicting conceptions of the good can be conducted. The most sophisticated theoretical account of a deliberative model of democracy is provided by Jürgen Habermas. Like Cohen, Habermas offers a characterization of an ideal deliberative procedure whose normative validity rests on a set of demanding pragmatic presuppositions. In contrast to Cohen, however, Habermas does not think that such an ideal deliberative procedure could be applied to society as a whole or to the entirety of its institutions. Rather, he conceives the ideal deliberative procedure as the core structure in a separate, constitutionally organized political system. For this reason Habermas advocates a two-track model of deliberative politics, according to which deliberative procedures operating in the formal decision-making domains of legislative and judicial activity are supplemented by informal processes of opinion formation taking place in the public sphere. Deliberative procedures in formal decision-making domains shape the processes of collective will formation with a view to the co-operative solution of practical questions, while informal opinion formation processes are geared to the identification and thematization of problems emerging from lifeworld experience. The two-track model of deliberative politics put forward by Habermas depends, therefore, on the successful interplay of democratically institutionalized will formation and informal opinion formation.

The chapter closes with an assessment of Fishkin's model of democratic deliberation. Fishkin's contribution focuses on the kinds of institutions required for the ideal of deliberative democracy to be realized in large-scale and technologically advanced societies. Such institutions must embody both political equality and deliberation. His institutional proposal centred around deliberative opinion polls embodies political equality, since everyone has an equal chance of being represented in the national sample of participants, and deliberation, since a selected group of citizens is immersed for an extended period of time in intensive, face-to-face debate. The advantage of a deliberative opinion poll over non-deliberative forms of polling is that it enables a representative sample of citizens to acquire an adequate level of information on a given issue, to listen to the contrasting opinions and perspectives of experts, and to test their own views and opinions through a process of common debate and discussion. Only after such an extended period of deliberation are the members of the sample 'polled', that is, asked to give their considered judgement on a given issue. By operating in a framework characterized by political equality, participation and non-tyranny, a collective process of deliberation occurs in which the group has a reasonable chance to form its collective, considered judgements on topics of public concern.

The theories of public deliberation put forward by Fishkin, Habermas, Cohen and Gutmann, together with Taylor's dialogic model of recognition, should be seen as providing the broad outlines of a model of normative justification that is more inclusive than the two alternatives based on the values of neutrality or perfectionism. Whether the emphasis is on the recognition of collective identities (Taylor), the adjudication of moral conflict (Gutmann), public reasoning on the common good (Cohen), formal and informal modes of collective opinion and will formation (Habermas) or the evaluation of issues of public concern (Fishkin), they all stress the importance of dialogue and deliberation for a more inclusive and just form of liberal society.

In Chapter 3 Maeve Cooke examines the merits of the main arguments commonly advanced in support of the deliberative conception of democracy. These arguments focus on (1) the educative power of the process of public deliberation, (2) the community-generating power of the process of public deliberation, (3) the fairness of the procedure of public deliberation, (4) the epistemic quality of the outcomes of public deliberation and (5) the congruence of the ideal of politics articulated by deliberative democracy with 'who we are'. She argues that, although most of these arguments express valid intuitions, the first four are insufficient as they stand and require help from the fifth argument if they are to be fully convincing.

The first argument holds that deliberative democracy should be advocated primarily because of the beneficial educative effects it has on citizens. John Stuart Mill and Hannah Arendt are often cited as proponents of the educative view: both see participation in public affairs as good in itself, and both believe that political participation improves the moral and intellectual qualities of individuals. Cooke maintains that the educative argument is insufficient as a justification of deliberative democracy for at least three reasons. The first can be seen by posing the question: what is it about deliberation – as opposed to participation – that produces beneficial educative effects on individuals? If the argument in favour of deliberation is to work it has to show that public deliberation produces beneficial educative effects that are superior to the benefits resulting from non-deliberative participation in public affairs. The problem here is that there is no uncontroversial standpoint from which such superiority may be measured. The second reason is that the beneficial effects of public deliberation cannot be the point of the deliberative ideal of democracy: such beneficial effects can accrue only if the individuals concerned take part in deliberation for other reasons. Thus the educative effects of public deliberation are at best side effects and cannot be the main point of, or provide the sole justification for, such deliberation. Finally, the educative argument is insufficient for a third reason, for it leaves open the question of what counts as improving the moral and intellectual qualities of individuals. In order for it to work, the educative argument has to presuppose the availability of some independent standard for evaluating the individual's moral and intellectual development. For that reason, too, it requires support from other arguments if it is to work as a justification of deliberative democracy.

The second argument in favour of deliberative democracy holds that public deliberation has a community-generating power. Like the educative argument, it is insufficient on its own, and for the same reasons. First, it runs against the problem of how to show that public deliberation is superior to non-deliberative participation in public affairs in generating a sense of community. Second, it faces the objection that the generation of a sense of community cannot be the point of public deliberation but only, at best, a beneficial side-effect. Third, it is insufficiently aware of the fact that not all communities are equally desirable and that some independent standard for evaluating communities is required. Like the educative argument, the community-generating argument requires the support of other arguments if it is to form part of a convincing defence of deliberative democracy.

The third argument in defence of deliberative democracy maintains that the procedure of public deliberation improves the fairness of democratic outcomes. This argument is based on a strictly proceduralist view according to which there are no non-procedural standards of fairness: if the procedure is fair, the outcome is fair. Thus, for advocates of strict proceduralism, such as Joshua Cohen and Seyla Benhabib, democratic decisions are fair or legitimate in so far as they are the product of fair deliberative procedures. Cooke argues that, as a justification of the deliberative ideal of democracy, the proceduralist argument is insufficient in at least two respects. The first is a feature of proceduralist conceptions of fairness in general, namely that they implicitly appeal to some standard that is external to the procedure. Cohen and Benhabib do in fact appeal to a conception of fairness that goes beyond a strictly procedural conception of impartiality (such as flipping a coin), but have yet to offer convincing arguments in support of their particular normative conceptions of fairness. The second respect in which the proceduralist argument is insufficient is that it can assign only a restricted role to democratic deliberation. In so far as they are strict proceduralists, Cohen and Benhabib can argue only that public deliberation makes the procedure itself more fair. But both Cohen and Benhabib hold a less restrictive view of deliberation: for Cohen deliberation improves the quality of decision making, while for Benhabib deliberative processes are essential to the rationality of democratic outcomes. Such arguments, however, are no longer about the fairness of the procedure but about the quality of the outcomes as judged by non-procedural epistemic standards. In sum, Cohen and Benhabib must either confine the role of democratic deliberation to improving the fairness of democratic procedures, or they must offer an explanation as to how deliberation contributes to the epistemic quality of democratic outcomes.

The fourth argument focuses on the epistemic role of public deliberation. In contrast to the third argument, which derives the quality of democratic outcomes from the procedures of public deliberation, the fourth argument distinguishes between the fairness of the procedure and the rationality of the outcome. It thus posits independent epistemic standards for assessing the quality of the results of deliberation. According to this argument, public deliberation contributes to the quality of democratic outcomes, which are assessed according to epistemic standards of validity. One of the leading advocates of this position, Jürgen Habermas, has defended the view that public deliberation has a cognitive dimension: it is concerned with finding the best way of regulating matters of public concern, where the 'best way' is judged according to objective standards of rationality. Furthermore, public deliberation contributes to the rationality of laws and their implementation. Cooke argues that Habermas's position encounters two main problems. The first is that it appeals to an epistemic standard of rationality whose basis is unclear. The second is that it does not explain how public deliberation contributes constructively to the rationality of outcomes.

As regards the first problem, Cooke claims that, unlike his theory of moral validity, Habermas's theory of democratic legitimacy does not rest on the criterion of universalizability: the validity of laws is not a function of their universalizability but of the fact that they are generally acceptable. However, *de facto* general acceptability cannot be the criterion of epistemic quality: some means of distinguishing between valid and invalid claims to general acceptability must be available. As regards the second problem, Cooke argues that since the universalizability test is not a criterion of the validity of legal norms, it is unclear why public deliberation is necessary: if general acceptability alone is required, voting would be sufficient. In sum, Habermas must clarify how public deliberation contributes to the epistemic quality of democratic oucomes in the absence of a test of genuine universalizability.

Having established the insufficiency of the preceding four arguments, Cooke turns to a fifth argument, one which stresses the congruence of the ideal of deliberative democracy with 'who we are'. This argument is part of an alternative strategy which could be described as anti-foundationalist and contextualist. Some versions of the fifth argument can be found in the divergent accounts of deliberative democracy put forward by Rawls, Habermas, Benhabib and Cohen. It posits the ideal of democracy as a fundamental principle of Western modernity and deliberative democracy as the elucidation of this ideal that is most congruent with 'who we are'. Such an argument, however, runs against the objection that its underlying strategy is too weak, for it appears to be compatible with a variety of widely diverging models of deliberative democracy. To meet this objection Cooke focuses on the two most divergent models, those articulated by Rawls and Habermas, and shows that the fifth argumentative strategy provides good reasons for preferring Habermas's model to that of Rawls.

After having outlined the points of agreement between the two authors, Cooke examines in detail four interconnected respects in which Rawls's model of deliberative democracy is less convincing than Habermas's. She claims, first, that Rawls's model makes use of a normative conception of public reason that is non-deliberative and, as such, fails to do justice to its own commitment to a deliberative ideal of democracy congruent with 'who we are'. Second, she argues that Rawls's demarcation of the public from the non-public gives rise to problems within his theory and leads to a contentious interpretation of the 'fact reasonable pluralism' that fails to fit with 'who we are.' Third, she notes that Rawls's model of deliberative politics points in the direction of a conception of personal autonomy that he explicitly rejects as an acceptable basis for his political conception of justice. Such a conception of personal autonomy ought to be central to a theory of deliberative democracy for it is a key element of 'who we are'. Lastly, she argues that Rawls's conception of political autonomy is too limited and insufficiently deliberative from the point of view of a deliberative ideal of democracy congruent with 'who we are'. Cooke shows that in each of these four respects Habermas offers a model of deliberative politics which is superior to Rawls's since it fits far better with our conception of 'who we are.'

By articulating and defending the fifth argumentative strategy Cooke is able to show the superiority of certain models of deliberative politics and to expose the weaknesses in others. The fifth strategy is not just the best available defence of deliberative democracy but can be put to good use in assessing the merits of diverging interpretations of the deliberative ideal.

In Chapter 4 Matthew Festenstein explores one of the key normative issues in the debate on deliberative democracy. Deliberative democracy, it is argued, entails special obligations among participants, that is, obligations which they owe to one another but not to those outside the deliberative process. These include the obligation to provide reasons that all can accept, to listen and respond to the reasons and arguments of others, and to try to arrive at a proposal acceptable to all. However, these obligations are not derivable in a straightforward fashion from the three central justificatory arguments for deliberative democracy. Its advocates are thus presented with a choice: either to amend the schedule of deliberative obligations or to derive them from another feature of deliberative democracy,

one which is not emphasized in the core justificatory arguments. Festenstein's contribution explores the latter strategy by
suggesting that deliberative democracy presupposes a notion of
community. Unlike other advocates of deliberative democracy,
however, Festenstein maintains that deliberative obligations
are grounded in a valuable social relationship rather than in a
shared sense of national identity.

Deliberative theorists have outlined a series of demanding
conditions to ensure the fairness of deliberative processes, such
as inclusiveness, equality of access, equality of power and
resources, and equal opportunity of political influence. In addition to these demanding conditions, citizens taking part in the
deliberative process are held to be under a distinct set of obligations. Festenstein highlights the three principal ones. First, the
obligation to offer arguments persuasive to all other participants in the deliberative process. Second, the obligation to
respond to the reasons and arguments of others *qua* reasons and
arguments: what matters in deliberation is not bargaining
power but only the force of the better argument. Third, the obligation to modify proposals in the light of the arguments and
reasons put forward in the deliberative process in order to arrive
at a commonly acceptable proposal. These three types of obligation fall in the category of 'special obligations' because they are
shared among participants in the deliberative process but are
not owed to outsiders. The idea that such obligations exist is not
in itself controversial. More controversial are the sources of
special obligations, whether they are best justified by appealing
to universalistic or particularistic values and norms.
Festenstein believes that no single model can account for the
variety of special obligations, but suggests that there is a plausible particularistic account of deliberative obligations.

In order to provide a background to his claim Festenstein
examines three arguments in support of deliberative democracy
to see whether they are successful in explaining why participants in public deliberation should fulfil their deliberative obligations. He contends that in each case there is a gap between the
reasons given for accepting deliberation as the yardstick of democratic legitimacy and the reasons for accepting that participants are under these obligations. The first argument in support
of deliberative democracy states that it is desirable by virtue of
the advantages which accrue to each participant from making
decisions in a deliberative way (e.g. each participant will benefit

from the pooling of private information and from the opportunity to redress bounded rationality). This prudential argument suggests that there are good (i.e. self-interested) reasons for adhering to the deliberative obligations. However, such an argument cannot provide a stable grounding for these obligations because the motivation for adhering to them – personal advantage – is also a motivation for flouting them, when it is not too costly to do so.

The second argument in support of deliberative democracy is epistemic: instead of viewing it as instrumental for the achievement of particular interests, it holds that it is the most reliable method of gaining knowledge of moral principles. The most plausible version of the epistemic argument is formulated not as an empirical claim but as a claim about the conditions for arriving at the truth and giving good reasons. The circumstances of public deliberation are seen as the necessary conditions for arriving at the right or best judgement of the public good. However, as Festenstein points out, there is a gap between accepting this argument and believing that participants should abide by their deliberative obligations. The outcome at which democratic deliberation aims is not, strictly speaking, a belief about the public good but a mutually acceptable proposal. If the goal of public deliberation is a mutually acceptable proposal, this is compatible with the parties agreeing to it not because it is supported by the best reasons but because it is the outcome of a negotiated compromise. The epistemic argument does not explain why we should compromise or moderate our reasons and arguments when we engage in public deliberation. There thus remains a gap between epistemic commitments and deliberative obligations.

The third justificatory argument envisages deliberation as a fair procedure. In contrast to the epistemic argument, which posits standards external to the deliberative process by which the justice of its outcomes may be judged, this argument claims that what makes the outcomes just is that they are the product of a procedure which is judged fair. However, as some critics have noted, the standard of fairness must be external to the procedure itself, otherwise we have no means of deciding between different claimants to procedural fairness (e.g. simple aggregation of votes, flipping a coin, etc.).[12] The standard answer is to claim that the deliberative character of the procedure distinguishes it as especially fair. Public deliberation is fair because it improves the quality of the preferences, opinions and reasons of the participants. If so, the procedural argument would seem to move either in the prudential or in the epistemic direction, depending on whether the improvement accrues to individual interests or to the quality of the reasons which provide the inputs to deliberation. In either case, the procedural argument fails to ground the deliberative obligations, because neither the prudential nor the epistemic arguments are sufficiently sensitive to important aspects of the idea of deliberative duties.

The three arguments just outlined focus on the structural aspects of the question 'Why deliberate?' Public deliberation, each argues, possesses advantages in enhancing the legitimacy of political decisions. Even if these arguments offer fruitful lines of inquiry, they are unsuccessful in answering the first-personal version of this question, namely 'Why should I deliberate?' That is, 'Why should I undertake the deliberative obligations?' The most plausible answer for Festenstein is to develop the particularistic account of special obligations, and to argue that the deliberative obligations are grounded in a valuable social relationship. The obvious candidate for such a relationship is citizenship, understood as an ethical rather than merely legal category. This argument requires that there is a non-instrumental value in being an equal member of a political community. If we accept this argument, certain obligations would flow from recognizing the relationship among civic equals as valuable. Citizenship could be seen not only as valuable on moral grounds but as partly constituted by the obligations to treat fellow citizens in particular ways. The key obligations here would consist in taking each other seriously as sources of political arguments and reasons, in taking each other's interests as a source of valid claims, conditioning our instrumental projects and particular moral opinions. These obligations would be discharged through public deliberation.

Festenstein then considers the argument advanced by David Miller that deliberative democracy and its associated obligations are best supported by a shared sense of national identity. According to this argument, national identity provides the motivational force impelling us to fulfil our deliberative obligations. Such an argument, however, needs to show how we can derive the deliberative obligations from an account of national identity. There have been several accounts designed to show that national identity has value for its members or constitutes a valuable form of social relationship. These accounts argue that national identity fosters trust, overcomes alienation, encourages solidarity and is a condition of individual autonomy. A shared national identity entails, in turn, certain obligations on its members: to give priority to fellow members' needs and to co-operate with them on deliberative terms. What national identity provides, then, is a concrete form of social and political identity which is valuable to its members in such a way as to generate special obligations. The problem with this argument, Festenstein notes, is that some national traditions may be resistant to practices of deliberation. If a national identity is non-deliberative in character, the duties which partly constitute it will not include the deliberative obligations. The alternative is to argue that the only form of valuable national identity is deliberative. However, if the argument is that the deliberative features of a national identity make it valuable to its members, it is not clear what the specifically national component would add, if we are seeking to derive the deliberative obligations. We may accept, then, that national identity has the benefits that recent nationalist writers have claimed for it, without finding in it a derivation of the deliberative obligations. Such obligations are best understood as special duties owed by citizens to one another, whose obligatory character derives from the value of the civic bond. The importance of deliberative democracy would reside in its contributing to a valuable form of social relationship whose ethical character could be affirmed by all citizens.

In Chapter 5 Michael Saward assesses the claim made by some interpreters that Rawls's idea of public reason and related notions bear a strong affinity with the idea of deliberative democracy. Rawls's device of the Original Position, which models an ideal dialogue on principles of justice, has provided the inspiration for Joshua Cohen's model of democratic deliberation. Such an undisputed line of influence is not sufficient, however, to establish the deliberative nature of Rawls's key ideas. There are fundamental reasons, Saward maintains, why the Rawlsian project cannot be genuinely deliberative. Moreover the basic categories of Rawls's theory can throw an unexpected light on deliberative models of democracy.

Saward formulates his argument in two steps. First, he shows that, despite claims by Rawls and some commentators, Rawls is not and cannot be a deliberative democrat. Second, if one asks how the ideal dialogue of the original position may be approximated in real-world conditions, one can reach conclusions about the institutional dimensions of deliberative democracy radically different from those reached by Rawls himself.

Saward begins by noting that Rawls's account of public reason has often been seen as a major statement of the idea of deliberative democracy. Rawls himself has maintained that public reason is a vital component of deliberative democracy. However, such a claim cannot be sustained: public reason and deliberation are quite different things, and Rawls's project is more accurately seen as non-deliberative. In order to establish this claim, Saward offers a list of the defining features of deliberative conceptions of democracy. First, voting must be preceded by formal deliberation among representative citizens. Second, there must be evidence of public facilitation of informal deliberation in a range of non-state civil forums. Third, deliberation in representative institutions must have a determinate impact on the shape of the final outcome. Lastly, formal deliberation must satisfy minimum procedural standards of equal respect and inclusiveness.

Saward examines key components of Rawls's account in order to show how they undermine this baseline vision of deliberative democracy. For Rawls, 'public reason' is either a set of reasons or a way of reasoning necessary to the adequacy of legislative outcomes on important political questions. Although at first glance it would appear that everyone should engage in public reason, since it is the reason of all those sharing the status of equal citizenship, it soon transpires that its guidelines apply primarily to judges, elected politicians, government officials and candidates for political office. Moreover, public reason is restricted to 'constitutional essentials and questions of basic justice' and must be distinguished from the non-public reasons people offer within the institutions of civil society. According to Rawls, when we reason in public on fundamental issues, we must reason in a certain way, by accepting certain contraints, because only by doing so can we render the exercise of political power legitimate.

Saward maintains that Rawls's notion of public reason refers not to a process of actual reasoning but to a solitary, inward-looking type of reflection. The key terms employed by Rawls to characterize public reason ('think', 'imagine', 'reflect') are more appropriate to an internal dialogue than to an actual process of public deliberation. Public reason is not an injunction actually to reason in public with fellow citizens; rather, it is a set of guidelines about how to think about fundamental constitutional issues in the public forum. Its content is derived from the original position: parties in the original position must adopt guidelines and criteria of public reason for applying the two principles of justice to the basic structure. But the original position is a purely hypothetical device: it is a place in which deliberation is ideal and inclusive, and thus cannot be an actual place. The metaphor of the original position (non-deliberative, hypothetical) is woven into the structure of the argument of *Political Liberalism* and later statements on public reason as well.

Saward argues that by locating the basis of public reason in the hypothetical device of the original position, Rawls renders public reason a thoroughly non-deliberative notion. Rawls's position is almost diametrically opposed to the dominant visions of deliberative democracy, each of which stresses the importance of actual and effective deliberation in various state and non-state forums. In order to establish this point, Saward highlights the key components of Rawls's idea of public reason and shows how they constitute a mirror image of the key components of the original position. Thus citizens with their reasonable comprehensive doctrines are equivalent to citizens with their considered convictions, while public reason is equivalent to reflective equilibrium in the demands it imposes upon citizens who aim to arrive at mutually acceptable principles of justice. Now, to the extent that Rawls has attempted to modify his original framework, as set out in *A Theory of Justice*, he is forced to make new assumptions about citizens that undermine the deliberative claims of *Political Liberalism*. Saward shows that with respect to four key assumptions (the motivation of citizens, the wide view of public reason, the duty of civility, and the political conception of persons as free and equal citizens), Rawls is forced to restore what was lost in moving from the original framework of *A Theory of Justice* to that of *Political Liberalism*. Each key assumption is introduced in order to retain control over the outcomes of ideal deliberation on principles of justice, but at the cost of undermining the deliberative claims of his later project.

In the concluding part of Chapter 5 Saward uses the device of the original position to explore the institutional aspects of deliberative democracy. The idea is to see how the key features of the original position may be approximated in practice. If we insist on actual (rather than ideal) deliberation, and do not worry about keeping control over the outcomes (as Rawls does), then some interesting conclusions about the institutions of deliberative democracy might follow. The two key descriptive features of the original position are (1) the assumption of self-interest and (2) the inducement to impartiality through the veil of ignorance. From a democratic perspective, five additional features are relevant: (1) generality (the outcomes reached will have general applicability); (2) inclusiveness (all interests are represented); (3) impartiality (all can endorse the fairness of the outcomes); (4) productivity (the original position unfailingly produces fair outcomes); and (5) the face-to-face character of ideal deliberations.

Saward suggests that we may use these features as regulative principles for the design of real-world deliberative institutions. There will clearly be some loss in the translation from the ideal to the real. We shall lose generality as well as inclusiveness, and there will be some loss of impartiality and productivity. But, keeping an eye on the regulative principles, it may still be possible to suggest a number of institutional mechanisms to render our democratic institutions more deliberative. With respect to the principle of inclusiveness, since not everyone can be included in face-to-face deliberations, the device of representation becomes crucial. Here Fishkin's deliberative opinion polls, based on a random sampling of the population to produce a representative body which deliberates on behalf of all, may represent one possible solution. Similarly, with respect to the principle of generality, Fishkin's deliberative polls will make it more likely that the outcomes reached by the deliberating body will reflect general concerns across the relevant population. But there are other, additional institutional devices which can be suggested in light of the regulative principles sketched above. Chief among them is a vibrant civil society with a network of civic associations and interest groups with the formal means of agenda setting. Voting according to rules that are broadly acceptable is also vital if the real-world equivalent of ideal deliberation is to produce fair outcomes. Thus, if one wanted to replicate as far as possible the features of the original position in the real world, one would have to produce an institutional vision that provided a mix of agenda-setting, deliberation and decision-making mechanisms. Although not entirely novel, the realization of such an institutional vision would accentuate the democratic character of current representative institutions and provide a defence of deliberative democracy quite distinct from that of the later Rawls.

Institutional perspectives

In Chapter 6 Judith Squires claims that the literature on deliberative democracy that emerged in the 1990s has little to say about decision making and nothing new to offer to debates about models of representative government. What it does offer is an account of how important it is to develop inclusive and vibrant informal public spheres for deliberation, to supplement the formal institutions of representative government. But it has yet to offer a sustained account of how these informal public spheres are to engage with the formal public sphere of government.

No comprehensive theory of democracy can focus on deliberation alone. There will always be a need for decision making. And deliberation is never used as the only procedure for making collective decisions: it is always supplemented by voting or bargaining. This means that deliberative democracy is not a proper 'model of democracy', only an ingredient within one. Advocates of deliberative democracy, if they are to offer a fully articulated theory of democracy, must say something specific about the relation between the deliberative and the decisional moments within the democratic process. They need to spell out in more detail how deliberation is to augment and improve existing procedures of aggregation, representation and decision making.

In order to explore this claim, Squires examines first those accounts that appear to endorse a bifurcated model of democracy, locating deliberation within an informal public sphere and decision making in the formal public sphere. She then considers those versions of deliberative democracy which avoid this apparent discontinuity by introducing the idea of regulated deliberation within formal institutions alongside the unregulated deliberation of the informal public sphere. The virtue of these versions of deliberative democracy is that they engage with issues pertaining to both democracy and constitutionalism, considering not only preference formation and informal group deliberation but also institutional decision making and the operation of the rule of law. But even such versions, she argues, have not yet provided a fully integrated account of the relation between the deliberative and decisional moments within the democratic process.

Advocates of deliberative democracy suggest that the idea of democracy revolves around the transformation, and not simply the aggregation, of preferences. Legitimate decision making is seen to emerge from deliberative procedures that are both rational and inclusive. Fair deliberative procedures, it is argued, can move a complex and differentiated political community towards decisions its members, including dissenters, ought to accept as legitimate. Theories of deliberative democracy claim to provide an answer to the problem of political justification in the face of moral disagreement. According to the ideal of deliberative democracy, the justification of political power must proceed on the basis of a free public reasoning among equals. Participants in democratic deliberation must defend their claims on the basis of reasons which are acceptable to all participants, rather than on the basis of mutual advantage. Most deliberative democrats reject the view that pluralism and social complexity are impediments to democracy. Public deliberation, the suggest, is uniquely suited to generating legitimate decisions in situations where no point of view commands universal assent. Pluralism and social complexity can, they argue, improve the public use of reason, rather than act as an obstacle to its operation.

Deliberative democrats are held to offer a conception of impartiality that is dialogical rather than monological. They suggest that, if the conditions of deliberation are met fully, the decisions reached will have greater legitimacy. The decisions are impartial in the sense of being inclusive and lacking bias. As a regulative ideal, this conception of impartiality has great merit. But there is a problem, Squires notes, in the institutional working out of the ideal within the models of deliberative democracy on offer. If one looks at the institutional arrangements proposed so far, they appear to embody not simply the dialogical conception of impartiality but rather a two-track model in which the monological and the dialogical have distinct roles and are located within clearly demarcated political domains. Rather than offering a distinct vision of democracy, deliberative democrats may simply be offering an augmented vision: unbiased or just decision making in the formal public sphere and inclusive deliberation in the informal public sphere. Habermas, for example, claims that political decisions in complex and plural societies can be rational and hence legitimate if decision-making procedures follow two tracks: they must be both open to inputs from an informal and vibrant public sphere and appropriately structured to support the rationality of the relevant types of discourse and to ensure implementation. This is a two-track model in which deliberation is located in the informal public sphere which acts as a 'context of discovery', and decision making is located in the formal public sphere, which acts as a 'context of justification'. Because it remains largely within the realm of ideal theory and entails little institutional design, the distinction does not offer much guidance as to how to establish or monitor the relation between these two types of public sphere. Moreover, by endorsing the separation between the context of discovery, which houses deliberation and generates dialogical impartiality, and the context of justification, which houses decision making and generates monological impartiality, there is a danger that the latter form of impartiality will subsume the former. This possibility would undermine the legitimation claims made for deliberation, based as they are on the dialogical rather than the monological conception of impartiality.

The assumption of discontinuity within some models of deliberative democracy presents a serious problem for its advocates. Each of the three central conditions stipulated for the ideal of deliberative democracy (inclusivity, rationality, legitimacy)[13] looks decidedly problematic in light of the endorsement of discontinuity. Members of the political community may all take part in deliberation on an equal basis, but elected representatives will make the decisions. Decisions may be influenced by deliberation, but will be determined by aggregation. And citizens may understand how deliberation proceeded and how aggregation took place, but they are unlikely to understand the structural relation between the two if it is left unspecified as 'influence'. Each of the inclusivity, rationality and legitimacy claims looks vulnerable.

Squires then considers the work of Iris Young, who stresses the importance of connecting the deliberation of informal public spheres with institutional decision-making and policy outcomes. In her most recent writings Young develops an account of political representation which is consistent with the norms of deliberative democracy. Like Habermas, she suggests that representatives should engage in regulated deliberations while remaining open to the unregulated deliberations taking place in informal public spheres. However, the procedures for specifying the relation between the two types of deliberation are left quite vague. Given this lack of specificity, what is the likelihood that deliberation within informal public spheres will influence the representatives in the formal public spheres? How could we evaluate the extent to which institutional decisions and policy outcomes had been influenced by the deliberations of informal public spheres?

Squires maintains that without being able to specify the relation between the two spheres deliberative democrats cannot claim to offer a comprehensive or coherent account of democracy. She concludes that, in order to redeem the claims of inclusivity, rationality and legitimacy, deliberative democrats ought to move from the realm of ideal theory and focus on the complex task of institutional design.

In Chapter 7 Smith and Wales address the question of how to institutionalize the principles and ideals of deliberative democracy. They begin by noting how, in the face of widespread dissatisfaction with contemporary democratic practices, renewed interest in deliberative forms of citizen participation has emerged. One of the main complaints against current forms of political representation in Western democracies is that the activities, backgrounds and interests of political representatives are seen as far removed from the lives and perspectives of citizens. Although periodic elections act as a constraint on the elected, the mandate that representatives enjoy extends over a period within which citizens have very little say on decisions made in their name. The principal–agent form of representation, so dominant within liberal democracies, rests on the fact that the political representative is able to deliberate and decide *for* others. But, as many critics have contended, the lack of presence or 'voice' of the politically marginalized in political decision-making processes means that their interests and perspectives are often excluded or inadequately addressed. Asymmetries of economic power and influence are reflected in the political sphere and undermine the principle of political equality on which representative democracy rests. Moreover, such power asymmetries undermine the apparent neutrality of social choice mechanisms, such as voting, which embody the liberal principle that the role of democracy is to aggregate individual preferences into a collective choice. Not only are such social choice mechanisms subject to strategic manipulation, but by taking preferences as given they fail to recognise that preferences are shaped by the institutional context. As Elster, Sunstein and others have argued, preferences are not exogenous to institutional settings. Hence, decision-making procedures should not be concerned only with aggregating preferences but also with the nature of the processes through which they are formed. The existing mechanisms of political representation are not designed to encourage engagement and the testing of preferences – citizenship is a passive affair which leads to a moral and political de-skilling of the electorate and the spread of cynical attitudes about public affairs.

Deliberative democratic theory can be seen as a response to these institutional and normative deficits and offers a challenge to contemporary liberal representative institutions. Although there is recognition that, given the complexity of modern societies, a division of political labour is necessary, deliberative democracy offers a possibility of a different form of that division, one in which increased opportunities for citizen participation are taken to be both feasible and desirable, and where citizen engagement forms part of a critical dialogue upon which more legitimate forms of political authority can be grounded. As with liberal theories, deliberative theories are concerned with creating institutions for the resolution of conflict, but recognize that preferences and value orientations can be transformed through a process of collective deliberation. A deliberative polity promotes political dialogue aimed at mutual understanding: citizens are motivated to resolve conflict by argument rather than by other means, and rely upon a deliberative, as opposed to a strategic or instrumental, mode of rationality.

Smith and Wales highlight three key features of deliberative democracy, namely that it promises more trustworthy and legitimate forms of political authority, more informed judgements and a more active account of citizenship. Legitimate forms of authority rest on two aspects of deliberative theory: inclusivity and democratic dialogue. Inclusivity refers to both presence and voice: all citizens are entitled to participate in the process of political dialogue and have an equal right to be heard.

Democratic dialogue encourages mutual respect and is orientated to the articulation of the common good. Taken together, inclusivity and democratic dialogue offer a basis for more legitimate and trustworthy forms of political authority. The second key feature of deliberative democracy is that it promises more informed judgements. Deliberation offers the conditions whereby citizens can widen their limited and fallible perspectives by drawing on each other's knowledge and experience; deliberation has the ability to lessen 'bounded rationality'. Finally, deliberative democracy offers a more active account of citizenship, one that recognizes that political engagement has the potential to transform the values and preferences of citizens in response to encounters with others.

Deliberative democratic theory can thus be seen to offer three criteria by which to judge existing political arrangements: inclusivity, deliberation and citizenship. But the question remains as to how democratic dialogue can be institutionalized. Smith and Wales distinguish a number of approaches to the institutionalization of democratic deliberation. The first is sceptical toward the institutions of the state, and focuses on the various associations of civil society as the natural location of deliberative politics. Smith and Wales argue that, while a vibrant civil society is an essential component of deliberative politics, the institutions of the state cannot be simply sidestepped. A second approach has suggested the supplementation of representative institutions with secondary associations, while a third has recommended the institutionalization of group representation and the need for deliberation to legitimize majoritarian decision-making rules. Smith and Wales acknowledge the value of these proposals, but argue that there is as yet few empirical case studies to substantiate the claims made on their behalf. The few case studies that have emerged have focused on the working of mainstream institutions, such as town meetings, workplace democracy, environmental planning and constitution making. Such studies are illuminating, but more valuable insights may be gained by investigating the development of novel democratic institutions such as citizens' juries, deliberative opinion polls, mediation and consensus conferencing. It is from the analysis of such innovative democratic designs, they argue, that we may learn more about the feasibility of institutionalizing opportunities for democratic deliberation.

Their chosen example is citizens' juries: such juries afford the opportunity for informed deliberation and active citizenship, and are a means of overcoming the growing divide between decision makers and the majority of the population. After having described the nature and function of citizens' juries, Smith and Wales assess them in light of the three criteria of inclusiveness, deliberation and citizenship. With respect to the first, they argue that citizens' juries approximate the ideal of inclusiveness by aiming for a broadly representative jury selection process which is able to draw on a wide range of experience and backgrounds. A number of problems are identified regarding the degree of inclusiveness. First, it is important for the composition of the jury to be fairly representative of the wider population; a simple random selection process is seen as superior to a method of stratified random sampling. Second, the population from which jurors are to be drawn should be appropriate to the nature and scale of the issue in question. Third, procedures must be in place such that all groups potentially affected by the decision have the opportunity to present evidence for the jury's consideration.

With respect to the ideal of deliberation, they assess the extent to which citizens' juries create the conditions for unconstrained and reasoned dialogue. They examine the problems faced by citizens' juries, such as the possibility of bias within the deliberative process, and the distortions that may arise at the agenda-setting stage. Even before the jury is selected there is a danger that issues, information and witnesses may be screened out of the process. Experiments with complete juror control have found that, in the initial stages, participants do not have enough knowledge of the subject to deal competently with the charge, the framing of the agenda or the selection of witnesses. In response to this problem, advocates of the jury process recommend that a steering group consisting of stakeholders should be established to develop the charge, select witnesses and set the agenda. An alternative suggestion is to bring together lay people to look at the charge in pre-jury focus groups, and to give to juries the power to alter the charge and call new witnesses as they deliberate and learn about the issues under consideration. Once jurors have come together, a number of features of the process encourage democratic dialogue and an orientation toward the common good. In most juries time is set aside at the start to draw up rules of conduct which emphasize the need to respect and listen to the arguments of others. Jurors are allowed to deliberate with only a few observers present, so that they may feel free to alter their positions in light of new evidence or arguments. The small size of the jury and the establishment of trust between participants are likely to enhance the deliberative quality of the proceedings. The role of the moderator is also crucial in fostering the discussion, encouraging an ethos of mutual respect and facilitating the decision-making process. There is growing empirical evidence that the process of deliberation has a significant effect on the participants: their preferences and judgements are markedly different from the pre-deliberative preferences of citizens which would have been aggregated within existing social choice mechanisms.

Finally, Smith and Wales assess the claim that citizens' juries, by encouraging a more active form of citizenship, have a positive effect on the values and attitudes of the participants. The empirical findings suggest that jurors become more open-minded and are more civically active long after the jury process has ended. The changes in preferences and attitudes during and after the jury process support the claims made for the transformative power of democratic deliberation. One of the important factors that facilitates attitudinal change is the sense of political efficacy gained by the participants, the extent to which they feel confident in their ability to participate and to influence the political process. Another important factor is the practice of drawing up a pre-jury contract between the commissioning body and the jury: under the terms of this contract, the commissioning body is bound either to act on the jury's recommendations or to give reasons why it has decided not to act. This not only increases the democratic legitimacy of the decision-making process but also gives jurors the sense that their deliberations will be taken seriously.

What lessons can be learned from citizens' juries? How does their practice stand up to deliberative democratic ideals? Smith and Wales argue that citizens' juries offer a good approximation to those ideals and should be seen as a valuable example of democratic innovation. However, they are not a remedy for all contemporary democracy's ills and need to be understood in a wider institutional context. At a minimum, citizens' juries should be seen as an important supplement to representative institutions, a way of bringing informed citizens' perspectives into the decision-making process. However, there is a need for further investigation of their relationship with both existing institutional forms and other innovative democratic designs such as referenda, deliberative opinion polls and mediation.

In Chapter 8 Shane O'Neill offers a normative assessment of a key aspect of the on-going cultural conflict in Northern Ireland. He examines the marching controversy at Drumcree and applies Habermas's discourse theory of rights to assess which of the conflicting claims should take priority. Rejecting the view that the claims are irreconcilable, he outlines four principles that offer a basis for just resolutions to conflicts over contentious marches in Northern Ireland.

O'Neill first sketches the political context in which the marching controversy must be understood. The problem at the root of the constitutional crisis in Northern Ireland has been the existence of a double minority. Nationalists have lived as a minority marginalized from the main institutions of the Northern jurisdiction set up by the partition of Ireland in 1921, while unionists have always been conscious of the fact that they remain a minority on the island of Ireland. So the apparent intransigence of many unionists may be explained by their insecurity within the United Kingdom and the fear that they may suffer the same kind of marginalization within a united Ireland that members of the nationalist minority claim to have suffered in Northern Ireland since partition.

The constitutional arrangement proposed by the Good Friday Agreement of 1998 is an attempt to solve this double minority problem. It seeks to protect both national communities from political domination. By setting up power-sharing arrangements and securing the principle of consent regarding any future change in constitutional status, the agreement aims to protect both national communities from discrimination and to ensure equal respect for both cultural traditions, no matter which of them is to find itself, at any particular time, in the minority.

Efforts to implement this constitutional settlement have been fraught with serious difficulties. One of the obstacles to the achievement of mutual accommodation between the two communities has been the controversy surrounding contentious marches organized by the Loyal Orders, especially with regard to the conflict at Drumcree. In stoking the fires of sectarian division such a conflict represents a serious threat to the political progress of the 1990s and to the spirit of accommodation required to make the new arrangements work. Portadown Orangemen insist that it is their right, as one of their civil and religious liberties, to parade through the mainly nationalist area surrounding the Garvaghy Road. Members of the Garvaghy Road Residents' Coalition have protested against the parade, which they view as a display of Protestant supremacy, and have asked the Orange Order to engage in direct talks with them. Both sides are insistent that they are defending their legitimate rights and both have appeared to be deeply entrenched in their positions. However, couching their claims in the language of rights opens up the possibility of their being involved in a complex debate about the nature of legally enforceable rights and the grounds of their justification. Their understanding of rights may be open to challenge, since claiming a right is not the same as justifying it.

In order to develop a convincing theoretical perspective on rights, O'Neill turns to the discourse theory of law of Jürgen Habermas. From the perspective of such a theory, legally enforceable rights are justified on the basis of inclusive and reasoned agreements among all those affected by the exercise. Rights make possible the on-going realization of a particular self-regulating legal community of free and equal citizens in its distinctive historical context. They are legitimated as the discursively agreed conditions of equal citizenship. There are certain basic categories of civil rights which are necessary to secure the conditions of equal citizenship: equal individual liberties, membership status, legal protection and communicative freedom. Citizens must also guarantee to one another rights to a basic minimum so as to render the exercise of civil rights effective for all. Finally, special rights may be granted to social groups so as to enable them to achieve equal membership status within the political community. In a deeply divided society such as Northern Ireland each national community should have the right to express its national, religious and cultural identity to an extent that is consistent with equal membership status for all citizens.

By securing the conditions for both private and public autonomy, rights make possible the realization of a self-regulating legal community of free and equal citizens. Following Habermas, O'Neill stresses that while legitimate laws must be consistent with human rights and constitutional principles, they can secure the conditions of equal citizenship only if they arc the result of a fair dialogical process that includes the different perspectives of all citizens on an equal basis. Once a law has been generated legitimately through fair democratic procedures, it is the role of the judiciary to protect and uphold the rights of the citizens by adjudicating in particular cases. Judges must apply the law in both an impartial and a contextually sensitive manner by basing their judgement on an objective reading of all the relevant facts.

Having outlined Habermas's discourse theory of law, O'Neill examines the arguments that could be put forward by those involved in the marching controversy at Drumcree. In seeking to assess the rational acceptability of the competing claims, he enters two provisos. First, an impartial judgement has to be based on an objective account of the empirical reality, one that is sensitive to the context in reflecting the perspectives of all affected. Second, the only just resolution will be one based on an impartial norm, one that all affected would have good reason to affirm as being appropriate to the context. Thus, in evaluating the claims, one must ask which of the positions expresses an impartially grounded norm that is sensitive to the context of the dispute.

O'Neill then provides, in the form of a virtual dialogue, a reconstruction of the best arguments that could be made on either side of the dispute at Drumcree. Joan, representing the position of the Orange Order, invokes a variety of familiar constitutional rights to justify the march down the Garvaghy Road, while Martha counters each of these arguments by defending the right of the residents to refuse to host the parade. Which of the positions comes closer to realizing the conditions of equal citizenship? Which can take on board the legitimate concerns of all as a basis for reasoned agreement? There is no doubt, O'Neill notes, that the rights invoked by Joan (religious liberty, freedom of expression, assembly and movement, protection of cultures from hostile forces) are important in securing equality of citizenship in a plural democracy like Northern Ireland. But the vital issue is how legitimate rights are to be applied in this context in a way that guarantees equal membership status to all citizens. Martha's arguments emphasize the need to set limits to the exercise of certain constitutionally valid rights in particular contexts. If the exercise of a right is incompatible with the equal membership status of other citizens, it cannot be legitimate in that context. By providing a more contextually sensitive account of the reality of the conflict, Martha is implicitly challenging Joan to broaden her perspective and to think of the matter from the standpoint of all those affected. By doing so she believes that she can convince Joan that these restrictions are impartially grounded in that they are based on principles that could be affirmed by all. The restrictions are needed to protect the equal membership status of the nationalist minority, just as they would be needed to protect a small unionist minority ghettoised into one area of a predominantly nationalist town.

In the final section O'Neill looks at ways in which the legitimate rights of the two national cultures in Northern Ireland can be protected without sacrificing either the civil and religious liberties of the Loyal Orders or the equal membership status of the nationalist citizens. With respect to ceremonial parades that are expressive of particular religious or national identities, he outlines four principles that would secure the conditions of equal citizenship in Northern Ireland. Each principle seeks to protect basic constitutional rights but restricts their exercise when it undermines the very grounds of their justification. All citizens should have good reasons to accept these restrictions, because they would secure equal membership status to all, no matter which of them are to find themselves, at a particular historical juncture, in the minority. In guaranteeing equal citizenship status the four principles provide a normative basis for the just resolutions to conflicts over contentious marches in Northern Ireland.

In the last chapter David Miller examines three of the most powerful critiques of the model of deliberative democracy. The advocates of such a model claim that it is *inclusive*, in the sense that each member of the political community takes part in decision making on an equal basis; that it is *rational*, in the sense that the decisions reached are determined by the reasons offered in the course of deliberation; and that it is *legitimate*, in the sense that every participant is willing to accept the outcome of a fair deliberative procedure. Each of these claims is used as a yardstick to evaluate current democratic arrangements; together they constitute a normative ideal of a fully democratic society based on fair deliberation among free and equal citizens. Such a normative ideal has faced three lines of criticism. The first originates from realist critics, who highlight the huge gap between the deliberative ideal and the actual practice of existing democracies. Large and complex societies, they argue, cannot be governed by deliberative assemblies, which, by their very nature, tend to be small and slow in reaching decisions. Moreover, even when deliberative assemblies may have a feasible role to play in decision making, there is no guarantee that they will not be used by powerful groups to advance their own interests. Politics must be seen as a struggle for the acquisition and maintenance of power, a struggle where deliberation plays a minor and ineffectual role, or serves to dress up the interests of the stronger. The second line of criticism comes from social choice theory. Here the argument is that the idea of a general will emerging from the deliberative process is an illusion. According to Arrow's 'impossibility theorem' there is no method of reaching a collective decision from an array of individual preferences that conforms to a set of conditions (such as anonymity and unrestricted domain) that we expect every democratic procedure to embody. Every procedure, including majority voting, is shown to be arbitrary and indeterminate, and this undermines both the rationality and the legitimacy claims of deliberative democracy.

Miller argues that neither the empirical criticism of the realists nor the formal criticism of the social choice theorists is fatal to the project of deliberative democracy. His main concern is to answer a third, more recent, line of criticism which claims that deliberative democracy is biased against groups that historically have been disadvantaged – the poor, ethnic minorities, women and non-white people. This is a serious criticism, because it challenges the view that deliberative democracy is capable of reaching decisions that are more socially just than those reached in existing liberal democracies, where the distribution of political power tends to reflect the distribution of social advantage. If valid, such a criticism would also call into question the claims about inclusivity, rationality and legitimacy made on behalf of deliberative democracy. Deliberative democracy may be formally inclusive, but if the debate by its very nature favours some groups at the expense of others it is not inclusive in a substantive sense. Similarly, if the reasons that count in deliberative settings are valid not for everyone but only for particular groups, the outcome cannot be described as rational. Finally, if the deliberative procedures rely on arguments and reasons that are not shared by members of disadvantaged groups, they cannot be regarded as legitimate.

In responding to this third line of criticism, Miller distinguishes two aspects, one having to do with inequality in deliberative institutions, the other with the bias of deliberative procedures. He considers the arguments of Lynn Sanders and Iris

Young to the effect that deliberative institutions are characterized by profound inequalities of access and by marked disparities of treatment. Disadvantaged groups, they claim, are faced not just with problems of unequal access to deliberative forums but with unequal treatment once they have gained entry into them. They may, for example, be reluctant to engage in political argument, feeling that they have no right to speak or that others will not take their interventions seriously. Sanders presents evidence that shows that women and members of disadvantaged groups tend to contribute less to group discussion and are less likely to have their views taken into consideration. In the case of juries, she contrasts an 'evidence-driven deliberation', which encourages the expression of a wide range of views and an attitude of open-mindedness on the part of the jurors, with a 'verdict-driven deliberation', which tries to move quickly to a yes/no decision by requiring jurors from the outset to become advocates of one or other position.

Miller's response is to note that good deliberation would require precisely that form of deliberation which corresponds to an evidence-driven jury: discussions ought to be open and exploratory at first, so that all views are taken into consideration, different options are assessed, and every participant is encouraged to engage with the perspectives of others. He makes the same point in response to Iris Young's claim that parliamentary debates and adversarial court procedures are characterized by styles of speech that are competitive, assertive and confrontational. Miller points out that deliberative theorists never claimed that parliamentary debates and adversarial courts are good examples of deliberative democracy at work. Rather, they maintain that political debate should be structured so that (1) as wide a range of views and arguments as possible is included, and (2) the final decision reflects the weight of reasons offered in its support and not the pre-established preferences or interest positions of powerful groups. Such a deliberative ideal can be approximated more or less exactly, depending partly on the structure and partly on the ethos of the deliberating body. In so far as the conditions for good deliberation correspond to forms of speech and argument characteristic of members of disadvantaged groups, a deliberative form of democracy would treat members of such groups far better, in terms of fairness and equal respect, than the institutions that Young rightly criticizes as inherently male-biased.

The second and deeper criticism levelled against deliberative democracy is whether the very idea of deliberation – that decisions be arrived at through a process of reasoned argument – is not biased against disadvantaged groups. Young claims that deliberation privileges speech that is formal and general, dispassionate and disembodied, while Sanders argues that deliberation requires a mode of discourse that is rational, restrained and orientated to shared problems, as against one that is impassioned, extreme and the product of particular interests. Both maintain that such norms of acceptable speech discriminate against women and ethnic minorities, whose perspectives and demands need to be presented in other ways. What disadvantaged groups need is not deliberation, but modes of discourse in which their distinct perspectives and concerns can emerge more clearly. Young mentions three such modes – greeting, rhetoric and storytelling – while Sanders mentions one – testimony – which closely resembles Young's notion of storytelling. Miller's response proceeds in two stages. He first considers the charge that (1) deliberation privileges speech that is rational and dispassionate at the expense of speech that is emotional and passionate; (2) it privileges formal and abstract reasoning at the expense of the concrete concerns of particular groups; and (3) it privileges speech that is moderate at the expense of speech that is extreme. He believes that none of these accusations is valid. With respect to the first, he argues that it relies on a false dichotomy between reason and emotion: political speech, to be convincing, requires both passionate expression and rational argument. With respect to the second, he argues that it creates again a false dichotomy: political argument often takes the form of linking the situation of a particular group with some general principle that has been applied in the past to other groups and now commands general assent. With respect to the third, he agrees that deliberation encourages participants to adopt moderate proposals as against radical ones, but he sees this as the inevitable outcome of democratic debate: participants in such debates must be willing to give up some of their initial claims for the sake of reaching agreement. Democratic deliberation allows each perspective to be considered on an equal basis, but cannot guarantee that any single or specific perspective will prevail at the end of the deliberative process.

Miller then considers whether the forms of discourse advocated by Young and Sanders (greeting, rhetoric, storytelling) are likely to serve the interests of disadvantaged groups better than familiar styles of deliberation. He claims that greeting cannot be a substitute for deliberation, and that rhetoric can be a divisive force in situations of conflict. As regards storytelling, he believes it suffers from three limitations. First, a person's life story becomes relevant to the wider community only when corroborated by a less personal account of the injustices suffered by her group. Second, adding together the testimony of many different individuals does not produce an overall perspective from which we can derive a solution to the problems highlighted by the various stories. A multiplicity of perspectives may give rise to conflicting accounts, in which case we may need the help of the social scientists to discover which perspective is nearest to the truth. Third, introducing unfamiliar perspectives into democratic debate may widen the perceived social distance between groups and thus weaken each group's commitment to deal justly with the others. One must strike a fine balance between emphasizing what you have in common with other members and the ways in which you are different, suffering from specific disadvantages.

Miller turns in the conclusion to the question posed by his title, and interprets it as saying, 'Is deliberative democracy materially fair to disadvantaged groups?' He believes that critics of deliberative democracy view the question as asking, 'Does deliberative democracy give adequate recognition to the perspectives of disadvantaged groups?' His concern is that fairness in the expressive sense may come at the expense of fairness in the material sense. If democratic deliberation is reduced to a talking shop in which each person has his own story to tell, one of the strongest weapons that disadvantaged groups have in their struggle for justice is rendered ineffective. For groups in this position, deliberative democracy offers the best chance of using political power to rectify social disadvantages.

Notes

1 See the survey article by James Bohman, 'The coming of age of deliberative democracy', *Journal of Political Philosophy*, 6: 4 (1998), pp. 400–25.

2 Jon Elster, 'Introduction', in J. Elster (ed.), *Deliberative Democracy* (Cambridge: Cambridge University Press, 1998), p. 1.

3 Thucydides, *The Peloponnesian War*, II, 40.

4 Edmund Burke, 'Speech to the Electors of Bristol on being Elected' (November

1774), in Iain Hampsher-Monk (ed.), *The Political Philosophy of Edmund Burke* (London: Longman, 1987), p. 110.

 5 J. S. Mill, 'Considerations on Representative Government' (1861), in J. S. Mill, *Three Essays*, intro. Richard Wollheim (London: Oxford University Press, 1975).

 6 John Rawls, *Political Liberalism* (New York: Columbia University Press, 1993; second edition 1996); Jürgen Habermas, *Between Facts and Norms* (Cambridge: Polity Press, 1996).

 7 Jon Elster, 'Introduction', in J. Elster (ed.), *Deliberative Democracy* (Cambridge: Cambridge University Press, 1998), p. 5.

 8 James Bohman and William Rehg, 'Introduction', in J. Bohman and W. Rehg (eds), *Deliberative Democracy* (Cambridge MA: MIT Press, 1997), p. ix.

 9 Joshua Cohen, 'Deliberation and democratic legitimacy', in A. Hamlin and P. Pettit (eds), *The Good Polity: Normative Analysis of the State* (Oxford: Blackwell, 1989), pp. 17, 21.

10 *Ibid.*, p. 19.

11 Bohman and Rehg, 'Introduction', p. ix.

12 David Estlund, 'Beyond fairness and deliberation: the epistemic dimension of democratic authority', in Bohman and Rehg, *Deliberative Democracy*, pp. 173–204.

13 See Chapter 9 below.

Part I

Normative perspectives

2

Political legitimacy and democratic deliberation

MAURIZIO PASSERIN D'ENTRÈVES

This chapter examines the question of legitimacy in democratic constitutional states from the standpoint of a theory of deliberative democracy. Its aim is to show that the validity of a conception of justice and the legitimacy of political institutions and public policies based upon it can be best defended on the basis of a normative theory of public deliberation. This theory, I shall argue, is superior to the two main normative models of justification that appeal to the ideal of neutrality (Rawls, Larmore, Nagel) or to the ideal of perfectionism (Raz, Galston, Kymlicka).

Justice in multicultural societies

The problem of justice and legitimacy has become particularly acute in societies characterized by the fact of pluralism. Pluralism refers to the existence of a variety of competing and often antagonistic and irreconcilable conceptions of the good life held by individuals and groups in contemporary Western societies. These competing conceptions of the good life have both an individual and a collective dimension, since they may refer to personal or to collective conceptions of the good, or be a partial combination of the two.

Although pluralism is not a uniquely modern phenomenon,[1] it has assumed greater political salience in societies composed of a number of distinct cultural groups claiming recognition of their unique collective identities (or their collective conceptions of the good). The type of recognition claimed by cultural groups, based on their ethnic, religious, gender or linguistic identity, is a claim pertaining to their collective sense of identity and their collective conception of the good. It therefore differs from the standard claim about recognition of individual identity, which liberal theory from Mill to Rawls has attempted to incorporate, more or less successfully, in its normative framework of justification. The emergence and increasing salience of multicultural groups claiming recognition of their collective identities represents, therefore, a challenge to the standard liberal model of justification. In what follows, I want to examine three responses to this challenge: the first is centred on the value of neutrality, the second on the value of autonomy and/or diversity, the third on the value of dialogue or deliberation.

Neutrality

Rawls is the best-known advocate of the model of neutrality, along with Larmore and Nagel.[2] Given the fact of reasonable pluralism, the aim is to find a basis of agreement that is neutral with respect to competing conceptions of the good life, whether individual or collective. This aim is achieved by the creation of an overlapping consensus among the variety of reasonable comprehensive doctrines, whether moral, religious or philosophical, embodying different conceptions of the good. The strength of this model lies in the acknowledgement of the fact of pluralism, seen as both inevitable and ineliminable, and in the effort to find a basis of agreement that is least controversial, since it is restricted to constitutional essentials and basic questions of justice and does not appeal to contestable comprehensive conceptions of the good. This is what Rawls calls the 'method of avoidance'. The weakness of this model lies in the strong distinction between public and non-public aspects of identity and the difficulty of defining a non-contestable notion of the 'reasonable'. The model assumes that individuals, in order to achieve an overlapping consensus on constitutional essentials, are able to set aside their personal or non-public conception of the good from the public conception of justice or the common good. For many individuals whose personal conception of the good is inextricably tied to the collective conception of the good of their group, this separation of private and public aspects of their identity is difficult to sustain. In effect, the individuals most likely to achieve and support an overlapping consensus are those for whom the separation of public and private aspects of identity is least troublesome, namely, liberal individuals.[3]

Liberal individuals have, as it were, a divisible conception of the self. But Rawls's theory aims to embrace non-liberal as well as liberal individuals, and there is some doubt as to whether his theory can successfully accommodate the former. Moreover, the very notion of what is 'reasonable' (reasonable doctrine, reasonable conception of the good, reasonable agreement) remains controversial, since its meaning varies in accordance with the different conceptions of the good (or reasonable comprehensive doctrines) held by various individuals and groups living in contemporary multicultural societies. Reasonableness thus remains a contested and contestable notion.

Perfectionism

Faced with these shortcomings of the neutrality model, some political thinkers have opted for a different model of justification, one based on perfectionist ideals, such as autonomy or diversity. They start by acknowledging the controversial – that is, non-neutral – character of liberal principles of justice and of the conception of the self that underlies them, and go on to defend liberal principles by arguing for their superiority with respect to available alternatives. By doing this, they engage on the terrain set by the communitarian critics of liberalism (MacIntyre, Sandel, Taylor, Walzer), because they eschew appeals to neutrality and defend liberalism as embodying a superior or normatively preferable conception of the good life. This strategy has been advocated, among others, by Joseph Raz, William Galston and Will Kymlicka.[4] Joseph Raz, for example, has argued that a liberal state should protect and foster all those forms of life that encourage autonomy. He believes that autonomy is a precondition of human well-being, since the value of an individual's life is enhanced if it is freely chosen from a range of available options. He also thinks that membership of a community is conducive to human well-being, because it determines the horizon of one's opportunities and helps to shape one's identity. He defends value-pluralism on the grounds that many different and incompatible ways of life are good for their members. Traditional communities which do not set a high value on freedom of choice may still be valid sources of identity for their members, and should therefore be respected and tolerated, provided that they do not oppress their members and allow them the option of exit. The liberal state is to be particularly valued because it makes available the conditions for the free pursuit of, and participation in, all those forms of life that are capable of being good for their participants. By securing certain rights to individuals and groups the liberal state makes available a range of valuable options that will permit every person or group to pursue their conception of the good, and thus secures the condition for human well-being. A similar argument has been put forward by Kymlicka in his liberal defence of group rights, which stresses the value of cultural membership and a secure cultural context for individual well-being. Other authors, such as Galston, have advocated the superiority of liberal principles by an appeal to the value of diversity, rather than autonomy. The liberal state accommodates diversity better than its rivals, since in its public principles, institutions and practices it affords maximum feasible space for the flourishing of individual and group differences, constrained only by the requirements of liberal social unity. What is common to these defences of liberal principles and institutions is a rejection of the model of neutrality in favour of a perfectionist model based on the values of autonomy or diversity. The strength of this perfectionist model of justification is that it engages in a substantive debate with the critics of liberalism and argues for the superiority of the liberal conception of the good *vis-à-vis* its possible competitors.[5] In doing so, it exemplifies what may be called a 'method of engagement' which sidesteps some of the difficulties of Rawls's 'method of avoidance'. It may indeed be a more straightforward way of defending liberal principles, since it disclaims any appeal to neutrality and enters self-consciously into a debate about the good. The weakness of this model, on the other hand, partly stems from its strength: it may allow greater debate about competing conceptions of the good life in the public-political domain, and will avoid claiming a spurious neutrality, but it will ultimately favour those individuals and groups whose conceptions of the good or well-being are predisposed to the value of autonomy and/or diversity. The perfectionist model may be a better way of defending liberal principles and institutions but is no less controversial or contestable than the model of neutrality. The aim of inclusiveness, of being able to accommodate the largest feasible range of competing and irreconcilable conceptions of the good, seems, in the end, unattainable with either model. But is this aim actually attainable? In what follows I will defend the model of deliberation or dialogue on the grounds that it is more inclusive than either the model of neutrality or that of perfectionism, but it is worth pointing out that such inclusiveness is a matter of degree. No model can achieve complete inclusiveness. Liberalism, as Taylor has put it, is also a 'fighting creed'.[6] The inevitable fact of exclusion of even the most expansive or accommodating forms of liberalism, such as that of Taylor, is what Donald Moon calls 'the tragedy of liberalism.'[7] The aim of complete inclusiveness is unattainable. There will always be tragic conflicts and tragic choices. But that should not stop us in our search for models of greater inclusiveness which will lessen the scope for tragic conflicts. The deliberative or dialogic model may provide a greater degree of inclusion, or so I shall argue, than either the neutrality or the perfectionist models.[8]

Deliberation

There are several lines of entry to the dialogic or deliberative model of justification. I shall describe briefly those put forward by Charles Taylor, Amy Gutmann and Dennis Thompson, Joshua Cohen, Jürgen Habermas, and James Fishkin.

Taylor argues in favour of a dialogic model of justification based on the recognition of the uniqueness of collective identities. He calls this model the 'politics of difference' to distinguish it from the standard liberal model which he terms the 'politics of equal dignity'. He characterizes their difference as follows:

> With the politics of equal dignity, what is established is meant to be universally the same, an identical basket of rights and immunities; with the politics of difference, what we are asked to recognize is the unique identity of this individual or group, their distinctness from everyone else. The idea is that it is precisely this distinctness that has been ignored, glossed over, assimilated to a dominant or majority identity.[9]

Thus, while the politics of equal dignity 'fought for forms of nondiscrimination that were quite "blind" to the ways in which citizens differ, the politics of difference often redefines nondiscrimination as requiring that we make these distinctions the basis of differential treatment'.[10] The example Taylor cites in defence of the politics of difference is that of the French-speaking community of Quebec. It should be granted special rights and immunities so as to be able to preserve its unique collective identity, and to maintain its cherished cultural distinctness from the majority of English-speaking Canada. Taylor's model of the politics of recognition is neither neutral nor perfectionist: it rests on the presumption of equal worth, namely that 'all human cultures that have animated whole societies over some considerable stretch of time have something important to say to all human beings'.[11] It is dialogic, in so far as it promotes cross-cultural exchange among different groups and collectivities. The aim of such an exchange is to enlarge our understanding of other cultures, so that we and they may learn something from the dialogic encounter. The aim, in other words, is to achieve a 'fusion of horizons,' to use Gadamer's well known formulation.

A similar stress on dialogue and deliberation characterizes the position of Gutmann and Thompson. They argue that controversial moral issues should not be excluded from public debate but should become the subject of collective deliberation. A liberal state, they maintain, 'must permit greater moral disagreement about policy and greater moral agreement on how to disagree about policy'.[12] The only constraints they advocate are procedural in character: 'Principles of accommodation [resting on the idea of mutual respect] govern the conduct of the moral disagreement on issues that should reach the political agenda.'[13] In a series of articles, culminating in their co-authored book entitled *Democracy and Disagreement*, they have offered a well articulated defence of the model of deliberative democracy. An important point they have emphasized is that deliberation

> may sometimes increase moral conflict in politics by opening up forums for argument that were previously closed . . . Deliberation encourages people with conflicting perspectives to understand each other's point of view, to minimize their moral disagreements, and to search for common ground, but it begins by opening politics up to a range of reasonable disagreement that is restricted by less deliberative politics.[14]

The advantage of deliberative politics over other models of justification (based on neutrality or perfectionism) is that

> in the absence of forums for deliberation mutual respect for reasonable differences is unlikely to be forthcoming and common ground is likely to be overlooked or devalued even by reasonable people since reason by itself, or reasoning by ourselves, rarely points us toward the conflicting perspectives of other reasonable people.[15]

An even stronger defence of deliberative democracy as the best institutional mechanism for the adjudication of conflicting moral and political perspectives is provided by Joshua Cohen. By deliberative democracy he means an association 'whose affairs are governed by the public deliberation of its members' and where political debate 'is organized around alternative conceptions of the public good'. Such an association requires broad and manifest equality among citizens and provides a basis for self-respect and the development of a sense of justice. Thus, when properly conducted, 'democratic politics involves *public deliberation focused on the common good*, requires some form of *manifest equality* among citizens, and *shapes the identity and interests* of citizens in ways that contribute to the formation of a public conception of common good'.[16] The idea is not to suppress difference, but to allow differences about competing conceptions of the public good to be debated in common deliberative forums that ensure the greatest degree of fairness to all participants. To this end Cohen sketches an ideal deliberative procedure that captures the notion of justification through public argument among equal citizens and serves in turn as a model for deliberative institutions. We should seek, he says, 'to mirror a system of ideal deliberation in social and political institutions'.[17] He stresses the fact that 'the ideal deliberative procedure is meant to provide a model for institutions to mirror . . . and not to characterize an initial situation [such as the original position] in which the terms of association themselves are chosen'.[18] Cohen's model of deliberative democracy is strongly normative in character and is partly indebted to Habermas's discourse theory of democracy. The relevance of such a normative theory of deliberative democracy is that it articulates the conditions under which a *fair debate* among competing collective identities and conflicting conceptions of the good can be conducted. The outcomes of debates carried out under conditions of deliberative fairness are democratically legitimate, since they are 'the object of a free and reasoned agreement among equals'.[19] Cohen's theory of deliberative democracy embodies, as all normative theories tend to do, an *ideal model* of fair deliberative procedures, but its explicit aim is to explore ways in which to institutionalize such an ideal, so as to make our social and political institutions more open to free public deliberation. It is not an ideal thought-experiment but an attempt to work out the fairest conditions for the adjudication of conflicting moral perspectives on the common good. Finally, the ideal of deliberative democracy is not a perfectionist doctrine, since it does not depend on a particular view of the good life (say, the life of active citizenship). Rather, 'it is organised around a view of political justification – that justification proceeds through free deliberation among equal citizens – and not a conception of the proper conduct of life'.[20]

The most sophisticated theoretical account of a deliberative model of democracy is provided by Jürgen Habermas. Like Cohen, Habermas offers a characterisation of an ideal deliberative procedure whose normative validity rests on the following criteria:

1 Processes of deliberation must take the form of an exchange of information and arguments backed by reasons.
2 Deliberations are inclusive and public: no one may be excluded in principle and all those affected have a right to take part.
3 Deliberations are free of any external or internal coercion that could detract from the equality of the participants.
4 Deliberations aim at rationally motivated agreement and can in principle be continued indefinitely or resumed at any time. *Political deliberations*, however, must be brought to a close by majority vote, given the institutional pressures to reach a decision. Since it is internally connected with a practice of deliberation, majority rule justifies the presumption that the decision adopted may be considered acceptable until further notice, namely until the minority convinces the majority of the correctness of its own views.
5 Political deliberations extend to all those matters that can be regulated in the equal interest of all, including matters, such as the unequal distribution of resources, that affect the equal and effective exercise of the right to participation in the political process.
6 Political deliberations, lastly, must also include the interpretation of needs, the articulation of collective identities, and the transformation of pre-political attitudes and preferences. In this respect, political deliberations must extend across the broad spectrum of moral, ethical and pragmatic discourses, as well as leaving a space for bargaining and fair compromises among conflicting and non-generalizable interests that take place in non-deliberative institutional settings. (A prime example would be corporatist forms of interests intermediation.)[21]

In contrast to Cohen, however, Habermas does not think that such an ideal deliberative procedure could be applied to society as a whole or to the entirety of its institutions. Rather, he conceives the ideal deliberative procedure as '*the core structure in a separate, constitutionally organised political system*', not as a model for all social institutions, not even for all government institutions.[22] The reason is that if, as he puts it, 'deliberative politics is supposed to be inflated into a structure shaping the totality of society, then the discursive mode of sociation expected in the *legal system* would have to expand into a self-organisation of *society* and penetrate the latter's complexity as a whole'. This is an impossible task, since 'democratic procedure must be embedded in contexts it cannot itself regulate'.[23] For this reason, Habermas advocates a *two-track model* of deliberative politics, according to which deliberative procedures operating in the formal decision-making domains of legislative and judicial activity are supplemented by informal processes of opinion formation taking place in the public sphere. Deliberative procedures in formal decision-making domains shape the processes of collective *will formation* with a view to the co-operative solution of practical questions, while informal *opinion formation* processes are geared to the identification, articulation and thematization of problems emerging from life-world experience. Thus, while the public of parliamentary bodies is 'structured predominantly as a *context of justification*', the general public of citizens located in the associational networks of civil society is structured primarily as a '*context of discovery*' made possible by a procedurally unregulated public sphere.[24] The division of labour between these two domains (formal institutions of deliberation and decision making which are procedurally regulated versus informal processes of opinion formation which are procedurally unregulated) is a fruitful one, in so far as 'democratically constituted . . . will-formation depends on the supply of informal public opinions that, ideally, develop in structures of an unsubverted political public sphere. The informal public sphere must, for its part, enjoy the support of a societal basis in which equal rights of citizenship have become socially effective'.[25] The two-track model of deliberative politics put forward by Habermas depends, in this respect, on the successful interplay between 'democratically institutionalised will-formation' and 'informal opinion-formation'.[26] The latter, operating in a procedurally unregulated fashion, is an essential complement to the former. As Habermas shows in a closely argued excursus, the alleged neutrality of the ideal deliberative procedure can be vindicated only if the formally regulated procedures of parliaments and courts are supplemented by the informal communications, debates and discussions taking place in the numerous public spheres of civil society.[27]

The last contribution to a theory of public deliberation I want briefly to advert to is that of James Fishkin. Fishkin's contribution focuses on the kinds of institutions required for the ideal of deliberative democracy to be realized in large-scale and technologically advanced societies. Such institutions must embody both *political equality* and *deliberation*. In his book *Democracy and Deliberation* (1991) and, more at length, in *The Voice of the People* (1995) he defends an institutional design based on the model of the deliberative opinion poll but also alludes to other institutional designs that embody both political equality and deliberation, such as the proposal of Philippe Schmitter and Claus Offe for every citizen to be given a 'representation voucher' and Bruce Ackerman's notion of a 'constitutional moment.'[28] His institutional proposal centred around the deliberative opinion poll embodies *political equality*, since everyone has an equal chance of being represented in the national sample of participants, and *deliberation*, since a selected group of citizens is immersed for an extended period of time (say, one or two weeks) in intensive, face-to-face debate.[29] The advantage of a deliberative opinion poll over non-deliberative or 'instant' forms of polling is that it enables a representative sample of citizens to acquire an adequate level of information on a given issue, to listen to the contrasting opinions and perspectives of experts, and to test their own views and opinions through a process of common debate and discussion. Only after such an extended period of deliberation are the members of the sample 'polled', that is, asked to give their considered judgement on a given issue. The results of a deliberative poll provide, in this respect, 'a statistical model of what the electorate *would* think if, hypothetically, all voters had the same opportunities that are offered to the sample in the deliberative opinion poll'.[30] Most important, the results of such a poll have a prescriptive, and not merely a predictive, force: 'Its results have prescriptive force because they are the voice of the people under special conditions where the people have had a chance to think about the issues and hence should have a voice worth listening to.[31] The topics under discussion in a deliberative opinion poll may vary: Fishkin suggests that deliberative opinion polls may be used to assess candidates in the American presidential primaries, but their more general purpose is to enable a selected but representative sample of people to evaluate and debate any issue that may be of public concern, such as welfare reform or the criminal justice system or voting rights legislation or campaign finance reform, to name but a few.

The point of deliberative opinion polls is to allow people to engage in a reasoned debate and to find some common ground on disputed moral, political or ethical questions. By operating in a framework characterized by political equality, participation and non-tyranny, Fishkin writes:

> a collective process [of deliberation] occurs in which the group has a reasonable chance to form its collective, considered judgments – to give its public voice, if you will, to the topic in question. Arguments on rival positions get an extended hearing, and each side has a chance to answer the other. The same information is available to all. People are present and engaged by the process. They do not merely listen. They also participate, in a context which is small enough that each can credibly believe that his or her individual voice counts. And they discuss the issues in an atmosphere of mutual respect, attempting to find common ground.[32]

The theories of deliberative democracy put forward by James Fishkin, Jürgen Habermas, Joshua Cohen and Amy Gutmann, together with Taylor's dialogic model of recognition, should be seen as providing the broad outlines of a model of normative justification, with its associated proposals for institutional reform, that is more inclusive than the two alternatives I have examined, based on the values of neutrality or perfectionism. Whether the emphasis is on the recognition of collective identities (Taylor), the adjudication of moral conflict (Gutmann), public reasoning on the common good (Cohen), formal and informal modes of collective opinion and will formation (Habermas), or the evaluation of issues of public concern (Fishkin), they all stress the importance of dialogue and deliberation for a more inclusive and just form of liberal society.

Notes

1 Nor is it a phenomenon that arises spontaneously or, as it were, 'naturally'. Rather, the formation of group identities, and the specific forms in which claims to recognition are articulated, are the result of a process of political mobilization and struggle and are shaped by the different kinds of institutional response they generate.

2 John Rawls, *Political Liberalism* (New York: Columbia University Press, 1993). See also Charles Larmore, *Patterns of Moral Complexity* (Cambridge: Cambridge University Press, 1987), and Thomas Nagel, *Equality and Partiality* (Oxford: Oxford University Press, 1991).

3 For a forceful reminder that liberal principles of justice are rationally acceptable, that is, justifiable in a strong normative sense only to liberal individuals, see Brian Barry, 'How not to defend liberal institutions', in R. B. Douglass, G. M. Mara and H. S. Richardson (eds), *Liberalism and the Good* (New York: Routledge, 1990), pp. 44–58, at p. 44: 'I want to ask what arguments are available to persuade people who are not liberals . . . that they ought nevertheless to subscribe to liberal institutions. I will examine four such arguments . . . and conclude that they are either limited in scope or dependent on dubious factual premises. The implication to be drawn is the rather depressing one that the only people who can be relied on to defend liberal institutions are liberals.'

4 Joseph Raz, *The Morality of Freedom* (Oxford: Clarendon Press, 1986) and *Ethics in the Public Domain* (Oxford: Clarendon Press, 1994); William Galston, *Liberal Purposes* (Cambridge: Cambridge University Press, 1991) and 'Two concepts of liberalism', *Ethics*, 105 (1995), pp. 516–34; Will Kymlicka, *Liberalism, Community, and Culture* (Oxford: Clarendon Press, 1989) and *Multicultural Citizenship: A Liberal Theory of Minority Rights* (Oxford: Clarendon Press, 1995).

5 A strong defence of the superiority of liberal views of the good and of a specific set of liberal virtues (such as tolerance, self-control, openness to change) is advanced by Stephen Macedo, *Liberal Virtues* (Oxford: Clarendon Press, 1990). It brilliantly exemplifies what I call a method of engagement but suffers from self-declared partiality to liberal principles and institutions. In fact it goes so far as to claim that 'Liberalism holds out the promise, or the threat, of making all the world like California' (p. 278).

6 Charles Taylor, 'The politics of recognition', in Amy Gutmann (ed.), *Multiculturalism: Examining the Politics of Recognition* (Princeton NJ: Princeton University Press, 1994), p. 62.

7 J. Donald Moon, *Constructing Community: Moral Pluralism and Tragic Conflicts* (Princeton NJ: Princeton University Press, 1993).

8 For an important statement about the importance of political inclusion, and the need to combine it with the requirement of rational agreement, see Shane O'Neill, 'The politics of inclusive agreements: towards a critical discourse theory of democracy', *Political Studies*, 48: 3 (2000), pp. 503–21.

9 Taylor, 'The politics of recognition', p. 38.

10 *Ibid.*, p. 39.

11 *Ibid.*, p. 66.

12 Amy Gutmann and Dennis Thompson, 'Moral conflict and political consensus', in R. B. Douglass, G. M. Mara and H. S. Richardson (eds), *Liberalism and the Good* (New York: Routledge, 1990), p. 125. This essay also appeared in *Ethics*, 100 (1990), pp. 64–88.

13 *Ibid.*, p. 126.

14 Amy Gutmann, 'The challenge of multiculturalism in political ethics', *Philosophy and Public Affairs*, 22: 3 (1993), p. 199.

15 *Ibid.*, p. 200. See also Amy Gutmann and Dennis Thompson, 'Moral disagreement in a democracy', *Social Philosophy and Policy*, 12: 1 (1995), pp. 87–110; 'Why deliberative democracy is different', *Social Philosophy and Policy*, 17: 1 (2000), pp. 161–80. For a more extended elaboration of their model of deliberative democracy see Amy Gutmann and Dennis Thompson, *Democracy and Disagreement* (Cambridge MA: Harvard University Press, 1996).

16 Joshua Cohen, 'Deliberation and democratic legitimacy', in A. Hamlin and P. Pettit (eds), *The Good Polity: Normative Analysis of the State* (Oxford: Blackwell, 1989), pp. 17, 18, 19.

17 *Ibid.*, p. 20.

18 *Ibid.*, p. 22.

19 *Ibid.*, p. 22.

20 *Ibid.*, p. 27. For a complementary paper to the one just discussed, focusing on the material preconditions of deliberative democracy, see Joshua Cohen, 'The economic basis of deliberative democracy', *Social Philosophy and Policy*, 6: 2 (1989), pp. 25–50. See also Joshua Cohen, 'Procedure and substance in deliberative democracy', in S. Benhabib (ed.), *Democracy and Difference: Contesting the Boundaries of the Political* (Princeton NJ: Princeton University Press, 1996).

21 Jürgen Habermas, *Between Facts and Norms: Contributions to a Discourse Theory of Law and Democracy*, trans. W. Rehg (Cambridge: Polity Press, 1996), pp. 305–6.

22 *Ibid.*, p. 305.

23 *Ibid.*, p. 305.

24 *Ibid.*, p. 307. The distinction between context of discovery and context of justification is drawn from Hans Reichenbach's theory of science. The former refers to those factors which are conducive to the generation of knowledge claims (such factors may be cognitive as well as non-cognitive), while the latter refers to those conditions under which knowledge claims are tested and accepted or rejected by the scientific community. (Such conditions, according to Reichenbach, are entirely cognitive in nature.) See Hans Reichenbach, *Experience and Prediction: An Analysis of the Foundations and the Structure of Knowledge* (Chicago: University of Chicago Press, 1938) and *The Rise of Scientific Philosophy* (Berkeley CA: University of California Press, 1951).

25 Habermas, *Between Facts and Norms*, p. 308.

26 *Ibid.*, p. 308.

27 See 'Excursus on the neutrality of procedures', in *ibid.*, pp. 308–14.

28 There have been a number of recent attempts to sketch the institutional requirements that would embody the ideal of deliberative democracy in complex and differentiated societies. See Marian Barnes, *Building a Deliberative Democracy: An Evaluation of Two Citizens' Juries* (London: IPPR, 1999); Joseph Bessette, *The Mild Voice of Reason: Deliberative Democracy and American National Government* (Chicago: University of Chicago Press, 1994); James Bohman, *Public Deliberation: Pluralism, Complexity, and Democracy* (Cambridge MA: MIT Press, 1996); Simone Chambers, *Reasonable Democracy* (Ithaca NY: Cornell University Press, 1996); John Dryzek, *Discursive Democracy* (Cambridge: Cambridge University Press, 1990) and *Deliberative Democracy and Beyond* (Oxford: Oxford University Press, 2000); John Elster, 'Arguing and Bargaining in Two Constituent Assemblies', Storrs Lectures, Yale Law School, 1991; Jane Mansbridge, *Beyond Adversary Democracy* (Chicago: University of Chicago Press, 1983); William Nelson, 'The institutions of deliberative democracy', *Social Philosophy and Policy*, 17: 1 (2000),

pp. 181–202; Carlos Nino, *The Constitution of Deliberative Democracy* (New Haven CT: Yale University Press, 1996); Anne Phillips, *The Politics of Presence* (Oxford: Clarendon Press, 1995); Michael Saward (ed.), *Democratic Innovation: Deliberation, Representation and Association* (London: Routledge, 2000); John Uhr, *Deliberative Democracy in Australia* (Cambridge: Cambridge University Press, 1998); John Urry, *Promoting Deliberative Democracy* (Cambridge: Cambridge University Press, 1998); Jorge Valadez, *Deliberative Democracy, Political Legitimacy, and Self-determination in Multicultural Societies* (Boulder CO: Westview Press, 2000); Iris Marion Young, *Inclusion and Democracy* (Oxford: Oxford University Press, 2000).

29 James S. Fishkin, *Democracy and Deliberation: New Directions for Democratic Reform* (New Haven CT: Yale University Press, 1991), p. 2.

30 *Ibid.*, p. 4. Fishkin argues that deliberative opinion polls may, in some respects, be considered as giant focus groups. They differ from conventional focus groups in being statistically representative of the entire population and in allowing a much greater degree of deliberation on the part of the participants. See *Ibid.*, p. 105 n. 7.

31 *Ibid.*, p. 4.

32 James S. Fishkin, *The Voice of The People: Public Opinion and Democracy* (New Haven CT: Yale University Press, 1995), p. 34. For a related discussion of democratic deliberation in relation to the question of political legitimacy see James S. Fishkin, *The Dialogue of Justice: Toward a Self-reflective Society* (New Haven CT: Yale University Press, 1992).

3

Five arguments for deliberative democracy

MAEVE COOKE

In its simplest terms, deliberative democracy refers to a conception of democratic government that secures a central place for reasoned discussion in political life. This conception has itself been the topic of much recent discussion, most of it favourable, with even its critics tending to acknowledge the intuitive attractiveness of democratic deliberation.[1] The new use of the label 'deliberative' by veteran political theorists John Rawls and Jürgen Habermas to describe their – quite dissimilar – normative conceptions of democracy is further evidence of its popularity.[2] Deliberative democracy, it seems, is in vogue. But does it *deserve* its current favourable reception? Why should we prefer a deliberative model to, for example, a non-deliberative participatory model or a purely procedural one? This chapter sets out to consider the merits of the main arguments commonly advanced in favour of the deliberative conception of democracy. It groups these under five broad headings.

The arguments focus respectively on (1) the *educative* power of the process of public deliberation (2) the *community-generating* power of the process of public deliberation (3) the fairness of the *procedure* of public deliberation (4) the epistemic quality of the *outcomes* of public deliberation, and (5) the *congruence* of the ideal of politics articulated by deliberative democracy with 'who we are'. Although most of these arguments express valid intuitions, the first four are insufficient – or deficient – as they stand. Even where they do offer good reasons for preferring the deliberative ideal of democracy, they require help from the fifth argument if they are to be fully convincing.

My discussion of deliberative democracy aims to show why the first four arguments are incomplete or unsatisfactory, requiring help from the fifth if they are to form part of a convincing defence of deliberative democracy. To this extent its concern is methodological. However, methodology is not purely a matter of abstract academic interest. In debates about deliberative democracy methodological issues merit attention for at least two reasons. First, since deliberative democracy is a normative conception that emphasizes public reasoning, it is particularly important that it can be defended publicly on the basis of good reasons. Second, we need arguments that can help us to choose rationally between the various deliberative models on offer today. For purposes of illustration I sketch how the fifth argumentative strategy enables us not only to justify the deliberative ideal of democracy but also to decide in a non-arbitrary way between two diverging interpretations of this ideal.

I opened with a preliminary specification of the main idea behind the deliberative conception of democracy. Clearly, this initial definition leaves many questions unanswered: questions about the kind of deliberation most appropriate for generating and testing laws, political principles and public policies,[3] about the proper domain and concerns of such deliberation[4] and about the social and institutional conditions that might facilitate it.[5] Although some of these questions will be touched on briefly in the course of my discussion, I make no attempt to treat them with the attention they deserve. Nor will I attempt a more adequate definition of deliberative democracy, for to do so would require a fuller treatment of these questions. I do, however, wish to elaborate on what is meant by 'deliberation'. By 'deliberation' I understand an unconstrained exchange of arguments that involves practical reasoning and always potentially leads to a transformation of preferences. Although public deliberation in this sense *aims* at rational agreement,[6] I freely acknowledge the likelihood that it will fail to result in consensus. The related question of whether public deliberation has a cognitive dimension – whether it is designed to produce knowledge of some sort – will be dealt with in the course of the discussion.

The process of public deliberation has an *educative* power

This argument holds that deliberative democracy should be advocated primarily because of the beneficial educative effects it has on citizens. J. S. Mill and Hannah Arendt are often mentioned as proponents of the educative view.[7] Despite some significant differences in their respective conceptions,[8] both Mill and Arendt see participation in public affairs as good in itself, not merely as instrumental in bringing about, or implementing, qualitatively better political decisions and laws. Furthermore, on this view, the benefits of participation in public affairs are primarily personal: participation improves the moral, practical or intellectual qualities of those who participate: it makes them not just better citizens – though clearly this is crucial – but also better individuals.

The educative argument is insufficient as a justification for deliberative democracy for at least three reasons. The first can be seen by posing the question: what is it about *deliberation* – as opposed to *participation* – that produces beneficial educative effects on individuals? If the argument from positive educative effects is to work as the main defence of deliberative democracy it has to show that participation in public deliberation produces benefits for the moral, practical or intellectual qualities of the participants that are *distinct from and superior to* the benefits resulting from non-deliberative participation in public affairs or, indeed, from non-participatory political action. *Distinguishing* the benefits of deliberative and non-deliberative participation seems relatively straightforward. A number of differences immediately spring to mind, for example, in the case of the former, learning how to present an argument cogently and, in the case of the latter, the feeling of achievement derived from helping to set up a residents' association group. Showing the *superiority* of deliberative participation is not so easy. The main difficulty here is that there is no uncontroversial independent vantage point from which such superiority may be measured. This undermines the usefulness of the educative argument as a principal strategy of justification and suggests that it is most convincing in conjunction with other arguments.

There is a second respect in which the educative argument is incomplete as a justification for deliberative democracy. The problem here is that the beneficial effects of participation in public deliberation cannot be the *point* of the deliberative ideal of democracy. It makes no sense to advocate participation in public deliberation solely for the sake of its beneficial effects on the moral character, practical abilities or reasoning powers of the individuals who participate. The beneficial effects can accrue only if the individuals concerned take part in deliberation for *other* reasons, for instance, in order to find out more about possible options, to reach a fair or a rational decision, or because they already uphold a particular ideal of citizenship. In short, the educative effects of participation in public deliberation are at best side effects; they cannot be the main point of, or provide the sole justification for, such deliberation.

Finally, the educative argument is insufficient in a third respect, for it leaves open the question of what counts as improving the moral, practical or intellectual powers of the individuals who participate in deliberative politics. Not all changes are for the better. The educative argument presupposes the availability of some independent standard for evaluating the individual's moral, practical or intellectual development. For this reason, too, it requires support from other arguments if it is to work as a justification of deliberative democracy.[9]

The process of public deliberation has a *community-generating* power

This justification is found most frequently among those who favour 'communitarian' versions of deliberative democracy,[10] for example the versions proposed by Benjamin Barber[11] or Charles Taylor.[12] The communitarian emphasis on the common good is often accompanied by the argument that the individual can become aware of, and consolidate, her co-membership in a collective form of life only by way of practices of public reasoning with others who owe their identities to the same values and traditions.

However, emphasis on the community-creating (or consolidating) power of public deliberation can also be found in 'liberal' versions of deliberative democracy, for example, in the version proposed by Joshua Cohen. Cohen claims that, by requiring justification on terms acceptable to others, deliberative democracy achieves one important element of the ideal of community, for it 'expresses the equal membership of all in the sovereign body responsible for authorising the exercise of that power'.[13]

The community-generating power of public deliberation is also an ingredient in 'discursive' versions of deliberative democracy, such as those proposed by Jürgen Habermas and Seyla Benhabib. These theorists conceive deliberation as a process of 'ideal role-taking' in which participants are forced to think of what could count as a good reason for all others involved in, or affected by, the decisions under discussion. On this view, not only does the discursive production of intersubjectively shared reasons have a motivating force, generating what Hannah Arendt calls 'communicative power'; the 'enlarged mentality' required for this operation is *itself* a form of solidarity.[14]

Like the educative argument for deliberative democracy, the argument that the process of public deliberation generates a sense of community or solidarity is insufficient. Moreover, it is insufficient for the same reasons. The community-generating argument runs up against the problems, first, of how to show that deliberative participation in public affairs is *superior* (in its community-generating effects) to non-deliberative participation; second, that the generation of a sense of community cannot be the *point* of participation in public deliberation but only, at most, a beneficial by-product; and third, that not all communities are equally desirable and that some independent standard for evaluating communities has to be available. Thus this argument too requires the support of other arguments if it is to form part of a convincing defence of deliberative democracy.[15]

This brings us to the third and fourth arguments. Unlike the first two, these direct our attention not only towards the *process* of public deliberation but also towards its *outcome*.

The *procedure* of public deliberation improves the fairness of democratic outcomes

This argument can be summarized as the view that the procedure of public deliberation improves the outcomes of the democratic process by making them more just, in the sense of more fair. In contrast to the fourth argument, which as we shall see posits non-procedural *epistemic* standards, the third argument advances a strictly proceduralist view. Contemporary examples of this argument can be found in the democratic theories of Seyla Benhabib and of Joshua Cohen.[16] The crucial point about strict proceduralism is that there are no non-procedural standards of fairness, the only permissible standards of adjudication are internal to the procedure itself. In other words, if the procedure is fair, the outcome is fair. Most of us are familiar with a basic version of this view of fairness: the position that democratic decisions are fair (and, on this view, also legitimate) in so far as they are produced by the fair procedure of majority rule.

As advocates of deliberative democracy Cohen and Benhabib upgrade the basic version to include deliberation. For them, democratic decisions are fair or legitimate in so far as they are produced by a fair deliberative procedure. Cohen, for example, writes that 'democratic procedures are the source of legitimacy'.[17] Benhabib, too, seems to share this view. She bases the practical rationality of the conclusions resulting from public deliberations on observance of the specified rational procedures of decision making,[18] and not on some standard of justice or fairness independent of the actual procedure.[19] It is important to note that neither Cohen nor Benhabib reduces fairness to what *actually happens* in democratic deliberative procedures.[20] Both hold normative conceptions of fairness, what Cohen describes as an ideal deliberative procedure[21] and Benhabib as a general moral theory based on a discursive model of validity.[22] However, in both cases ideal fairness provides a standard for assessing only the procedure, that is, the formal conditions of participation and argumentative exchange operating in actual deliberative procedures (for instance, whether everyone potentially affected by the outcome is equally entitled to participate or whether force other than that of the better argument is exerted). It provides no additional standards for assessing the quality of the results of deliberation.

As a justification of the deliberative ideal of democracy the proceduralist argument, too, is incomplete. As it stands it is insufficient in at least two respects. The first is a feature of proceduralist conceptions of fairness in general. David Estlund highlights the difficulty here by means of a coin flip example:

> A problem for [what he calls] the fair proceduralist approach is that, while democratic procedures may indeed be fair, the epitome of fairness among people who have different preferences over two alternatives is to flip a coin. Nothing could be fairer. In so far as we think this is an inappropriate way to decide some question, we are going beyond fairness.[23]

I take Estlund's point to be that the popular view, that the decisions resulting from majority rule are fair because the democratic procedure used to arrive at them is fair, implicitly appeals to some standard that is *external* to the democratic decision-making procedure. Otherwise why not simply flip a coin? This seems correct. However, Estlund's criticism is not straightforwardly applicable to Cohen and Benhabib, for, as we know, they both explicitly appeal to normative conceptions of procedural fairness. Nonetheless, his criticism does draw attention to a fundamental difficulty. Like the popular view that majority rule is fair, Cohen and Benhabib make use of a conception of fairness that goes beyond a strictly *procedural* conception of impartiality (e.g. flipping a coin). A more precise formulation of their respective positions would be that fair procedures produce fair outcomes that are in some normative sense fairer than other outcomes. To show this, however, they require additional arguments to explain why we should prefer the particular normative conceptions of fairness on which their theories rely. Both Cohen and Benhabib do hint at such arguments; however, this part of their respective accounts of democratic legitimacy is not well developed.[24]

There is a further respect in which the third argument requires help from other arguments. Without such help, the deliberative proceduralist view can assign only a restricted role to democratic deliberation. We can see this in the case of Cohen and Benhabib. In so far as they are strict proceduralists Cohen and Benhabib can coherently argue only that public deliberation makes the procedure itself more fair: they have to confine the normative value of democratic public deliberation to the conditions governing participation in, and the conduct of the processes of, such deliberation. Although far from redundant, this is clearly a restricted view of democratic deliberation. Equally clearly, Cohen and Benhabib hold a less restricted view. Cohen explicitly states that deliberation is concerned with the interests, aims and ideals that comprise the common good.[25] Indeed, at times he appears to advance a version of epistemic proceduralism. This is apparent, for example, in his clear implication that the results of voting[26] will be qualitatively better – more just or fair in some epistemic sense – if voting takes place subsequent to public deliberation on the issues involved; [27] or again, when he writes that 'outcomes are democratically legitimate if and only if they could be the object of free and reasoned agreement among equals'.[28] Benhabib, too, seems to swing between strict (deliberative) proceduralism and epistemic (deliberative) proceduralism. For example, she gives three reasons as to why deliberative processes are essential to the practical rationality of collective decision-making processes: (1) deliberative processes impart new information (2) deliberative processes help individuals to order their preferences coherently, and (3) deliberative processes impose a certain reflexivity on individual preferences and opinions, forcing participants to adopt an 'enlarged mentality'.[29] However, despite her explicit rejection of non-procedural epistemic standards and consequent apparent commitment to strict proceduralism, it is evident that these reasons pertain not to the fairness of the procedure but to the quality of the outcome as judged by non-procedural epistemic standards.[30]

But Cohen and Benhabib cannot have it both ways. They must *either* confine the role of democratic deliberation to improvement of the fairness of democratic procedures *or* they must provide a better explanation of how deliberation contributes constructively to the epistemic quality of democratic outcomes. We can now turn to the fourth argument, for it is precisely the constructive epistemic role of deliberation that is at issue here.

Public deliberation contributes constructively to the *practical rationality* of democratic *outcomes*

In contrast to the third argument, which derives the quality of democratic outcomes from the *procedure* of public deliberation, the fourth argument distinguishes between the fairness of the procedure and the rationality of the outcome. It thus posits independent epistemic standards for assessing the quality of the results of deliberation. Some theories of democracy posit such epistemic standards of rationality *without* asserting any connection between public deliberation and the epistemic quality of decisions and laws.[31] The fourth argument, by contrast, is distinguished by its claim that public deliberation contributes constructively to the quality of democratic outcomes (to be assessed according to epistemic standards of rationality). This argument forms part of Habermas's theory of deliberative democracy.

According to this theory – which Habermas is now careful to distinguish from his theory of moral validity (discourse ethics) – public deliberations have a cognitive dimension: they are concerned with finding the best way of regulating matters of public concern, whereby the 'best way' is judged according to standards of rationality that have a certain objectivity.[32] Often, of course, compromises are necessary. Compromises can be submitted to a fairness test only from the point of view of *how* they are reached, not from the point of view of their *content* – in other words, only from the point of view of procedural standards of fairness. On Habermas's view, however, public deliberation does not *aim* at compromises, it merely accepts them in situations in which agreement is not forthcoming; its aim is to produce results that are objectively rational. Furthermore, public deliberation in some way constructively contributes towards the rationality of democratic laws and policies, and their implementation.

I see two main problems with Habermas's argument. The first is that it appeals to an epistemic standard of rationality whose basis is quite unclear. The second is that it does not explain how public deliberation contributes constructively to the rationality of outcomes.

One way of presenting these problems is to contrast Habermas's theory of democratic legitimacy with his theory of moral validity. For our present purposes, there are two important asymmetries between these theories. The first has to do with the *epistemic* status of the outcomes of democratic and moral discourses respectively. The second has to do with the role of *deliberation*.

1. Habermas conceives moral claims in analogy with truth claims. On his view both truth claims and moral claims are cognitive claims that, if vindicated, have an objective, epistemic status. The epistemic quality of moral norms depends on three elements: (a) the procedure of discourse, which has to be conducted in accordance with exacting standards of fairness; (b) the principle of universalizability, which functions as a rule of argumentation requiring participants to check the equal general acceptability of their individual interests; and (c) the discursively achieved consensus that the disputed norm or principle is equally in the interests of all affected. Thus participation in moral discourse (public deliberation on moral matters) contributes constructively to the validity of moral norms and principles. By contrast, the legitimacy of democratic laws depends on only two ingredients: (a) the procedure of discourse, which has to be conducted according to exacting standards of fairness, and (b) a discursively achieved consensus that the laws are acceptable to all affected. In the case of moral discourses, the epistemic status of the outcome depends on whether the norms and principles in question are genuinely universalizable: the discursive procedure is designed to ensure this. In the case of democratic discourses, by contrast, the epistemic status of the laws that emerge is a

function not of their genuine universalizability but of the fact that they are generally acceptable.[33] However, *de facto* general acceptability cannot be the criterion of epistemic quality: if generally acceptable laws are to lay claim to any kind of objective epistemic status, some means of distinguishing between valid and invalid claims to general acceptability has to be available. In contrast to moral claims, where the universalizability principle acts as a test of objective validity, legitimate laws are not subject to this test. The only other independent test of the validity of laws consonant with Habermas's theory is whether or not they result from a fair procedure: this view of legitimacy would be what I have described as a strict proceduralist one, and would, as such, make the element of consensus redundant. But this is clearly not Habermas's position. If it was, his distinction between fair bargaining processes, which result in fair compromises, and legal discourses, would make no sense.[34] Similarly, his remarks on majority rule, in particular that it retains an internal relation to the search for truth, would be unintelligible.[35]

2. The second of the above-mentioned asymmetries between moral and legal norms has to do with the role of deliberation. As we have seen, in the case of moral norms, public deliberation, which has the function of testing the universalizability of interests, contributes *constructively* to their validity. But since the universalizability test is not a *criterion* of the validity of legal norms,[36] it is unclear why public deliberation is necessary. If general acceptability alone is required, voting (or indeed a coin flip) would be sufficient. In short, either Habermas must clarify how public deliberation contributes constructively to the epistemic quality of democratic outcomes or he must provide some other kind of justification of the value of democratic deliberation.

Once again, the insufficiency of the argument here points to the need for an additional argument – or perhaps an alternative strategy. The fifth argument pursues such a strategy, one that could be described as anti-foundationalist and contextualist. As I understand it, an anti-foundationalist, contextualist approach to justification has three main aspects: (*a*) it disputes the authority of timeless, objective truths as a non-controvertible foundation for science, law, political principles, morality and so on; (*b*) it acknowledges the inescapable contextualization of reason and of validity in general, and (*c*) it recognizes the fallibility of all claims to knowledge, including those of strictly philosophical inquiry. For reasons I cannot develop here, I regard this kind of anti-foundationalist, contextualist approach to justification as the most viable option for us today in the wake of the subjectivist and linguistic turns of Western modernity.[37] This brings me to the fifth argument.

Deliberative democracy elucidates an ideal of democracy that is most *congruent with 'who we are'*

The strength of this argument is that it relies on an anti-foundationalist, contextualist strategy. Of course, this in itself is not sufficient: the argument must also be convincing. Below I mention some reasons in support of it.

Some version of the fifth argumentative strategy can be found in accounts of deliberative democracy as divergent as those of Rawls,[38] Habermas,[39] Benhabib[40] and Cohen.[41] (The list could be extended: it clearly includes Richard Rorty,[42] for example, and probably Ronald Dworkin.[43]) It posits the ideal of democracy as a fundamental principle that is in a sense uncircumventable for inhabitants of modern Western modernity and deliberative democracy as the elucidation of this ideal that is most congruent with 'who we are'.

The argument that deliberative democracy elucidates the ideal of democracy most congruent with 'who we are' thus has two main elements: (1) that there are certain key normative conceptions of knowledge, of the self and of the good life that are so central to modern Western history and traditions that we can no longer meaningfully choose whether to accept or reject them, and (2) that a deliberative model of democracy makes best sense of these normative conceptions.

The following four examples could be mentioned in support of the claim that for inhabitants of Western modernity some normative conceptions of knowledge, of the self and of the good life are not simply a matter of choice but are constitutive of their deepest self-understandings:

1 The view that there are no authoritative standards independent of history and cultural context that could adjudicate claims to epistemic validity, particularly in the areas of science, law, politics and morality, and that knowledge in these areas should be construed fallibilistically.
2 The view that autonomous reasoning is a valuable part of human agency.

3 The view that publicity is important, especially in the realms of law and politics.
4 The view that everyone is in principle deserving of equal respect as an autonomous moral agent with a distinct point of view.

The ideal of deliberative democracy fits well with these normative conceptions. If there are no authoritative standards of scientific, legal, political or moral validity independent of history and cultural context, and if knowledge is still deemed possible in these areas, then some alternative means of deciding between rival justifications has to be found. If, in addition, knowledge in these areas is construed fallibilistically – that is, if it is seen as never final and conclusive but always open to challenge and revision in light of new evidence and arguments – open-ended, unconstrained rational argumentation seems the most appropriate forum for adjudicating rival claims.

This 'desacralized' view of knowledge, which goes hand in hand with the secularization of authority and which is acknowledged to be one of the defining characteristics of Western modernity, helps to explain the value attached to autonomous reasoning, in particular to two of its main ingredients, rational accountability and objectivity of judgement.[44] By 'rational accountability' I mean the individual's readiness to accept responsibility for her judgements, (self-) interpretations and life history as expressed in a willingness and ability to provide reasons in support of her claims to validity and to enter into an open-ended, unconstrained discussion of these reasons, if necessary.[45] By 'objectivity of judgement' I mean the individual's ability to engage in a critically detached, informed, perceptive and flexible way with her surroundings, with other persons and with her own judgements, (self-) interpretations and life history.

The desacralization of knowledge also helps to explain the value attached to publicity, both in the weaker sense that rational outcomes must be capable of being made public and in the stronger sense that justifications themselves should be public. However, for a more adequate account of the value attached to publicity in the latter, stronger sense, we need to draw on a further principle: the principle of equal respect for citizens as autonomous moral agents with a distinct point of view.

Equal respect in this sense means that *everyone* is deemed capable (in principle) of making an informed and insightful judgement on moral matters; more precisely, that no one's argument should be discounted on grounds of race, sex, class, and so on. This implies that in rational discussions in which moral arguments are advanced (and such arguments are always in principle relevant in discussions of laws, political principles and public policies), every citizen's contribution must be seen as worthy of consideration.

We may note that this in turn suggests a conception of political autonomy in terms of an ideal of self-authorship: citizens are held to be politically autonomous in so far as they can see themselves as authors as well as subjects of the law (political principles, public policies and so on). If combined with the desacralization of knowledge it suggests, in addition, a deliberative interpretation of self-authorship. For, if there are no timeless, authoritative standards of legal, political or moral validity, then in order for citizens to be able to see themselves as authors in this sense, they must be able to see the law, political principles and public policies as the outcome of a process of public deliberation whose aim is the best possible justification of the proposals under discussion.

These four elements of the modern Western self-understanding – the view that claims to validity are a matter for open-ended, unconstrained rational discussion, the value attached to autonomous reasoning and to publicity and the principle of equal respect for citizens as autonomous moral agents with a distinct point of view – can be combined to provide a strong argument in favour of deliberative democracy, for they imply the need for an environment in which all citizens have an equal opportunity, and are equally encouraged, to contribute to public deliberation on matters of common concern. Furthermore, since one central purpose of such deliberation is to discuss the merits of arguments with the aim of producing outcomes that have the best possible justification, no restriction may be placed on the kinds of reasons deemed permissible in a given case nor may the outcome of deliberation be determined in advance; deliberation so conceived is thus unbounded in principle and has an in-built transformatory potential.

With these brief remarks I have indicated some reasons supporting the fifth argument. However, this argument must not only be convincing, it should also be useful. Even if accepted as correct, the fifth argument runs up against the objection that its underlying strategy is too weak to be helpful, for it appears to be compatible with a variety of widely diverging models of deliberative democracy. Indeed, I myself have claimed that some version of the argument can be found in the models proposed by Rawls, Cohen, Benhabib and Habermas – models that clearly diverge in significant respects. Since of the foregoing the two that diverge most widely are proposed by Rawls and Habermas, I focus on them in dealing with this objection. To meet the objection fully it is necessary to show that the fifth argumentative strategy permits a rational decision in favour of one or other of these models, of some combination of the two, or against both of them. I argue that it provides good reasons for preferring Habermas's model to Rawls's.

One possible explanation of the differences between Rawls and Habermas with respect to deliberative democracy is that each gives different and equally convincing interpretations of – or, at least, different weightings to – the key elements of our history and traditions with which the deliberative ideal is supposed to be congruent. Such an explanation would undermine the usefulness of the fifth argumentative strategy, for it would make it too weak to be helpful in deciding between the various deliberative models on offer today. Fortunately, therefore, I disagree with such an explanation.

An alternative explanation seems to me both more plausible and more promising. This explanation acknowledges the significant overlap between Rawls's and Habermas's respective evaluation of our history and traditions, and, furthermore, explains the differences between their conceptions in terms that allow us to choose between them in a non-arbitrary way.

For our present purposes, it is important to note that Rawls and Habermas are in agreement regarding the centrality of the four elements of modern Western history and traditions I have mentioned above. My contention in the following is that Rawls's interpretation of these elements is less convincing than Habermas's. Furthermore, that a sympathetic reading of Rawls's theory of deliberative democracy – one that attempted to remedy its main deficiencies – would produce a theory that closely resembled Habermas's, at least with respect to its deliberative components.

The respective conceptions of Rawls and Habermas concur on the following points:
1 Both acknowledge the absence of authoritative standards for adjudicating legal and political validity claims independently of cultural context and history, while recognizing the need for alternative epistemic standards.

2 Both support a principle of equal respect for citizens as moral agents with a distinct point of view.
3 Both point towards an ideal of personal autonomy according to which rational accountability is a valuable part of human agency. (Rawls disputes that his conception is committed to any such ideal: I shall come back to this.)
4 Both stress the importance of publicity in the realms of law and politics and uphold an ideal of political autonomy as self-authorship.

Corresponding to these four points of agreement I see four (interconnected) respects in which Rawls's model of deliberative democracy is less convincing than Habermas's. (The latter is used mainly for purposes of contrast in the following.) In all four respects the arguments that I bring to bear against Rawls's model either appeal directly to the fifth argument or are consonant with its anti-foundationalist, contextualist strategy.

The four respects in which Rawls's model of deliberative democracy is less convincing than Habermas's are:
1 It makes use of a normative conception of deliberation to which it fails to do justice. Furthermore, this normative conception of deliberation *should* be central to a theory of deliberative democracy for it fits best with 'who we are'.
2 Rawls's demarcation of the public from the non-public gives rise to problems within his theory. Furthermore, this demarcation is connected with a contentious postulate of the irreconcilability of ethical differences that produces, in turn, a contentious interpretation of 'the fact of reasonable pluralism' and a conception of tolerance that fails to fit with 'who we are'.
3 Rawls's conception of deliberative politics points in the direction of a conception of personal autonomy that he explicitly rejects as an acceptable basis for his political conception of justice. Furthermore, this conception of autonomy *should* be central to a theory of deliberative democracy for it is a key element of 'who we are'.
4 Rawls proposes a normative conception of political autonomy that is too limited and insufficiently deliberative from the point of view of a deliberative ideal of democracy congruent with 'who we are'.

In conclusion I want to deal briefly with each of these points.

1. Not only is Rawls's political theory of liberalism usually included in the broad family of normative models of deliberative

democracy, he himself now explicitly identifies it as a member.[46] Claiming that his political theory of liberalism is concerned with well-ordered constitutional democracies understood also as deliberative democracies, he clearly implies that his idea of public reason subscribes to the deliberative ideal. Nonetheless, closer inspection reveals that its deliberative features are not obvious. The idea of public reason requires of citizens to consider what kinds of reasons they may reasonably give one another when fundamental political questions are at stake.[47] However, only one of its aspects makes any reference to public *reasoning*. This is the aspect of reciprocity: the citizens must check the compatibility of the principles of political justice they advocate and vote for with the comprehensive doctrines of all other citizens. The condition of reciprocity ties in with the duty of civility, which requires citizens to be able to explain to one another on fundamental questions how the principles and policies they advocate and vote for can be supported by the political values of public reason. It can be seen from this that the Rawlsian 'condition of reciprocity' and 'duty of civility' outline a conception of public reasoning that is not deliberative in the sense of 'deliberation' I introduced initially (that is, deliberation as the free exchange of arguments involving practical reasoning and always potentially leading to a transformation of preferences). By contrast with this specification, public reasoning is presented by Rawls as an essentially 'monological' or *private* process in which citizens work out for themselves whether the advocated political principles are reasonable in the sense of capable of being reasonably accepted by all. What is missing from the Rawlsian conception of public reasoning is its dynamic, transformatory dimension: for Rawls, public reason is not a dynamic process of reasoning that *generates* normative agreement through the transformation of preferences but an idea imposing a *constraint* on publicly acceptable political principles.[48] Given this depiction of public reason as a process that can in principle be carried out privately, Rawls's explicit comparison of his conception with Rousseau's is not surprising. But Rousseau, as is well known, proposes a model of democratic politics that *rejects* public deliberation.[49] For this reason it can be argued that Rawls's non-deliberative interpretation of the idea of public reason fails to do justice to its own commitment to a deliberative ideal of democracy.

Rawls himself seems implicitly to have acknowledged this

deficiency. In his most recent work there is evidence of a shift towards a more transformatory conception of deliberation. Rawls now specifies what he calls the wide view of public reason, which allows that reasonable comprehensive doctrines may be introduced in public political discussion at any time, provided that in due course proper political reasons – and not ones supported solely by comprehensive doctrines – are presented sufficient to support whatever the comprehensive doctrines are introduced to support.[50] The broad view of public reason is less 'monological' than his original one, because it opens the way for the parties in a dispute to explain to one another how their views do indeed support their basic values.[51] However, although it moves in the direction of the normative conception of deliberation referred to in the foregoing, the transformatory dimension of public reason is still underplayed. The main purpose of introducing comprehensive doctrines into public political discussion appears to be *reassurance*: political opponents reassure each other of their respective allegiance to basic constitutional and political values; they do not anticipate, or even hope for, modification of their own or of their opponents' views.[52]

Rawls's – still inadequate – shift away from a 'monologically' construed conception of deliberation towards a more transformatory one supports my general thesis in this chapter: that the fifth argument gives us non-arbitrary grounds for preferring a more extensively and vibrantly deliberative model to a more restricted and cautious one. As I have already suggested, some of the key normative conceptions shared by inhabitants of Western modernity concerning knowledge, the self and the good life provide the basis for maximizing unconstrained public deliberation that has an in-built transformatory potential. Thus, in so far as Habermas's model of deliberative politics can be said to promote such unconstrained, transformatory public deliberation, it may claim to be more in tune with 'who we are' and in this respect superior to Rawls's model.

A transformatory potential is a central element of Habermas's twin-track theory of democracy. This twin-track theory is designed to allow for the dynamic interplay between particular needs and concerns and general laws and policies.[53] On his view, public deliberation is important both in the formally organized processes of political decision making and legislation, and in the 'anarchic' processes of will formation in the public sphere; he also insists on the need for constant interpenetration of the two dimensions: prevailing laws and policies must constantly be open to challenge (on grounds of their probable ethical bias) by objections formulated in 'anarchic' processes of will-formation.[54] In addition, he emphasizes that no topic is immune to thematization and critical scrutiny in public deliberation.[55] In short, citizens engaged in public deliberation along both tracks of democratic decision making and will formation should be prepared to discuss *any* of their preferences, and to modify them as a result of valid objections. Admittedly, Habermas's deliberative model of democracy does not quite live up to its own promise. In particular, its account of (ethical-) political discourses is inadequate and misleading. However, its shortcomings are not so much structural as problems of execution and, as I have argued elsewhere, can be remedied fairly easily.[56]

2. Rawls's demarcation of the public from the non-public gives rise to problems within his theory and opens it to objections from the fifth argument. Rawls insists that the idea of public reason applies only to the basic structure of society. By this he means a society's main political, social and economic institutions and how they fit together into one unified system of social co-operation from one generation to the next.[57] He usually specifies the subject of public reason as 'constitutional essentials' and 'matters of basic justice', emphasizing that its principles do not apply to the 'background culture',[58] understood as the many associations of civil society – churches and universities, scientific societies, professional groups and so on.[59] However, he also insists that the idea of public reason is not a view about specific political institutions or policies but rather a view about the *kinds of reasons* on which citizens are to rest their political cases in making their political justifications to one another.[60]

There are two main problems with Rawls's position here. First, his claim that public reason does not apply to the 'background culture' is unsustainable. This is evident from some of his own examples, for instance, his remarks on the family as part of the basic structure.[61] Rawls rejects as a misconception the objection that, since the family is an association within civil society, the principles of public reason do not apply to it and thus fail to secure justice for women and children. While reiterating his position that the principles of political justice do not apply to such associations (thus, like churches, families do not have to be democratic), he claims that they do impose certain constraints. Specifically, they guarantee the basic rights and liberties, and the freedom and opportunities, of all family members. Rawls also formulates his position in this regard as the need to distinguish between the point of view of people as citizens and their point of view as members of families and other associations. However, this distinction is ultimately unsustainable. Tellingly, Rawls ends his argument with an approving reference to Mill's critical comment on the family. Mill claimed that the family in his day was a school for male despotism, inculcating habits of thought and ways of feeling and conduct incompatible with democracy. Rawls draws from this the conclusion that the principles of justice can plainly be invoked to reform the family.[62] But is hard to see how they could be invoked in that way *without* applying directly to the internal life of the family – which is precisely what Rawls denies.[63] Furthermore, if the principles of justice are applicable to the family on the grounds that families inculcate the political virtues required of citizens in a viable democratic society, then people must also be able to invoke them in order to reform the churches, universities and other associations of civil society wherever these inculcate habits of thought and ways of feeling and conduct that are incompatible with democratic values. And again, it is very difficult to see how this could be done without profoundly affecting the internal life of the churches, universities and other associations.[64] It seems clear, therefore, that – contrary to what Rawls himself claims – the principles of political justice *do* require families, churches and so on to be democratic in significant ways, for otherwise they could not promote habits of thought and ways of feeling and conduct that are compatible with democratic values.

The second problem has to do with the psychological burdens the demarcation of the public from the non-public imposes on citizens. Rawls's citizens are expected to be divided selves, offering different kinds of reasons in support of their convictions in official forums, in which constitutional essentials and matters of basic justice are under discussion, than they may offer in discussions within the many associations that are part of the background culture. In the former case, they may offer only reasons that they might reasonably expect others, as free and equal citizens, reasonably to accept; in the latter case, they may also offer reasons rooted in their particular comprehensive doctrines. Thomas McCarthy puts his finger on the difficulty here: '[on Rawls's conception] political discussion would have to be radically transformed whenever the venue changed in relevant ways, even if the very same people were discussing the very same issues. . . . The conceptual, psychological, cultural and institutional problems this avoidance strategy raises are formidable.'[65] Moreover, these problems are not solved by Rawls's specification of the broad view of public reason for, as we know, citizens may introduce reasons rooted in their comprehensive doctrines only where in due course these can be shown to be compatible with political reasons. It is easy to think of cases, such as political discussions of policies on abortion or treatment of animals or the environment, where the deep convictions held by some citizens provide them with strong reasons to reject the proposed policy – reasons, however, that they could not reasonably expect other citizens to accept. In such discussions, therefore, the citizens concerned would have to impose a considerable check on their deepest convictions. The psychological difficulties here give rise to further problems – for example, moral problems concerning the appropriate treatment in a given case of those obliged to accept political reasons that override their deepest convictions. This problem is compounded by the fact that, in any society with a diversity of comprehensive doctrines, the psychological burdens are unlikely to be distributed evenly. For, given the fit between the idea of public reason and certain 'liberal' conceptions of the self and the good life (in particular, as I argue below, an ideal of autonomous agency), the psychological burden will be lightest for those whose deepest convictions are fundamentally compatible with these 'liberal' conceptions.[66] This is not to deny that Rawls may be right to grant priority to publicly acceptable reasons when it comes to laws and public policies: the point is that his conception as it stands fails to take sufficiently seriously the psychological burdens that this prioritization may impose on citizens, and the moral and other kinds of problems that may arise from it.

Rawls's demarcation of the public from the non-public is connected with a contentious interpretation of the 'fact of reasonable pluralism'. As is well known, the distinguishing feature of Rawls's political conception of liberalism is that it is freestanding: it is presented as independent of, and as not derived from, any of the comprehensive doctrines subscribed to by the citizens who find it reasonable.[67] Rawls uses the image of a module: the political conception is a module that fits into and can be supported by various reasonable comprehensive doctrines in the society regulated by it. On its own this freestanding character is not problematic; it becomes so only in conjunction with his peculiarly *static* interpretation of the 'fact of reasonable pluralism'. Rawls takes this to mean that differences between comprehensive views are irreconcilable.[68] Accordingly, his conception calls for a kind of tolerance of ethical differences that accepts them unquestioningly as incapable of resolution, exempting them from public deliberation rather than attempting to overcome them productively.

The fifth argument offers at least two reasons for rejecting Rawls's interpretation of 'the fact of reasonable pluralism'. The first is that Rawls's postulate that ethical differences are irreconcilable in principle is not in itself a key normative element of modern Western history and traditions, nor does it evidently follow from any other such element. The most likely candidate in this regard would be the principle of tolerance, for this is indeed a central normative conception formative of the modern Western self-understanding. But the principle of tolerance merely enjoins us to live peacefully alongside those whose comprehensive doctrines are unacceptable and distasteful to us. It does not advocate the withdrawal of comprehensive doctrines from the hermeneutic endeavours – or indeed the critical objections – of others, nor tell us that normative convergence between currently opposed comprehensive doctrines is in principle impossible. Indeed, it seems not only possible but desirable to combine the principle of tolerance with a plea for hermeneutic openness and for unconstrained critical exchange between mutually opposing comprehensive doctrines since, for reasons already indicated, such a deliberative (in the sense of transformatory) interpretation of the principle of tolerance fits well with 'who we are'.

A second reason for rejecting Rawls's interpretation of the 'fact of reasonable pluralism' (together with its accompanying conception of tolerance) is that it is at odds with the modern Western understanding of personal autonomy, which is in turn a key normative element of 'who we are'. The value of personal autonomy is sometimes disputed by communitarian and by feminist thinkers. In my view, however, their criticisms apply only to certain *interpretations* of the concept of autonomy and offer no compelling reasons for rejecting it as an ideal. Elsewhere I have argued for a reconceptualization of personal autonomy that takes on board the valid objections raised by feminists and others.[69] Most important for our present purposes, personal autonomy on my proposal involves an orientation towards evaluative conceptions of the good. Through its connection with 'strong evaluation' autonomy is given an intersubjectivist interpretation: it calls for rational accountability concerning personally held conceptions of the good life. The individual agent who aspires to autonomy must be willing and able to give a rational account to others of her subjectively held strong evaluations. In doing so she appeals to a conception of validity that cannot be understood in a purely subjectivist manner but has a context-transcendent, or 'objective', moment. However, under conditions of modernity ascertaining the 'objectivity' of strong evaluations is considerably complicated by the absence of timeless, universally acknowledged standards for adjudicating validity. 'Objectivity', if it is possible at all, now has to be construed in an anti-foundationalist and contextualist way. This entails recognition of the contexualized and essentially fallible character of reason and suggests the need for critical engagement with all relevant arguments advanced in unconstrained intersubjective processes of rational deliberation. Thus, by virtue of its connection with strong evaluation, personal autonomy has an inherent intersubjective dimension that enjoins individuals to open their subjectively held evaluative conceptions to rational challenge by others. This aspect of personal autonomy calls, in turn, for a conception of privacy as a space that is essentially permeable.[70] Rawls's demarcation of the public and the non-public, which grants protection against uninvited criticism to comprehensive doctrines, thus undermines the intersubjective aspects of ethical agency and as a result does not fit well with a notion of personal autonomy that is a key normative element of 'who we are'.

For reasons mentioned in the last section, Habermas's model is superior to Rawls's in its interpretation of the 'fact of reasonable pluralism' for it allows for the productive interchange between, and possible modification of, opposing ethical views. For the same reason it also fits better with the ethical aspect of personal autonomy, which opens up comprehensive doctrines to challenge on the basis of good reasons and allows for a conception of privacy that immunizes no topics against thematization in public debate.

3. Rawls's model points in the direction of a conception of personal autonomy that he explicitly rejects as an acceptable basis for his political conception of justice. Rawls equips his citizens with two moral powers, a capacity for a sense of justice and a capacity for a conception of the good.[71] Correspondingly, they are both reasonable and rational: they are reasonable agents who desire for its own sake a social world in which they, as free and equal, can co-operate with others on terms all can accept and who, moreover, are ready to discuss the fair terms that others propose; they are also rational agents who have the capacity to form, to revise and rationally to pursue a conception of their rational advantage or good.[72] According to Rawls, however, such agents are not personally autonomous. He insists that his political conception relies only on an idea of *political* autonomy. It does not affirm the moral value of personal autonomy, for to do so would undermine the constraint of reciprocity.[73] This is because 'many citizens of faith reject [the moral value of personal] autonomy as part of their way of life' and thus could not reasonably accept it as part of a political conception of justice.[74]

It is not easy to make sense of Rawls's objection to affirming the moral value of personal autonomy as part of his political conception of justice. In particular, it is not easy to understand his statement that many 'citizens of faith' reject it. This statement is puzzling, for it is clear that the ideal of personal autonomy is incompatible only with *certain kinds* of religious faith. More specifically, it is incompatible only with doctrines that deny that divine authority has to pass through the filter of human reason, that human beings are unique moral agents capable of reasoning, and that all human beings are equal in this respect. It is hard to imagine why reasonable and rational agents as defined by Rawls should deny any of these principles; consequently, it is hard to understand why reasonable and rational agents who are also 'citizens of faith' should find the ideal of personal autonomy unacceptable. This difficulty is compounded by the fact that religious conviction *per se* is not seen by Rawls as an impediment to accepting his political principles. Indeed, one of the main points of his political liberalism is to show that there need be no conflict between religious faith and the political principles of justice, provided only that the religious doctrines in question are reasonable.[75] He is also clear as to what this entails. This can be seen from his 'perfect example of an overlapping consensus', in which he distinguishes between 'reasonable' and 'unreasonable' religious convictions: drawing on the work of Abdullahi Ahmed An-Na'im, Rawls shows how an Islamic justification for constitutionalism can overlap with secular and other justifications to endorse a constitutional regime. [76] Here the main point he takes from An-Na'im's argument is that only Muhammad's early Mecca teachings, and not the later Medina teachings, are compatible with arguments endorsing a reasonable constitutional democracy, for only the former support equality of men and women and complete freedom of choice in matters of faith and religion. This is an unambiguous example of how some religious comprehensive doctrines can be regarded as reasonable whereas others cannot.

Most interesting for our present purposes is that Rawls here seems to acknowledge the *psychological* importance of consistency between citizens' comprehensive doctrines and the political principles of justice. Otherwise his insistence that an overlapping consensus is possible only between those who hold reasonable comprehensive doctrines would make no sense.[77] We would therefore expect him to recognize a similar psychological need for consistency between the normative ideal of agency underlying his conception of political autonomy and the various normative ideals of agency affirmed by citizens in their 'non-public' lives. Since he does not, we must seek some explanation.

One possibility is that Rawls does not perceive any lack of consistency. His position may be that the attributes of agency presupposed by the notion of political autonomy are sufficiently consistent with the attributes of agency his citizens affirm in their non-public lives. There would thus be no gap or discrepancy of the kind indicated and thus no significant psychological problems. However, Rawls's explicit statements to the effect that his citizens are not required to value personal autonomy seem to rule out this interpretation. Nor can the problem be dismissed as a quibble about the meaning of personal autonomy. Although there are many interpretations of this ideal, there are certain core convictions common to all of them. One of the least controversial of these is the conviction that human beings themselves must be able to endorse their conceptions of the good, which means: have good reasons for affirming them. (I have argued that, under conditions of modernity, this conviction becomes what I have called rational accountability: a readiness to supply reasons in support of one's claims, if challenged.) We may note that Rawls offers a formulation of *political* autonomy that appeals to the need for rational justification (though not to the requirement of rational accountability): political autonomy requires citizens to be able fully to endorse the constitution and the laws to which they are subject.[78] In other words, when his citizens don their political cap and assume their role as public reasoners, they are guided by the normative idea of reasonableness – by the view that being able rationally to justify the validity of the laws that govern their lives is important. However, Rawls is quite clear that this normative idea need not be operative in their non-public lives. When citizens doff their political caps and revert to their various roles in non-public life, they are required only to be rational (in his sense). Admittedly, they are expected to possess a *capacity* for reasonableness, but that, presumably, may lie dormant in non-public life. We will recall that 'rationality' as defined by Rawls does not require agents to justify their validity claims to anyone – not even to themselves. Indeed, we have seen that, on his account, rational and reasonable agents may even have moral (for example, religious) reasons for *rejecting* the normative idea of rational justification with respect to the conceptions of validity they hold in their non-public lives.

From the foregoing it is evident that Rawls allows for a possible gap between the attributes of agency valued by citizens when acting or reasoning publicly and those valued when they act or reason non-publicly. Moreover, he seems unperturbed by it. I think he is wrong to be unconcerned. In the previous section I criticized his failure to take seriously the psychological difficulties (and attendant moral and other problems) that arise when citizens are required to offer different kinds of reasons as public reasoners from those they may wish to give as non-public ones. A similar criticism can be made here. In so far as Rawls's citizens affirm the value of political autonomy while conceivably rejecting the parallel non-public value, they will be 'divided selves' with the psychological and other problems entailed by that. Against this Rawls could argue that no serious psychological difficulties arise from the division. But such an argument would be undermined by the fact that he elsewhere appears to acknowledge the need for psychological consistency: as indicated, the very idea of an overlapping consensus is premised on the need for citizens to perceive compatibility between political principles and their comprehensive doctrines.

In short, Rawls runs into problems if he does not attribute a commitment to personal autonomy to his citizens, whereas no obvious problems ensue if he does so. For, as we know, Rawls sees no conflict in principle between religious faith and political principles. Moreover, the objection that it would make his political conception of justice unnecessarily exclusionary is unconvincing, for it seems to disregard the fact that Rawls's conception *already* excludes those who are not reasonable. Indeed, it seems to imply that a non-exclusionary conception of political justice is possible. But against this it can be argued that *all* political systems are exclusionary to some degree. If this argument is correct, it is more important to address the moral and other kinds of problems arising as a result of political and social exclusion than to bemoan a given conception's failure to live up to an impossible ideal.[79] In short, Rawls's political conception of justice could only benefit from explicit acknowledgement that citizens must recognize the value of personal as well as political autonomy. This does not, of course, mean that they have to embrace an interpretation of autonomy that relies on an atomistic, voluntaristic, or otherwise discredited, picture of human agency.[80]

Habermas's conception is superior to Rawls's also in this third respect. In his theory there is no tension between citizens' commitment to the ideal of political autonomy and their normative conceptions of human agency. He defines political autonomy in terms of citizens' capacity 'to view themselves jointly as authors of laws to which they are subject as individual addressees'.[81] Political autonomy as self-authorship is then presented as co-original with, and as presupposed by, a conception of private autonomy,[82] at the core of which is a normative notion of human agency as rationally accountable.[83]

There are, in addition, reasons external to Rawls's theory for acknowledging the connection between deliberative democracy and personal autonomy. In the last section I mentioned an independent reason for preferring a model of democracy that is guided by a normative conception of human agency as personally autonomous: that such a conception of agency is a key element of modern Western traditions and history and the conceptions of self and of the good life that have emerged from them.[84] As Habermas puts it, it is the 'dogmatic' core of the deliberative paradigm.[85] Interestingly, with this formulation Habermas draws explicitly on the fifth argumentative strategy:

his explanation of why such dogmatism is harmless is that it merely expresses the idea that autonomy is not a matter of choice for us who have developed our identities in particular socio-cultural forms of life.[86]

4. In addressing the third respect in which Rawls's model of deliberative democracy is less preferable than Habermas's I have already touched on the fourth one. This has to do with the ideal of political autonomy. I contend that Rawls's model produces a conception of political autonomy that is less congruent with 'who we are' in two main respects. First, in so far as it limits the exercise of political autonomy to matters pertaining to the 'basic structure', that is, to constitutional essentials and matter of basic justice. Second, in so far as it is in principle 'monological', that is, not internally dependent on the process of public deliberation. Since these two objections reiterate arguments advanced in the foregoing with regard to other aspects of Rawls's theory, there is no need to say much about them here. For the sake of clarity, however, I shall briefly set out the main points of criticism, once again by contrast with Habermas's conception.

Rawls and Habermas share an interpretation of political autonomy as self-authorship. Citizens are politically autonomous when they are able to see themselves jointly as authors of laws to which they are subject as individual addressees. Although the metaphor of self-authorship is encountered more frequently in Habermas's writings,[87] it is also suggested by Rawls's various formulations of political autonomy – for example, where he defines citizens as politically autonomous when they fully endorse the constitution and the laws to which they are subject;[88] moreover, Rawls appears to accept the metaphor of self-authorship when comparing his conception of political autonomy with Habermas's.[89] Despite this apparent agreement, however, there are two significant differences between their conceptions. In each case, Habermas's conception can be said to be preferable in that it is more congruent with the normative conceptions of knowledge, the self and the good life that are part of the evaluative horizon of Western modernity.

First, Rawls's conception accords a more limited place to political self-authorship. Citizens are deemed politically autonomous if they are able to express their interest in self-authorship with regard to constitutional essentials and matters of basic justice. Self-authorship in other areas of social life (for instance, in the area of public policy making or informal public opinion formation, not to mention the many associations of civil society) is seen as irrelevant. By contrast, Habermas extends the interest in self-authorship to *all* areas of democratic decision making and opinion formation – to matters under discussion in the informally organized domains of the public sphere as well as in the more formal organs of government. If, as I have argued, the ideal of autonomy with its core value of rational accountability is a key normative conception within Western modernity, then a model of politics that places value on its maximal exercise in all areas of social life fits best with 'who we are'. This constitutes one reason for preferring Habermas's conception of political autonomy to Rawls's.

Second, Rawls's conception of political autonomy has no explicitly deliberative component. As we have seen, the normative ideal of self-authorship requires citizens to be able to endorse the reasonableness of a law or political proposal. On Rawls's account, however, such endorsement does not have to be the result of a public process of deliberation but can take place 'monologically', that is, by each citizen privately. By contrast, at least on the reading I favour, Habermas's conception of political autonomy is directly tied to the actual process of public deliberation. To be sure, at least two different interpretations of Habermas's conception are possible here: one that ties political autonomy to the (epistemic) rationality of democratic *outcomes* and one that ties it to the *process* of public deliberation. I have already called attention to some problems connected with the view that deliberative procedures contribute constructively to the epistemic rationality of democratic outcomes – problems that will be encountered by any interpretation of political autonomy that ties it conceptually to the epistemic validity of democratic outcomes. For this reason I wish to avoid a reading of Habermas's conception of political autonomy that defines it in such terms. On an alternative reading, political autonomy is defined in terms of *participation* in actual processes of legislation and political decision making. The ideal of self-authorship requires citizens to be able to accept laws and policies as valid for reasons they themselves can accept as valid. We might say: political autonomy as conceived by Habermas aims for the closest possible convergence of legitimacy with justification.[90] Public deliberation is necessary in order to maximize such convergence, for it is an attempt to find the laws, principles and public policies that can be justified as most appropriate. Given the absence of authoritative standards for adjudicating such justifications, citizens have no way of knowing whether or not the laws, principles and policies that are eventually agreed on are epistemically valid. Nonetheless, public deliberation *aims* to ascertain what is objectively right in the given context (even if there is no way of knowing whether this has been achieved) and is necessary for the kinds of reasons mentioned by Benhabib: to facilitate the exchange of information, for the coherent ordering of preferences and for the enlargement of mentality. This is the sense in which public deliberation is a cognitive process. Citizens engage in this cognitive exercise because they have an interest in political self-authorship, that is, in minimizing the gap between legitimacy and justification. However, it is the *process* and not the outcomes of public deliberation that is the locus of political autonomy. Thus, in contrast to what Benhabib herself implies, the cognitive dimension of public deliberation cannot be explained in terms of democratic procedures (nor, indeed, as she sometimes, with Habermas, suggests, in terms of democratic outcomes): it becomes intelligible only through reference to the *process* of democratic deliberation. Connected with this is a normative conception of political autonomy that calls on citizens to look for the best justifications of the laws, principles and policies that govern their lives and to seek these justifications through processes of public deliberation. The desire for public processes of reasoned justification – for what I have called rational accountability – thus constitutes the heart of deliberative democracy. If, as I have argued, the deliberative ideal of democracy fits best with 'who we are', it is because of this emphasis on rational accountability – and not because it offers a vision of perfect ethical harmony which holds out hope that ethical disagreements could, someday, finally be overcome.

Conclusion

My discussion in the foregoing has had two main aims. First, to show that even good arguments in favour of deliberative democracy (such as, for example, the 'educative' and 'community-generating' ones) depend, in the end, on a fifth argument – the argument that the principles of deliberative democracy incorporate normative conceptions of knowledge, of the self and of the good life that are most congruent with 'who we are'. With respect to this first aim, I see three further tasks as particularly important: (1) to defend more adequately the centrality of the normative conceptions of knowledge, of the self and of the good life that I have identified by offering a convincing explanation of why they have often been disregarded in the history of Western modernity, most notably in the twentieth century by National Socialism and fascism; (2) to explain how a contexualist strategy of the kind I have proposed can avoid reducing normative standards of validity to mere cultural preferences;[91] and (3) to defend more adequately the deliberative ideal of democracy by showing that the dangers to which it is prey – in particular, manipulation of public processes of deliberation for sectional strategic purposes – do not undermine its basic principles but rather can be accounted for, and responded to, within the deliberative conception itself.

My second main aim was to show how the fifth argumentative strategy can be used to argue for the superiority of certain models of deliberative democracy and to expose the weaknesses in others. Although in these pages I have confined myself to discussion of the respective merits of just two of the conceptions of deliberative democracy currently on offer, my thesis, of course, goes further. In my view, the fifth argumentative strategy can be used as a basis for critically examining all other contemporary conceptions of deliberative democracy and for deciding between them, if necessary. It provides a basis, for example, for rejecting certain 'communitarian' conceptions on the grounds that they reject the value of personal autonomy or for rejecting certain 'liberal' models on the grounds that they postulate individual liberties that are conceived not as *political* rights but rather as antecedent to, and for ever removed from, the process of political deliberation. As such it is not just the best available defence of deliberative democracy, it can be put to good use in contemporary debates on the merits of diverging interpretations of the deliberative ideal.

Notes

1 See, for example, J. Johnson, 'Arguing for deliberation', in J. Elster (ed.), *Deliberative Democracy* (New York: Cambridge University Press, 1998), pp. 161–84, and L. Sanders, 'Against deliberation', *Political Theory*, 25: 3 (1997), pp. 347–76.

2 J. Rawls, '"The idea of public reason" revisited', *University of Chicago Law Review*, 64: 3 (1997), pp. 765–807 (at p. 772); J. Habermas, 'Three normative models

of democracy', *Constellations*, 1: 1 (1994), pp. 1–10, and J. Habermas, *Between Facts and Norms*, trans. W. Rehg (Cambridge MA: MIT Press, 1996), especially chapter 7.

3 For example, questions about whether deliberation should be public rather than private, collective rather than individual, and carried out by citizens themselves or by representatives on their behalf.

4 For example, questions about whether deliberation should be restricted to the judiciary, parliament and other governmental forums or extended to the less formal organizations and groupings of civil society; in addition, questions about whether its principles should apply only to constitutional essentials and matters of basic justice or should extend to public decision making and opinion formation in general.

5 For example, questions about the kind of substantive equality required if it is to function effectively and about the kind of educational arrangements that would help to foster it.

6 Cf. M. Cooke, 'Are ethical conflicts irreconcilable?', *Philosophy and Social Criticism*, 23: 2 (1997), pp. 1–19.

7 See, for example, the introduction to J. Bohman and W. Rehg (eds), *Deliberative Democracy* (Cambridge MA: MIT Press, 1997), p. xiii, and J. Fearon, 'Deliberation as discussion', in Elster, *Deliberative Democracy*, pp. 44–68 (at p. 59). The frequent inclusion of Mill and Arendt in the ranks of advocates of deliberative democracy is strange, for both are concerned primarily with participatory public action rather than public deliberation.

8 Mill's picture of participation is more individualistic: he stresses the importance of the *personal* discharge of some public function, local or general; see J. S. Mill, 'Representative Government', in his *Utilitarianism, On Liberty, and Considerations on Representative Government* (London: Dent, 1972), p. 207. Although Arendt, like Mill, sees the benefits of participation as accruing to the individual, she differs from Mill in her emphasis on 'acting in concert', that is, on the community-generating power of participation; see H. Arendt, *On Violence* (London: Allen Lane, 1970), p. 44.

9 It should be clear from this that I do not reject the educative argument as a partial justification of deliberative democracy. Quite the opposite: I believe that there is a need for institutional arrangements that foster participation in public affairs on account of its educational benefits.

10 For a discussion of three models of deliberative democracy (the 'liberal', the 'communitarian' and an alternative 'discursive' model) see R. Forst, 'The rule of reasons: three models of deliberative democracy', *Ratio Juris* (forthcoming).

11 Cf., for example, B. Barber, *Strong Democracy* (Berkeley CA and Los Angeles: University of California Press, 1984), pp. 232–3.

12 Cf., for example, C. Taylor, 'Cross-purposes: the liberal–communitarian debate', in N. Rosenblum (ed.), *Liberalism and the Moral Life* (Cambridge MA: Harvard University Press, 1989), pp. 159–82.

13 J. Cohen, 'Procedure and substance in deliberative democracy', in S. Benhabib (ed.), *Democracy and Difference* (Princeton NJ: Princeton University Press, 1996), p. 102.

14 Cf. Habermas, *Between Facts and Norms*, pp. 147–8, also p. 308; S. Benhabib, 'Toward a deliberative model of democratic legitimacy', in Benhabib, *Democracy and Difference*, pp. 71–2.

15 Again, this is not to deny that the community-generating effects of deliberative democracy provide good arguments in favour of deliberative democracy. Quite the

opposite: there is a need for institutional arrangements that foster its community-generating aspects.

16 Cohen and Benhabib clearly also draw on other kinds of argument in their attempts to justify deliberative democracy. As indicated, both appeal to the community-generating power of deliberation. In addition, as suggested below, both appear to propose an epistemic argument (whereby democratic outcomes are deemed valid according to some non-procedural epistemic standard). Finally, both also seem to pursue the fifth argumentative strategy (whereby deliberative democracy is justified because it is most congruent with 'who we are').

17 J. Cohen, 'Deliberation and democratic legitimacy', in Bohman and Rehg, *Deliberative Democracy*, pp. 67–91 (at p. 73).

18 Thus she writes, 'in many instances the majority rule is a fair and rational decision procedure . . . it is not the sheer numbers that support the rationality of the conclusion, but the presumption that if a large number of people see certain matters a certain way as a result of following certain kinds of rational procedures of deliberation and decision making, then such a decision has a presumptive claim to being rational unless shown to be otherwise' (Benhabib, 'Toward a deliberative model of democratic legitimacy', p. 72). Earlier in the same essay she implies that the ideal discourse model is useful only from the point of view of the procedural constraints it imposes on actual deliberative procedures and not from the point of view of testing the epistemic validity of their outcomes (p. 70).

19 Benhabib's 'interactive universalism' departs from Habermas's moral theory in giving up the latter's insistence on consensus. Correspondingly, her model of deliberative democracy focuses on the conditions governing participation in deliberation rather than on the epistemic status of its outcome. See my critical discussion of this aspect of Benhabib's approach in M. Cooke, 'Habermas and consensus', *European Journal of Philosophy*, 1: 3 (1993), pp. 260–4.

20 David Estlund fails to appreciate this. See D. Estlund, 'Beyond fairness and deliberation: the epistemic dimension of democratic authority', in Bohman and Rehg, *Deliberative Democracy*, pp. 173–204.

21 Cohen, 'Deliberation and democratic legitimacy', pp. 73–5.

22 Benhabib, 'Toward a deliberative model of democratic legitimacy', p. 70.

23 Estlund, 'Beyond fairness and deliberation', p. 176.

24 Cohen, for example, claims that democracy is 'a fundamental political ideal' (see 'Deliberation and democratic legitimacy', p. 68); however, he fails adequately to account for its normative status. Benhabib, too, hints at an account of the normative status of her version of fair proceduralism when she associates her approach with those of Rawls and Habermas, both of whom share the 'assumption that the institutions of liberal democracies embody the idealised content of a form of practical reason' ('Toward a deliberative model of democratic legitimacy', pp. 68–9).

25 Cohen, 'Deliberation and democratic legitimacy', p. 77.

26 We should note that neither Cohen nor Benhabib maintains that fair democratic decisions must result from consensus reached in actual processes of public deliberation: both accept that fair decisions may result from a vote, subject to some form of majority rule. See Cohen, 'Deliberation and democratic legitimacy', p. 75, and Benhabib, 'Toward a deliberative model of democratic legitimacy', p. 72.

27 He writes that 'the results of voting among those who are committed to finding reasons that are persuasive to all are likely to differ from the results of an aggregation that proceeds in the absence of this commitment' (Cohen, 'Deliberation and democratic legitimacy', p. 75).

28 *Ibid.*, p. 73.

29 Benhabib, 'Toward a deliberative model of democratic legitimacy', pp. 71–2.

30 Benhabib acknowledges that a deliberative model suggests a necessary but not sufficient condition of practical rationality as procedures can always be misapplied,
misinterpreted and abused ('Toward a deliberative model of democratic legitimacy', p. 72). However, on the strictly proceduralist view, deliberation is not evidently even a necessary condition of the practical rationality of the outcome.

31 David Estlund's epistemic proceduralism is an example here. See Estlund, 'Beyond
fairness and deliberation'.

32 Habermas frequently refers to the cognitive dimension of democratic deliberation.
See, for example, Habermas, *Between Facts and Norms*, pp. 147 and 151.

33 See, for example, *ibid.*, pp. 124–5, 154–7, 450–4.

34 *Ibid.*, pp. 166–8.

35 *Ibid.*, p. 179.

36 Habermas acknowledges that some legal norms do satisfy the criteria of moral
validity; for example, human rights that are positively valid as constitutional
norms may also be justifiable as *moral* rights, i.e. as morally justified norms of
action (see *ibid.*, pp. 454–6). However, this does not undermine his point that legal
norms are addressed only to the members of a specific political community and not
to human beings in general.

37 I argue, however, that it must be supplemented by an 'objectivist' account of socio-
cultural learning. See M. Cooke, 'Between "objectivism" and "contextualism": the
normative foundations of social philosophy', *Critical Horizons*, 1: 2 (2000), pp.
193–227.

38 Cf. J. Rawls, 'Kantian constructivism in moral theory', *Journal of Philosophy*, 77:
9 (1980), p. 519: 'what justifies a conception of justice is not its being true to an
order antecedent to and given to us, but its congruence with our deeper understanding of ourselves and our aspirations, and our realization that, given our
history and the traditions embedded in our public life, it is the most reasonable
doctrine for us'.

39 Cf. Habermas, *Between Facts and Norms*, especially chapters 3 and 4.

40 See Benhabib, 'Toward a deliberative model of democratic legitimacy', pp. 68–9.

41 See Cohen, 'Deliberation and democratic legitimacy', p. 67, where democracy is
described as a 'fundamental political ideal'.

42 See R. Rorty, 'Idealizations, foundations, and social practices', in Benhabib,
Democracy and Difference, pp. 333–5.

43 See R. Dworkin, *Law's Empire* (Cambridge MA: Harvard University Press, 1986).

44 Elsewhere, I have argued in favour of an interpretation of personal autonomy in
terms of four main elements: rational accountability, independence in the sense of
objectivity, purposive rationality and exercise of the capacity for strong evaluation.
For a summary of my argument see M. Cooke, 'A space of one's own: autonomy,
privacy, liberty', *Philosophy and Social Criticism*, 25: 1 (1999), pp. 23–53, especially pp. 25–30.

45 Here I endorse Habermas's position that rational accountability is a central ingredient of modern conceptions of autonomy. See M. Cooke, 'Habermas, autonomy
and the identity of the self', *Philosophy and Social Criticism*, 18: 3–4 (1992), pp.
269–91. The place of rational accountability within my normative conception of
personal autonomy is outlined in Cooke, 'A space of one's own'.

46 See Rawls, ' "The idea of public reason" revisited'.

47 *Ibid.*, p. 766.

48 Benhabib refers to it as a regulative principle. See Benhabib, 'Toward a deliberative theory of democratic legitimacy', p. 76.

49 Cf. J-J. Rousseau, 'The Social Contract', in G. D. H. Cole (ed.), *The Social Contract and Discourses* (London: Dent, 1973), especially Book 2, chapters III and VI. In clarifying the difference between the will of all and the general will Rousseau argues *against* public deliberation (see p. 185). Furthermore, he argues that in order for the people to see the good, public guidance in the shape of a legislator – as opposed to public processes of deliberation – will be necessary (see p. 193).

50 Rawls, 'The idea of public reason', in J. Bohman and W. Rehg (eds), *Deliberative Democracy*, pp. 135–6, and Rawls, '"The idea of public reason" revisited', pp. 783–7.

51 Cf. Rawls, '"The idea of public reason" revisited', pp. 785–6.

52 *Ibid.*

53 Habermas, *Between Facts and Norms*, pp. 312–14.

54 See Habermas's example of women's struggle against false and repressive interpretations of their needs (J. Habermas, 'Struggles for recognition in constitutional states', *European Journal of Philosophy*, 1 (1993), pp. 128–55 (at pp. 132–3), and *Between Facts and Norms*, pp. 418–27).

55 Habermas, *Between Facts and Norms*, pp. 312–13.

56 See Cooke, 'Are ethical conflicts irreconcilable?', pp. 9–16.

57 J. Rawls, *Political Liberalism* (New York: Columbia University Press, 1993), pp. 11–15.

58 Rawls, '"The idea of public reason" revisited', pp. 767–8.

59 Rawls, *Political Liberalism*, p. 220.

60 Rawls, '"The idea of public reason" revisited', p. 795.

61 *Ibid.*, pp. 787–94.

62 *Ibid.*, p. 788.

63 He denies this explicitly on at least two occasions: see *ibid.*, pp. 789 and 790.

64 Rawls denies that the principles of political justice may apply to the internal life of a church, see *ibid.*, p. 789.

65 T. McCarthy, 'Kantian constructivism and reconstructivism: Rawls and Habermas in dialogue', *Ethics*, 105 (1994), p. 52.

66 Cf. my argument concerning liberalism's inevitable exclusions in M. Cooke, 'Authenticity and autonomy: Taylor, Habermas and the politics of recognition', *Political Theory*, 25: 2 (1997), pp. 258–88.

67 Rawls, *Political Liberalism*, p. 12.

68 See, for example, Rawls, '"The idea of public reason" revisited', p. 766, where he glosses the fact of reasonable pluralism as follows: 'Citizens realize that they cannot reach agreement or even approach mutual understanding on the basis of their irreconcilable comprehensive doctrines.' Similarly, in the same article he emphasizes that political liberalism is primarily concerned with conflicts deriving from irreconcilable comprehensive doctrines as opposed to ones deriving from differences in status, class position and so on, or to ones deriving from the burdens of judgement (pp. 804–5).

69 See M. Cooke, 'Questioning autonomy: the feminist challenge and the challenge for feminism', in R. Kearney and M. Dooley (eds), *Questioning Ethics* (London: Routledge, 1998), pp. 258–82.

70 See Cooke, 'A space of one's own'.

71 Rawls, *Political Liberalism*, pp. 18–20 and 103–4.

72 *Ibid.*, pp. 49–52. Rational agents are not solely self-interested; they lack, however, the form of moral sensibility that underlies the desire to engage in fair co-operation as such, and to do so on terms that others as equals might reasonably be expected to endorse.

73 Although Rawls tends to formulate his position as one that does not affirm the value of autonomy, it is clear from the context that he means the moral value of personal autonomy.

74 Rawls, 'The idea of public reason', pp. 132–3. Cf. also Rawls, *Political Liberalism*, pp. 98–9; Rawls, '"The idea of public reason" revisited', p. 778.

75 This is especially clear in Rawls's '"The idea of public reason" revisited', pp. 780–3.

76 *Ibid.*, pp. 782–3 n. 46.

77 Cf. *ibid.*, p. 801.

78 Cf. J. Rawls, 'Reply to Habermas', *Journal of Philosophy*, 92: 3 (1995), p. 155.

79 See Cooke, 'Autonomy and authenticity'.

80 See Cooke, 'Questioning autonomy'.

81 J. Habermas, 'Reconciliation through the public use of reason', *Journal of Philosophy*, 92: 3 (1995), p. 130.

82 *Ibid.*, pp. 126–31; see also *Between Facts and Norms*, pp. 127–31.

83 Cf. Cooke, 'A space of one's own', especially pp. 38–48.

84 This is often disputed by communitarian and by feminist critics. Against this I argue that we need to reconceptualize personal autonomy in order to take on board some of the valid objections that have been levelled against it (see Cooke, 'Questioning autonomy'). In an apparently new twist to the critique of autonomy S. Mendus criticizes modern political philosophy for giving centrality to the value of autonomy on the grounds that to do so is to neglect what is most important in people's lives. She targets in particular the interpretation of autonomy as self-authorship, arguing that such authorship is secondary to successful *reading* of one's self and situation. Against Mendus it could be argued that her analysis in fact reveals the importance of a reworked conception of autonomy – one that includes the ability to interpret one's self and environment objectively, that is, in an informed and insightful manner. See S. Mendus, 'Out of the doll's house', *Philosophical Explorations*, 1 (1999), pp. 59–69.

85 Habermas, *Between Facts and Norms*, pp. 445–50.

86 *Ibid.*, p. 446.

87 Cf. Habermas, 'Reconciliation through the public use of reason', p. 30, and Habermas, *Between Facts and Norms*, p. 126.

88 Rawls, 'Reply to Habermas', p. 155.

89 *Ibid.*, pp. 153–5.

90 Cf. *ibid.*, pp. 175–6, for a helpful discussion of this distinction.

91 See Cooke, 'Between "contextualism" and "objectivism"'.

4

Deliberation, citizenship and identity

MATTHEW FESTENSTEIN

The theory of deliberative democracy is usually viewed as an account of the legitimacy of political decisions. It expresses an ideal of democratic decision making as a process of reasoned public discussion of arguments for and against some proposal with the aim of arriving at a judgement which is generally acceptable. Arguments for deliberative democracy have overwhelmingly been concerned with establishing that democracy conceived as a process of this sort possesses a legitimacy lacking from democratic procedures which are understood merely as mechanisms for the aggregation of private interests or preferences. According to the latter conception:

> Voters pursue their individual interest by making demands on the political system in proportion to the intensity of their feelings. Politicians, also pursuing their own interests, adopt policies that buy them votes, thus ensuring accountability. In order to stay in office, politicians act like entrepreneurs and brokers, looking for formulas that satisfy as many, and alienate as few, interests as possible. From the interchange between self-interested voters and self-interested brokers emerge decisions that come as close as possible to a balanced aggregation of individual interests.[1]

By contrast, proponents of deliberative democracy argue that the process of public debate, discussion and persuasion prior to the aggregation of votes is crucial to the legitimacy of the outcome. Key arguments advanced on its behalf include: that this process informs and improves the preferences which lie behind votes; that it allows the public to approach more closely the right or best answer to the problem facing voters; and that the process of public deliberation embodies a standard of fairness in decision making. The literature on deliberative democracy has been concerned to flesh out the details of this contrast, to offer a fuller specification of the reasons to prefer deliberative democracy, and to suggest ways in which this ideal conception may be employed, as a critical criterion or standard for institutional reform.[2]

The purpose of this chapter is different, although it is an exploration (as with so much of this literature) of the normative foundations, rather than knotty institutional detail, of deliberative democracy. In outline, the argument is this. Deliberative democracy, as it is usually conceived, entails 'special obligations' among participants in deliberation: that is, obligations which they owe to one another but not to those outside the deliberative process. These include the obligation to provide reasons in the deliberative process which all can accept, to listen to and sincerely respond to the reasons and arguments of others, and to try to arrive at a proposal acceptable to all. However, these obligations are not straightforwardly derivable from the three central justificatory arguments for deliberative democracy. This presents a choice: either to amend the schedule of deliberative obligations, on the one hand, or to derive them from another feature of deliberative democracy, which is not emphasized in the core justificatory arguments.

The final section explores this latter strategy by suggesting that deliberative democracy, if it is understood along the lines initially sketched, presupposes a notion of community. I differentiate this perspective from the argument, persuasively set out by David Miller, that deliberative democracy requires, or benefits from, a shared national identity. This is the claim that special obligations may derive from a facet of the identity, and particularly the national identity, of participants in the deliberative process: as Miller puts it, a successful deliberative democracy rests on:

> the idea of a community with a shared way of life which serves as a source of ethical standards and as a framework within which people will want to justify their decisions to one another by reference to shared criteria of justice . . . If our concern is with the politics of the state, the community in question must be the nation'.[3]

In the final section I suggest some reasons why, even if one follows the 'special obligations' line taken here, this latter claim needs to be diluted heavily if it is to be plausible.

Deliberative obligations

In fleshing out the deliberative conception certain attributes are usually ascribed to the citizens who engage in this process of discussion.[4] First, there is a shared commitment to continued coexistence: this is a strategy of 'voice', not 'exit'. Second, they possess diverse and conflicting goals, ideals, and interests, which they wish to further through democratic politics. There is no presumption that citizens possess what Jon Elster calls a non-instrumental view of politics, which views political activity as beneficial regardless of the success or failure of that activity.[5] Citizens may view political activity in this way, but the standard conception of deliberative democracy does not require that they do so. Nor is there a presumption that a regime of deliberative democracy will eradicate these differences. As Amy Gutmann and Dennis Thompson write of one sort of difference, moral conflict, 'moral disagreement is a condition with which we must learn to live, not merely an obstacle to be overcome on the way to a just society'.[6] Third, citizens share a commitment to furthering these goals specifically through public deliberation, which they recognize as conferring legitimacy on the policy or law arrived at.

Public deliberation is usually understood as a stylized process of discussion or debate. The focus of this chapter is on the terms in which this discussion is meant to proceed. Deliberative theorists have emphasized the need for inclusiveness and equality of access to the process. If, as Bernard Manin writes, 'a legitimate decision . . . is one that results from the deliberation of all', the need to ensure that all in fact do or may take part in the deliberative process becomes paramount.[7] The focus of this chapter is not directly on the equality of opportunity to influence political decisions, although it has an indirect bearing on how we understand the relationship between the norms of deliberation and political equality. Instead the concern here is with what the deliberative process must be like if it is to be distinguished from a process of discussion which is non-deliberative. Deliberative theorists converge on the following demanding conditions for this process, although, as I shall argue, they do so from different directions. Citizens taking part in the deliberative process are held to be under a peculiar set of obligations.[8] These include:

1. *The obligation to offer arguments persuasive to all other participants in the deliberative process.* On the standard

conception of deliberative democracy, participants in the deliberative process are required not only to offer arguments but to offer arguments persuasive to all: there is no presumption then that some members of the deliberating body do not count. As Joshua Cohen puts it, deliberation aims at finding 'reasons persuasive to all who are committed to acting' on its results, and participants are committed to 'providing reasons that they sincerely expect to be persuasive to others who share that commitment'.[9] This is not of course to impose the impossible requirement that one's arguments should agree with all the beliefs of one's interlocutors: the point is precisely to change their minds, at least with respect to the proposal at issue. There is plainly a question here about the limits of the duty to offer generally persuasive arguments: if I persist in failing to draw the simplest inference from your arguments or base my reception of them on bizarre or horrible assumptions, how long should you pour resources in trying to communicate your reasons to me? But I want here to accept this obligation provisionally as an intelligible as well as essential component of deliberative democracy.

2. *The obligation to respond to the reasons and arguments of others qua reasons and arguments.* What is meant to matter in deliberation is not bargaining power but only the force of the better argument: participants give their reasons 'with the expectation that those reasons (and not, for example, power) will settle the fate of their proposal'.[10] This exercises a crucial equalizing function in the deliberative process. If participants are not under this duty they are free to respond to the relative bargaining strength of others, with the result that those positioned so as to stymie the process of decision making, to help build a coalition, or offer an attractive deal, will benefit at the expense of those who lack such bargaining resources. This obligation then means that the arguments and point of view of the weak are taken into consideration, although there is no presumption that a position of weakness in itself confers any particular authority on their arguments or point of view. Here too there is a question about limits: ought one to take seriously into consideration any point of view or argument – say, that of a proponent of slavery?[11] Some writers suggest that there are features of the process of public deliberation which help to 'launder' it of horrible proposals and insupportable reasons.[12] Others insist on the necessity of 'entry rules', pre-political normative criteria which

mark out certain points of view as unreasonable and therefore not admissible into public deliberation.[13] Setting aside the important question of limiting cases, however, deliberative theorists agree on the requirement that participants take seriously the arguments of all.

3. *The obligation to modify proposals in the light of the arguments and reasons put forward in the deliberative process in order to arrive at a commonly acceptable proposal.* Here too it is necessary to distinguish this from the implausible demand that participants are required always to arrive at an agreement which is wholly satisfactory to all. Some theorists cast a reasoned agreement as a regulative ideal, which, although it may not be possible in actual cases, should nevertheless inform the conception of actual deliberation.[14] Others stress that the fairness of the procedures themselves gives the outcomes normative weight.[15]

Only on a narrowly rationalist interpretation of deliberation is this obligation collapsed into the first two. From this perspective, the emergence of good reasons for some proposal is a sufficient condition for the parties to deliberation to agree on it. If all the good arguments favour redirecting resources away from the building of trunk roads and into the improvement of railways the latter policy has been vindicated in deliberation. However, this misconceives deliberation in an important way, since the good reasons given for a proposal are often not a sufficient condition for convergence on it. For public deliberation is not usually understood purely as a process of exchange of reasons, filtering out the bad ones, but as a forum in which the point of view of each is taken seriously. But taking someone's point of view seriously in this context cannot be a matter of listening to her patiently and then explaining to her why she is wrong, lacking in good reasons for her point of view. Rather, each person's point of view should be accommodated in the outcome. This is often not possible, but it is part of the ideal of deliberative democracy that the participants should aim at this mutual accommodation.

The obligation to arrive at a commonly acceptable outcome is distinct from the obligation to offer and respond to reasons. Believing this need not imply any thesis about the irreparable cognitive defects of fellow citizens. An alternative ground for believing in the distinctness of this obligation is the claim that reasons may not determine the acceptability of particular proposals – in any case requiring a decision there may be lacking 'uniquely determinate solutions rationally compelling upon all'.[16] One basis for this claim about underdetermination is value pluralism, the thesis that there are important human values which are plural, unrankable, incommensurable and often incompatible.[17] From this standpoint, there may be good reasons to support strict privacy laws and good reasons too to support press freedom, but there is no presumption that there exists a unique and rationally compelling determination of which policy should be pursued. As several authors have emphasized, this pluralism may characterize the relationship among particular virtues (prudence, spontaneity), political ideals (liberty, equality, community) and moral theories (deontology, consequentialism). If pluralism holds for one or more of these dimensions we have a reason to reject the claim that good reasons furnish a sufficient condition for convergence.

It does not follow that good reasons do not constitute a necessary condition for the kind of convergence which is acceptable to deliberation. Pluralism does not imply that there are no reasons to prefer one course of action to another, only that there is no presumption that there is a uniquely determinate solution which rationally compels each of us. The deliberative theorist can hold that the outcome of deliberation must be reasoned, and not merely the product of arbitrary plumping for one alternative rather than another: embracing pluralism does not require rejecting the first two obligations.

Value pluralism is not the only ground for resisting the rationalist interpretation of public deliberation. The other, independent reason is that for deliberation to be democratic requires 'respecting the voices of individual citizens in the formation of the popular will. Respecting them requires not only taking individuals each to be important sources of political argument that ought to be heard, but also accepting their claims as to some extent "self-originating", or as not requiring any basis or justification'.[18] This may appear anathema to public deliberation, with its emphasis on reasons and arguments. Yet public deliberation, as initially sketched above, is not only a process of clarifying technical and moral beliefs but also an arena in which one attempts to further one's desire and interests, and in which participants together try to find ways in which differing and sometimes conflicting interests and desires can be accommodated.

This conception of deliberation finds space for the notion of deliberating towards a reasoned compromise. Indeed, it is arguable that a deliberative resolution to many or most political controversies involves an ineradicable element of compromise as the 'bread and butter of democratic deliberation'.[19] Participants accommodate each other's ends, not only by conceding the force of good reasons but by acknowledging that the claims put forward in deliberation may (*ceteris paribus*) have a force by virtue of being the claims of fellow citizens. Compromise may take the form of splitting the difference, as in a wage dispute. But it may take the form of an arrangement which seeks to recognize the arguments on each side of a dispute as they emerge and change in the process of public deliberation.

The deliberative obligations, as outlined here, do not determine the scope of democratic decision making – whether this process should govern many or only a few decisions – or the extent to which there are external constraints (considerations of justice or rights, for example) on deliberative decisions. However, it is intended to indicate the unity of these obligations: for deliberative democrats, one cannot pick and choose among them, for example, by generously offering reasons to persuade others while self-righteously refusing to modify one's own position in response to their reasons and arguments. A further point to make here is that the concern of this chapter is with public deliberation only in the relatively narrow sense summed up in these obligations. Critics of deliberative democracy often insist that it is incomplete and glosses over the 'vulgar fact that under democracy deliberation ends in voting. And it is the result of voting, not of discussion, that authorizes governments to govern, to compel.'[20] The question of the relationship of deliberation to the legitimacy of the outcomes of votes is one which vexes the justificatory accounts of deliberative democracy which I examine in the following section. But my interest here is only with the degree to which they support the deliberative obligations, and accordingly I focus only on the process of political dialogue.

A potentially more damaging objection is that these obligations impose an incoherent set of demands on an agent. The requirements to offer reasons and arguments to all, to respond sincerely to the reasons and arguments of others, and to arrive at a mutually acceptable proposal, it may be argued, pull in different directions. On one side, deliberation has a cognitive face:

it is about what should be done, and the arguments and reasons offered concern which policy or proposal should be adopted. On the other side, it attempts to accommodate the wishes, projects and desires of the citizens, and aims at a resolution that is appropriately sensitive to these considerations too. So what do I do, as a deliberative citizen? I can try to offer you good reasons, and to respond to the good reasons which you offer me, or I can try to further my interests and to accommodate yours within some mutually satisfactory proposal. The disjunction here would signal not a logical inconsistency but a pragmatic conflict on the part of someone who attempts to combine both enterprises. There are conceptions of practical reason which argue that it is quite possible to reason about one's interests and goals and for collectivities to reason jointly about their interests and goals.[21] But if we accept the claim about underdetermination argued above, then there remains an important distinction between the two ways of relating to fellow citizens. I do not want to offer a general argument here to resolve this tension, which it seems must arise at least in some cases: when others remain immune to your good reasons, you eventually give up trying to convince them of these reasons' superiority and start trying to reach an accommodation with your fellow citizens which reflects those good reasons as far as possible. This too seems like the bread and butter of democratic deliberation, seen from a first-personal point of view.

If the account of deliberative democracy in this section is right, then deliberation entails what have been called 'special obligations': these are obligations shared among members of an association or community which are not owed to outsiders. The idea that such obligations exist is not in itself controversial: parties to a contract have special obligations to one another; parents have particular responsibility for the welfare of their children; a lifeguard has particular responsibility for the swimmers on his beach.

Far more contentious are the sources of special obligations – whether, in general, they are what Robert Goodin calls assigned responsibilities, 'merely devices whereby the moral community's general duties get assigned to particular agents'.[22] On an alternative view, special obligations derive from valuable features of the particular social relationship which exists among the agents bound by these obligations to one another.[23] The latter idea requires a normative (or, as Mason puts it, 'moralized') conception of social relationships, the goods of which put its members under those obligations necessary to sustain it.[24] This is a large question for moral and political theory: special obligations come in different shapes and sizes and it is *prima facie* implausible to insist that a single model of either the universalistic or particularistic sort will account for them all. The section after next considers one suggestion: that there is a plausible particularistic account of the deliberative obligations.

Arguments for deliberation

This overview of three key arguments for deliberative democracy is not intended as a full reconstruction or critique of these positions. I am not concerned here with what Cheryl Misak calls 'the problem of justification', the challenge to give reasons to persuade a sceptic that these are the appropriate terms on which to take part in political life.[25] The focus here is only on the extent to which each account is successful in explaining why participants in public deliberation should fulfil their deliberative obligations. My argument is that in each case there is a gap between the reasons given for accepting deliberation as the touchstone of democratic legitimacy, and the reasons for accepting that participants are under these obligations.

One line of support for deliberative democracy argues that it is desirable by virtue of the advantages which accrue to each participant from making decisions in this fashion. For this model, first, each participant will benefit from the pooling of private information which flows from the revelation of individual preferences and other beliefs, provided that there exists an effective norm of sincerity. Second, each participant will benefit from the opportunity to redress her 'bounded rationality', the limited and fallible capacity for reflection and calculation which each of us possesses by exposure to a larger range of viewpoints, considerations and styles of reasoning.[26] Participants' reflective capacity is improved not only through listening to others but also through the discipline of formulating arguments acceptable to all. The prudential model suggests that there are reasons for adhering to the deliberative norms which were expressed above as obligations.

The instability in such a grounding for these norms lies in the fact that the motivation for adhering to them, personal advantage, is also a motivation for flouting them when it is not too costly to do so. This leads directly to a sceptical counter-argument to these prudential considerations. If political speech is understood as motivated by individual interest, it should be understood as a strategic instrument deployed in order to gain an advantage for the speaker. Furthermore, as a resource speech is relatively cheap, and 'speakers have every incentive to conceal information, manipulate and deceive, while maintaining the appearance of credibility'.[27]

There are two responses to this scepticism, each of which recalls that speakers are prudentially motivated agents not merely in the short term but in the long run, and each of which relies on a claim about the pragmatics of discussion. The first is that exposure as a liar is not costless, but destroys future credibility.[28] Exposure is likely in the kind of forum envisaged by deliberative democrats, where there is 'recurrent public interaction about knowable information among multiple senders and multiple receivers, not onetime private interaction about unknowable information in a dyad'.[29] The second response is that in the long run a participant will be encouraged to mimic and perhaps ultimately to adopt the norms which guide deliberation. Since it is difficult to offer purely egoistic reasons for adopting a particular measure in a process of public discussion ('It's good for me' is unlikely to be a widely persuasive argument), she must frame them in the interests of all, and give reasons which all can appreciate. In this way, she must 'launder' her egoistic preferences for public presentation. This in turn may carry with it a psychological corollary: lip service to the common good means that 'one will in time be swayed by considerations about the common good'.[30]

I do not want to deny that there are norms endogenous to the process of deliberation, which are fostered by the pragmatics of public discussion, or that these are 'transformative' for those who take part.[31] It has been objected that this account of the norms of deliberation expresses an optimistic view of this process, which may also (or instead) be characterized by conformism or the covert pursuit of self-interest.[32] My argument here is only that this claim about the pragmatics of deliberation, if true, does not provide us with the grounding for the deliberative obligations which is the objective here. These arguments trace the likely effects of participating in the deliberative process over time, but they do not explain why we should shoulder the burdens expressed in the deliberative obligations when not to do so would incur minimal costs. Imagine that the deliberative forum contains a small minority whose views tend not to prevail: a religious group, for example, whose ideas are only narrowly shared, seen as mistaken, etc., by the rest of society. (This example need presuppose no homogeneity on the part of the majority, or the minority.) The votes of this group are unlikely to be decisive on most issues, and their arguments are usually based on premises which the rest cannot accept, no matter how attentively they listen. Yet this minority does not wish to split the association, its behaviour is sincere and not filibustering, and it continues to participate, in its awkward and cranky fashion. Why bother to tailor one's arguments so as to include them? The deliberative obligations sketched above include the duty precisely to do this. But it is not clear that the pragmatic arguments here offer a secure motivational counterpart to this obligation. If members of the majority are unlikely to gain anything from taking the time to listen and respond to this group, and to frame arguments in terms which might win this group's acceptance, why should they do so?

One response is that they should not; that is, that the majority are under no obligation to do so, since that minority are not themselves putting enough into the deliberative process. From the perspective of public deliberation, however, the reasons that one has to treat a group in this way are not the reasons that one has *qua* seeker of private advantage. The latter reason for breaking with the norm is that this group is never likely to be decisive (for example, its members always abstain) and therefore there is no advantage in tailoring one's arguments to include it, or in seeking to compromise to accommodate it. The point of view expressed in the deliberative obligations is different. If this group is ultimately to be overlooked, it is not because there is no advantage in trying to persuade its members; rather, it is because the arguments and considerations which appeal to everyone else find no purchase with this minority, and are highly unlikely ever to do so. I am not arguing that from the perspective of public deliberation the majority must give up on this cranky minority, or even that they may do so. My point here is only that, if one takes this to be one of the cases which falls beyond the deliberative pale, the reasons for doing so expressed in the pragmatic argument still appear different from the reasons embodied in the deliberative obligations. Even where these two points of view intersect, it is not the case that we find in the pragmatic arguments a successful derivation of the deliberative obligations, since it mislocates their normative status.

Like the prudential argument, the epistemic case for deliberative democracy is also instrumental, conceiving deliberation as a means to a logically independent end.[33] According to this line of thought, although public deliberation improves the beliefs and reasons of particular participants, it does so in a way that makes decisions more responsive to considerations of justice or the public good. Instead of viewing deliberative democracy as instrumental for the achievement of particular interests and goals, it holds that it is 'the most reliable procedure for obtaining access to the knowledge of moral principles'.[34] Polities containing a lot of debate on deliberative terms tend to arrive at juster democratic decisions. The core intuition is famously expressed by Mill:

> The whole strength and value then of human judgement, depending on the one property that it can be set right when it is wrong, reliance can be placed on it only when the means of setting it right are kept constantly at hand. In the case of the person whose judgement is really deserving of confidence, how has it become so? Because he has kept his mind open to criticism on his opinions and conduct. Because it has been his practice to listen to all that could be said against him; to profit by as much of it as was just, and to expound to himself, and on occasion to others, the fallacy of what was fallacious. Because he has felt, that the only way in which a human being can make some approach to knowing the whole of a subject, is by hearing what can be said about it by persons of every variety of opinion, and studying all the modes in which it can be looked at by every character of mind.[35]

On this view, public discussion tracks a conception of the public good which while it is logically independent of this process is epistemically dependent on it. If there was another epistemic route to the public good (policy experts, animal entrails) we could consult that, which would give us 'epistocracy'.[36]

On the face of it, this appears to be an empirical claim, the extension of a hypothesis about factual or scientific enquiry to democratic politics. But it is not clear that we can make sense of this claim in empirical terms. The presupposition of the epistemic argument is that we have no other epistemic access to the public good. If we did, we could use that to establish what the good in fact is. How then can we judge whether or not deliberative democracy successfully tracks that good? In a more plausible version, the epistemic argument is not an empirical claim, but an argument about the conditions for arriving at the truth and giving good reasons. The circumstances of public deliberation are seen as the necessary conditions for arriving at the right or best judgement of the public good. As Misak puts it, 'if you want to have your beliefs governed by reasons, then you will have to expose yourself to different reasons, different perspectives, different arguments. You will have to engage in debate and deliberation'. Furthermore, 'a case can be made that any opponent is committed to having her beliefs governed by reasons, so any opponent is committed, whether he acknowledges it or not, to debate and deliberation.'[37] This hinges on strong claims: that there is a truth about the public good, and that openness to varieties of experience, which is successfully captured in deliberation, is a necessary condition of arriving at this truth.

Here too I do not want to take issue with these claims about deliberation, or about cognitivism in moral enquiry. However, there is a gap between accepting these claims and believing that participants should abide by their deliberative obligations. This can be understood as a difference in the kind of 'convergence constraint' operative in enquiry and the constraint at work in public deliberation.[38] The outcome at which democratic deliberation aims is not, strictly speaking, a belief about the public good at all but a mutually acceptable proposal. This may embody many particular conceptions of the good, or none, and it may be judged in terms of the conception(s) of the good implied by it; but the outcome of the deliberative process is not itself necessarily a belief. As it was framed in the previous section, the goal of public deliberation is a commonly acceptable proposal, toward which participants deliberate, offering reasons and arguments, reforming their initial positions, and so on. This is compatible with the parties to deliberation arriving not at a proposal which is supported by the strongest reasons but at a negotiated compromise.

The resulting outcome may not be one which embodies a conception of the public good with which anyone in fact agrees. Participants may insist that the public good was quite satisfactorily expressed in their own original proposals, with its supporting reasons, or by some other view which emerged. However, public deliberation demands both reasoning and argument and the goal of arriving at a commonly acceptable proposal. The epistemic argument does not explain why we should compromise or moderate our proposals and arguments in public discussion. Mill's point is not that we should moderate our views in order to reach a reasonable and acceptable compromise – that is a route to conformism. (He does make the rather different point that often a reasonable compromise between extremes is close to the truth about social matters.)[39]

This difficulty is not overcome by Cohen's strategy in his seminal essay 'Deliberation and democratic legitimacy' of defining democratic legitimacy as the product of an ideal process of deliberation: 'outcomes are democratically legitimate if and only if they could be the object of a free and reasoned agreement among equals. The ideal deliberative procedure is a procedure which captures this principle.'[40] Actual deliberation seeks to 'mirror' or approximate key features of this ideal, in order that its results may carry democratic legitimacy. As David Estlund has pointed out, this is an epistemic argument, since the ideal procedure is logically independent of the actual procedure, but the latter is meant to give us access to the good reasons which are constituted by the ideal.[41] Formulating the epistemic case this way gets us no further with grounding the obligation to arrive at a mutually acceptable proposal when reasons give out.

Indeed, the gap between epistemic commitments and deliberative obligations is only made clearer by a rider which Cohen adds to his conception of the ideal deliberative procedure. Arguing that this ideal is not only procedural but incorporates substantive liberal and egalitarian values, he claims that:

> In an idealized deliberative setting, it will not do simply to advance reasons that one takes to be true and compelling. Such considerations may be rejected by others who are themselves reasonable. One must instead find reasons that are compelling to others, acknowledging those others as equals, aware that they have alternative reasonable commitments, and knowing something about the kinds of commitments that they are likely to have – for example, that they may have moral or religious commitments that impose what they take to be overriding obligations.[42]

The kind of reasons which the deliberative process will block includes the view that 'some are worth less than others or that the interests of one group are to count for less than those of others'.[43] But, as the passage cited indicates, it is not merely the basic interests which are to be ring-fenced by this consideration, but the reasonable moral commitments of fellow citizens. Prude may not then argue that a particular film ought to be banned on the ground that it violates standards of decency, according to her moral commitments, for a ban for that reason violates the reasonable moral commitments possessed by her fellow citizens, Lewd and Libertarian. Rather, she must strive to find commonly acceptable reasons to justify her proposal: perhaps viewing the film has grave psychological consequences, the reality of which both Lewd and Libertarian may concede without abandoning core tenets of their respective outlooks.[44] If an actual deliberative process is swayed by reasons which violate these standards it fails to 'mirror' the reasoned agreement which (it was argued) constitutes a democratically legitimate outcome. This then constitutes an *a priori* constraint on the kinds of reason which may be offered in actual processes of deliberation.

This raises again the debate about conceptualizing entry requirements on reasons, part of which here includes the controversy over how to understand reasonableness for political purposes. The point to underline here is that this entry requirement imposes only a negative obligation on citizens in the deliberative process: they must not offer reasons which violate these canons of reasonableness. This leaves hanging the obligation in actual deliberation to try to arrive at a commonly acceptable outcome.

The third justificatory account envisages deliberation as a fair procedure. In contrast to the epistemic argument, which posits standards external to the deliberative process by which the justice of its outcomes may be judged, this argument claims that what makes the outcomes just is that they are the product of a procedure which is judged fair: there is no appeal to standards of justice external to the deliberative process itself. This abandons the premise that the public good and deliberative democracy are logically independent. According to this argument, public deliberation is valuable as a condition of the justice of the outcomes that are decided on through public deliberation: 'because it comes at the close of a deliberative process in which everyone was able to take part . . . the result carries legitimacy'.[45] In contrast to the epistemic account, for this approach what counts as a just outcome is one that has emerged from the ideal deliberative process.

Fairness, in the sense of impartiality among participants,

may be claimed by other procedures. The mere aggregation of votes, or even flipping a coin, can claim to be fair means of deciding between different inputs or 'voices'. The standard of fairness must be external to the procedure itself; otherwise we have no means of deciding between these various claimants to procedural fairness.[46] The obvious move here is to claim that the deliberative character of the procedure distinguishes it as especially fair.[47] In general, the argument runs, public deliberation is fairer because it improves the quality of preferences, opinions, and reasons, in ways discussed with reference to the pragmatic argument. This is a slightly odd response, since improving the quality of the inputs is not what is usually meant by a procedure's being fair; what is usually meant is that the procedure deals impartially with whatever inputs confront it. The procedural argument could be interpreted as claiming that public deliberation possesses an advantage which is not possessed by non-deliberative procedures, namely that it improves the inputs in these ways. If so, the procedural argument would seem to move either in the prudential or (as Estlund has argued) the epistemic direction,[48] depending on whether this benefit is interpreted as accruing to individual interests or to the quality of reasons which provide the inputs. On the prudential interpretation, deliberation is especially fair by virtue of allowing each participant to gain an equally clear and reflective understanding of his ideas and interests, in contrast with modes of social decision making in which there is no opportunity to improve understanding. This counteracts unfair inequalities in information and rationality which in turn affect how each participant understands and pursues his own interests. On the epistemic interpretation, deliberation is especially fair since it exposes each participant to the best reasons and arguments, and in doing so tends to overcome unfair inequalities in rationality. Either way, the standard of improvement is independent of the procedure's outcomes. If it were not, the idea of improvement, and so the argument for the benefits of a deliberative procedure, would be rendered vacuous, since 'improvement' would mean merely 'more closely approximating whatever the procedure ultimately issues in'.

The fairness argument needs to show that each citizen is under the deliberative obligations. Positing an individual interest in the fairness of social arrangements is not enough, however. This interest must be such that it is uniquely or especially expressed in public deliberation. The two obvious routes to this are through the pragmatic and epistemic arguments, but these do not successfully ground the deliberative obligations: the way each of these conceptualizes deliberation and its duties is insensitive to some important aspects of this idea.

Citizenship and identity

The pragmatic, epistemic and fairness arguments focus on the systemic or structural dimension of the question 'Why deliberate?' A practice of decision making by public deliberation, each argues, possesses advantages in enhancing or constructing the legitimacy of political decisions. Even if these arguments offer fruitful lines of enquiry, they are unsuccessful in answering the first-personal version of this question: why should I deliberate? That is, why should I undertake the deliberative obligations? The fairness argument must specify the nature of the individual interest in fairness on deliberative terms. The epistemic argument limits itself to the duty to improve the reasons underlying decisions about the public good, and so overlooks the obligation to arrive at a commonly acceptable proposal where reasons do not determine one. The pragmatic argument seems best equipped to address the first-personal question, but does so at the expense of eliding the distinction between a pragmatic norm and an obligation.

An alternative response is to develop the particularistic account of special obligations, and to argue that the deliberative obligations are grounded in a valuable social relationship. This makes no general argument either that this particularistic account holds for all special obligations or that all valuable social relationships imply special obligations – only that it is plausible in this case to hold that special obligations are grounded in a valuable relationship. The obvious candidate for such a relationship here is citizenship, understood as an ethical rather than merely legal category.[49] This argument requires that there be some value in citizenship which is not only instrumental: that citizenship is valuable for a person not only because a slice of the social cake then accrues to her. We need to accept that there is a non-instrumental value in being an equal member of community of decision making about common affairs. To accept this is not to believe that political participation on the part of citizens must be non-instrumental, carried out for its own sake.[50] I may participate in order that my preferred policies are adopted. But there is a non-instrumental good in my being able to take part in this way in a community which makes decisions about its common affairs. The bad of apartheid or second-class citizenship is not only that those stigmatized in this way cannot press their particular interests through, although that is a severe wrong; it is also that they do not enjoy equal civic status with citizens of their own or other countries, where that is itself a value.

If we accept this, certain obligations flow from recognizing the relationship as valuable. There is an analogy here (as Andrew Mason has argued) with friendship: the good justifies the obligations which are at least partially constitutive of it.[51] Friendship is morally valuable for its own sake, as an expression of mutual concern, but part of what it is to be a friend is to be under certain obligations (for example, not to exploit confidences). Similarly, citizenship may be seen as not only valuable on moral grounds but as partly constituted by the obligation to treat fellow citizens in particular ways. The key relevant obligations for our purposes here are that we should take each other seriously as sources of political arguments and reasons, and also take each other's interests as sources of claims on us, conditioning our instrumental projects and particular moral opinions. These obligations then are discharged through public deliberation. This is not to say that they are the only obligations, and particularistic accounts of duties of citizenship have also emphasized a broader concern for the needs of fellow citizens, a topic about which neutrality is possible here.[52] The value of the friendship analogy is in allowing us to see how a valuable relationship may have attached to it associated constitutive duties, rather than in suggesting that citizenship may have the same or the same kind of value as friendship. (The latter is voluntary, for example.) All that is needed is a way of understanding that others qua citizens are sources of claims on us *qua* citizens, not that there is any stronger emotional bond.

None of this is uncontentious. But deliberative democracy needs an account of the deliberative obligations, and this fills that gap. A different line of argument which comes close to this is Miller's argument that social justice and deliberative democracy should be seen as underpinned by shared national identity. Here he finds support from those authors who hold that special obligations are derivable from identity rather than from what I have more broadly called valuable social relationships. Yael Tamir, for example, writes that 'deep and important obligations flow from identity and relatedness'.[53] Furthermore, there is a line of thought which insists that democracy requires, or flourishes best under, conditions of national identity.[54] There are two nationalist arguments to be considered here. The first is an argument about the motivating force of national identity, and the second is about the character of national community.

The first claim is that 'only a common nationality provides the sense of solidarity' that democratic politics requires.[55] National identity provides the right motivating background to ensure that we identify and fulfil our deliberative obligations. As a derivation of these obligations, this is subject to the objection that it misplaces their normative status, in the same way as the pragmatic argument about the mechanisms endogenous to deliberation. But if the argument is only that national identity provides the motivational force impelling us to fulfil our deliberative obligations, it is substitutable by the endogenous arguments, which suggest an alternative mechanism, internal to public deliberation, which motivate participants to fulfil their obligations. If there are mechanisms endogenous to the process itself which provide this motivational support, the need to invoke national identity as a motivational factor recedes. In one respect, national identity may be superior to the endogenous mechanisms. The latter inculcate social norms in self-interested individual participants, but the efficacy of those norms depends on their serving the long-term interests of the participants. If national identity provides a more direct route to the establishment of these norms, then the norms will be less vulnerable to alternative strategic assessments on the part of disaffected participants. What follows from this is not clear, however, since a policy designed to promote (say) a particular common culture in the deliberative process may be even more alienating. What can be concluded is the relatively weak point that, where national identity acts as a motivating force for deliberation, *ceteris paribus* it is beneficial from a deliberative standpoint – but fleshing out the *ceteris paribus* clause here entails some cautious ethical and practical judgement.

The fundamental issue is whether or not we can derive the deliberative obligations from an account of national identity. There have been several philosophical accounts designed to show that national identity has value for members or constitutes a valuable form of social relationship.[56] These accounts argue that national identity fosters trust, overcomes alienation, encourages solidarity and/or is a condition for the exercise of individual autonomy. So, the argument runs, this relationship in turn entails certain obligations on those members: to give priority to fellow members' needs, and to co-operate politically with them on deliberative terms. What national identity supplies, then, is a concrete form of social and political identity which is valuable to its members in such a way that it generates special obligations. The argument of the nationalist need not be that national identity of any sort or character will entail these obligations. National traditions may be resistant to practices of deliberation. Miller assuages the concern that the emphasis on national identity as the basis of political community leads to the 'sanctification of merely traditional ethical relations' by arguing that 'to the extent that national identities, and the public cultures that help to compose them, are shaped by processes of rational reflection to which members of the community can contribute on an equal footing, this no longer applies'.[57]

But if a national identity is non-deliberative in character the duties which partly constitute it do not include the deliberative obligations. If there are valuable but non-deliberative forms of identity, even if there are also valuable and deliberative ones, what is valuable in a national identity is not its connection with deliberation, and the claim about the constitutive role of the deliberative obligations fails. The alternative is to argue that the only form of valuable national identity is deliberative. However, the identity is presumably valuable by virtue of its deliberative character, or of some characteristic intimately related to deliberation: it would be odd to argue that only deliberative national identities are valuable by virtue of characteristics which have nothing to do with their deliberative character. If the argument is that the deliberative features of a national identity make it valuable to its members, it is not clear what the specifically national aspect of those characteristics adds, if we are seeking to derive the deliberative obligations. We can accept, then, that national identity has the benefits that nationalist writers have wanted to claim for it without finding in it a derivation of the deliberative obligations. (But we need not accept the former claims.) There is some weight to the first nationalist argument about the motivating character of national solidarity, but the consequences of that for how we should conceive of and conduct public deliberation are not clear.

Conclusion

The theory of public deliberation is a normative theory of social and political decision making under conditions of pluralism. As a practical enterprise it involves on the part of participants both responsiveness to reasons and the search for mutually satisfactory outcomes, commitments which I set out as deliberative obligations. The key justificatory arguments for deliberative democracy overlook these obligations, in the sense that they provide no grounds for them, while concentrating on desirable systemic features of public deliberation. Rather than viewing the deliberative obligations as derivations from the fairness, epistemic or pragmatic arguments for deliberation, we should understand these duties as special obligations owed by citizens to one another, whose obligatory character derives from the value of this civic bond. Finally, I suggested some arguments to resist assimilating this relationship to one of national identity, although the latter may play *ceteris paribus* a motivating role in strengthening commitment to these obligations. I think that understanding public deliberation in this way clarifies both the attractiveness and the difficulty of deliberative democracy. Its attractiveness lies not only in the character of the decisions produced, which the fairness, pragmatic and epistemic arguments emphasize, but also in its contributing to a valuable form of social relationship. Yet the difficulty of this ideal is that it relies on that social relationship's meeting the ethical standards that it sets for itself: that citizenship is not merely a legal category in which most of us are involuntarily impressed but an ethical relationship whose value we can affirm.

Notes

Earlier versions of this chapter were given at the MANCEPT Conference on Deliberative Democracy, University of Manchester, March 1999, and in the Department of Sociological Studies, University of Sheffield, October 1999. I am grateful to participants at both these venues, and particularly to John Horton and David Miller.

1 Jane Mansbridge, *Beyond Adversary Democracy* (New York: Basic Books, 1980), p. 17.

2 For helpful overviews see James Bohman and William Rehg (eds), *Deliberative Democracy: Essays on Reason and Politics* (Cambridge MA: MIT Press, 1997); James Bohman, 'The coming of age of deliberative democracy', *Journal of Political Philosophy*, 6 (1998), pp. 400–25; Jon Elster (ed.), *Deliberative Democracy* (New York: Cambridge University Press, 1998); John Dryzek, *Deliberative Democracy and Beyond: Liberals, Critics, Contestations* (Oxford: Oxford University Press, 2000).

3 David Miller, 'Group identities, national identities, and democratic politics', in John Horton and Susan Mendus (eds), *Toleration, Identity and Difference* (Basingstoke: Macmillan, 1999), p. 120.

4 Joshua Cohen, 'Deliberation and democratic legitimacy', in Bohman and Rehg, *Deliberative Democracy*, pp. 72–3; David Miller, 'Citizenship and pluralism', *Political Studies*, 43 (1995), pp. 432–50; Henry Richardson, 'Democratic intentions', in Bohman and Rehg, *Deliberative Democracy*, p. 376.

5 Jon Elster, 'The market and the forum: three varieties of political theory', in Bohman and Rehg, *Deliberative Democracy*, p. 19.

6 Amy Gutmann, and Dennis Thompson, *Democracy and Disagreement* (Cambridge MA: Harvard University Press, 1996), p. 26.

7 Bernard Manin, 'On legitimacy and political deliberation', *Political Theory*, 15 (1987), p. 352. See also Anne Phillips, *The Politics of Presence* (Oxford: Oxford University Press, 1995); Cohen, 'Deliberation and democratic legitimacy'; James Bohman, *Public Deliberation: Pluralism, Complexity, and Democracy* (Cambridge MA: MIT Press, 1996); James Bohman, 'Deliberative democracy and effective social freedom: capabilities, opportunities, and resources', in Bohman and Rehg, *Deliberative Democracy*, pp. 321–48; Jack Knight and James Johnson, 'What sort of equality does deliberative democracy require?', in Bohman and Rehg, *Deliberative Democracy*, pp. 279–320.

8 Nothing is intended here by calling these 'obligations' rather than 'duties', although some accounts of normativity distinguish these.

9 Cohen, 'Deliberation and democratic legitimacy', pp. 75–6.

10 *Ibid.*, p. 74. See also Miller, 'Group identities, national identities, and democratic politics', pp. 119–20.

11 Cf. James Johnson, 'Arguing for deliberation: some sceptical considerations', in Elster, *Deliberative Democracy*, pp. 169–70.

12 Dryzek, *Deliberative Democracy and Beyond*, pp. 45–7.

13 Amy Gutmann, 'The challenge of multiculturalism in political ethics', *Ethics*, 102 (1993), pp. 171–206; Gutmann and Thompson, *Democracy and Disagreement*.

14 Cohen, 'Deliberation and democratic legitimacy', p. 75.

15 Seyla Benhabib, 'Toward a deliberative model of democratic legitimacy', in Seyla Benhabib (ed.), *Democracy and Difference: Contesting the Boundaries of the Political* (Princeton NJ: Princeton University Press, 1996), pp. 67–94; Thomas Christiano, 'The significance of public deliberation', in Bohman and Rehg, *Deliberative Democracy*, pp. 243–78.

16 Steven Lukes, *Moral Conflict and Politics* (Oxford: Clarendon Press, 1991), p. 20.

17 There is now a large and quite well known literature on this: for a recent guide see Ruth Chang (ed.), *Incommensurability, Incomparability, and Practical Reason* (Cambridge MA: Harvard University Press, 1997), and Richard Bellamy, *Liberalism and Pluralism: Towards a Politics of Compromise* (London: Routledge, 1999), for a relevant exploration in this context.

18 Richardson, 'Democratic intentions', p. 358.

19 *Ibid.*, p. 352; Bellamy, *Liberalism and Pluralism*, pp. 12–13, 37–8, 93–114.

20 Adam Przeworski, 'Deliberation and ideological domination', in Elster, *Deliberative Democracy*, p. 142.

21 For one relevant conception see Matthew Festenstein, *Pragmatism and Political Theory* (Oxford: Polity Press; Chicago: University of Chicago Press, 1997); Henry S. Richardson, 'Truth and ends in Dewey's pragmatism', in Cheryl Misak (ed.), *Pragmatism, Canadian Journal of Philosophy* supplementary volume (Calgary: University of Calgary Press, 1999), pp. 109–48.

22 Robert Goodin, 'What is so special about our fellow countrymen?', *Ethics*, 98 (1988), p. 678.

23 Michael Hardimon, 'Role obligations', *Journal of Philosophy*, 91 (1994), pp. 333–63; John Horton, *Political Obligation* (Basingstoke: Macmillan, 1992); Yael Tamir, *Liberal Nationalism* (Princeton NJ: Princeton University Press, 1993); Bhikhu Parekh, 'A misconceived discourse on political obligation', *Political Studies*, 41 (1993), pp. 236–51; David Miller, *On Nationality* (Oxford: Oxford University Press, 1995); Richard Dagger, 'Membership, fair play and political obligation', *Political Studies*, 48 (2000), pp. 104–17.

24 Andrew Mason, *Community, Solidarity and Belonging: Levels of Community and their Normative Significance* (Cambridge: Cambridge University Press, 2000), pp. 32–3, 99–112.

25 Cheryl Misak, *Truth, Politics, Morality: Pragmatism and Deliberation* (London: Routledge, 1999), chapter 1.

26 E.g. Benhabib, 'Toward a deliberative model of democratic legitimacy', p. 71; Carlos Nino, *The Constitution of Deliberative Democracy* (New Haven CT: Yale University Press, 1996), p. 113; Bohman, *Public Deliberation*, p. 27; James Fearon, 'Deliberation as discussion', in Elster, *Deliberative Democracy*, pp. 45–9.

27 Dryzek, *Deliberative Democracy and Beyond*, p. 37; Przeworski, 'Deliberation and ideological domination'.

28 Gerry Mackie, 'All men are liars: is deliberation meaningless?', in Elster, *Deliberative Democracy*, pp. 97–122.

29 *Ibid.*, p. 84.

30 Elster, 'The market and the forum', p. 12.

31 Mark Warren, 'Democratic theory and self-transformation', *American Political Science Review*, 86 (1992), pp. 8–23; Mark Warren, 'The self in discursive democracy', in Stephen K. White (ed.), *The Cambridge Companion to Habermas* (Cambridge: Cambridge University Press, 1995), pp. 167–200.

32 Cf. Elster, 'The market and the forum', pp. 13–18.

33 David Estlund, 'Beyond fairness and deliberation: the epistemic dimension of democratic authority', in Bohman and Rehg, *Deliberative Democracy*, p. 180.

34 Nino, *The Constitution of Deliberative Democracy*, p. 107.

35 John Stuart Mill, *On Liberty and other Essays*, ed. John Gray (Oxford: Oxford University Press, 1991), p. 25.

36 Estlund, 'Beyond fairness and deliberation', p. 183.

37 Misak, *Truth, Politics, Morality*, p. 106.

38 *Ibid.*, p. 99.

39 Mill, *On Liberty*, pp. 52–3.

40 Cohen, 'Deliberation and democratic legitimacy', p. 73.

41 Estlund, 'Beyond fairness and deliberation', p. 180.

42 Joshua Cohen, 'Procedure and substance in deliberative democracy', in Bohman and Rehg, *Deliberative Democracy*, p. 414.

43 *Ibid.*, p. 414.

44 I do not think that this account is committed to the claim that Prude, Lewd and Libertarian must aim to converge on the *same* reason for the policy adopted; but compare Gerald Postema, 'Public practical reason: an archeology', *Social Philosophy and Policy*, 12 (1995), p. 70; Gerald Gaus, 'Reason, justification, and consensus: why democracy can't have it all', in Bohman and Rehg, *Deliberative Democracy*, p. 206.

45 Manin, 'On legitimacy and political deliberation', p. 359.

46 Estlund, 'Beyond fairness and deliberation', pp. 176–7.

47 Benhabib, 'Toward a deliberative model of democratic legitimacy', pp. 68, 71–2.

48 Estlund, 'Beyond fairness and deliberation', pp. 179–80; Maeve Cooke, 'Five arguments for deliberative democracy', *Political Studies*, 48 (2000), pp. 951–2 (Chapter 3 of this volume).

49 This argument then has some affinity to republican accounts of the value of citizenship, e.g. Miller, 'Citizenship and pluralism'; Philip Pettit, *Republicanism* (Oxford: Oxford University Press, 1997); Quentin Skinner, *Liberty before Liberalism* (Cambridge: Cambridge University Press, 1998); Bellamy, *Liberalism and Pluralism*; Mason, *Community, Solidarity, and Belonging*, pp. 96–114.

50 The latter claim is the target of Elster, 'The market and the forum'.

51 Mason, *Community, Solidarity, and Belonging*, pp. 109–10.

52 *Ibid.*, p. 111.

53 Tamir, *Liberal Nationalism*, p. 41. See also Horton, *Political Obligation*, p. 157; Richard Rorty, *Contingency, Irony, and Solidarity* (Cambridge: Cambridge University Press, 1989), p. 195.

54 Margaret Canovan, *Nationhood and Political Theory* (Cheltenham: Edward Elgar, 1996), chapter 3.

55 Miller, *On Nationality*, p. 98. Mill is a famous forerunner: 'Free institutions are next to impossible in a country made up of different nationalities. Among a people without fellow-feeling, especially if they read and speak different languages, the united public opinion necessary to the working of representative institutions cannot exist' (Mill, *On Liberty*, p. 428).

56 As well as Miller's work, see, e.g., Avishai Margalit and Joseph Raz, 'National self-determination', *Journal of Philosophy*, 87 (1990), pp. 439–61; Tamir, *Liberal Nationalism*; Will Kymlicka, *Multicultural Citizenship* (Oxford: Oxford University Press, 1995); Canovan, *Nationhood and Political Theory*; Robert McKim and Jeff McMahan (eds), *The Morality of Nationalism* (Oxford: Oxford University Press, 1997); Paul Gilbert, *Philosophies of Nationalism* (Boulder CO: Westview Press, 1998).

57 Miller, *On Nationality*, p. 70.

5

Rawls and deliberative democracy

MICHAEL SAWARD

It seems very reasonable to link the ideas of Rawls on public reason and related notions with the idea of deliberative democracy. Apart from the fact that in recent writings Rawls himself makes the connection explicitly,[1] we can ask whether any real compulsion to attach 'deliberation' and 'democracy' could have arisen at all without powerful contemporary forebears – Rawls and Habermas above all – emphasizing dialogical approaches to political principles and institutions.[2] Rawls's device of the original position famously models an ideal dialogue on principles of justice; Cohen's influential deliberative model[3] clearly springs directly from these Rawlsian roots. The original position provides a means to assess different interpretations of social justice, while deliberative democracy brings together different preferences in order to subject them to the test of public and open scrutiny. One can agree that these chains of influence are real and still question fundamentally whether some of the links are strong enough to sustain them. Benhabib[4] pursues this task briefly, noting among other things that Rawls's idea of public reason is about limits on how to reason rather than a process of actual reasoning in public. But it is worth paying closer attention to the issue in order to draw out (1) fundamental reasons why the Rawlsian project as Rawls presents it *cannot be* genuinely deliberative, and (2) the light that can be thrown on deliberative models of democracy by looking at basic Rawlsian categories in new ways.

This chapter offers arguments to support the following conjectures: (1) despite claims by Rawls and some commentators, Rawls is not and cannot be a deliberative democrat; the evidence for this can be gleaned by focusing on various interpretations of the structure of Rawls's arguments in *A Theory of*

Justice (1972) and *Political Liberalism* (1993) respectively; and (2) if we ask more directly how the ideal dialogue of the original position might be approximated in real-world conditions, we can reach suggestive conclusions about institutions and deliberative democracy radically different from those reached by Rawls himself.

Layered ambiguities: Rawls on public reason

Rawls's account of 'public reason' has been cited as a 'major statement' of the 'idea of deliberative democracy', one which tries to work out 'the philosophical details of political justification based on deliberation and public reason'.[5] Rawls himself has written that public reason as he understands it is one vital ingredient of 'deliberative democracy'.[6] However, as I shall argue, this link cannot be sustained; public reason and deliberation are quite different things. Rawls's vision is more accurately seen as non-deliberative – even anti-deliberative – unless we stretch the meaning of deliberation well beyond what any of the major deliberative theorists[7] intend it to mean.

These claims require a clear distinction between deliberative and non-deliberative conceptions of democracy (to put it in black-and-white terms). Alas, we are not helped in this task by the stipulative and contestable nature of the definitions of deliberative democracy offered by key theorists. It rapidly becomes clear that 'deliberative democracy' means many things. Authors like Cohen,[8] Dryzek,[9] Gutmann and Thompson[10] and Fishkin[11] define and to varying degrees elaborate divergent conceptions of deliberative democracy. Some see it as discussion over issues in state forums, others in non-state contexts; some see it as a vital adjunct to existing democratic practices like voting, others as elevating 'talk' well above traditional mechanisms. Even in reasonably full conceptions of democracy that are not tagged as deliberative or which on the face of it do not emphasize deliberation, reason giving and political dialogue (such as that of Dahl[12]) it is clear that deliberation of various types is envisaged and valued. However, it is not the raw presence of deliberation in a conception of democracy (or in a real system reflective of the features of such a conception) but rather its *status* and *role* that defines the deliberative/non-deliberative boundary.[13]

Can we set out reasonable defining features of deliberative conceptions despite these understandable grey areas?[14] I believe so, if we specify a conception of democracy as 'deliberative' if it stipulates that (1) voting must be preceded by formal and actual deliberation among representative citizens, (2) there must be evidence of successful public facilitation of free deliberation in a range of non-state civil forums, (3) deliberation of the first sort in particular must have a determinate impact on the shape of the final outcome, such that (for example) the outcome can be justified and accounted for in terms of themes or arguments that were prominent in the deliberative process concerned, and (4) that the formal deliberations in particular satisfied minimum procedural standards of equal respect and inclusiveness.

I will (briefly) explore key parts of Rawls's account in order to show how in fact it undermines even this baseline vision of deliberative democracy. This matters because the influence of Rawls on the world of political ideas is understandably huge, given his achievements, and his impact on real institutional design and decision making is not negligible.

For Rawls, 'public reason' is either *a set of reasons* or *a way of reasoning* (it makes a real difference which it is – this is the first significant ambiguity) necessary to the adequacy of legislative or constitutional outcomes on important political questions. In Rawls's view of 'public reason', so central to his project in *Political Liberalism*, who gets to 'reason', and where and how? Initially, it is everyone: 'Public reason is characteristic of a democratic people: it is the reason of its citizens, of those sharing the status of equal citizenship.'[15] But in fact Rawls sees it as applying in particular to a more narrowly circumscribed set of issues and group of actors. On this view, it is not something that all need engage or indulge in, at least not constantly or compulsorily – it is primarily something that applies to, and should act as a constraint upon, judges, elected politicians, government officials and candidates for political office.[16]

Public reason is also seen by Rawls as applying not to 'political' questions generally, but to 'constitutional essentials and questions of basic justice'; it has to do with higher, constitutional arrangements rather than more mundane, within-politics issues. It is distinguished from the 'non-public' reasons people offer for the political stances they adopt on a variety of issues within the institutions in civil society, such as churches, universities, etc.[17]

So when we reason in public on fundamental issues, we must reason in a certain way, by accepting certain constraints. But, Rawls asks – taking the broad view of who should honour public reason's constraints – 'Why should citizens in discussing and voting on the most fundamental political questions honour the limits of public reason?'[18] His reply, from within 'political liberalism', is that 'our exercise of political power is proper and hence justifiable only when it is exercised in accordance with a constitution the essentials of which all citizens may reasonably be expected to endorse in the light of principles and ideals acceptable to them as reasonable and rational'.[19]

Let us break this key argument down into its constituent parts:

1 Reasonable and rational people, aware of pluralism . . .
2 will find certain principles/ideals acceptable to them . . .
3 therefore they will endorse a constitution which embodies these principles/ideals.
4 If political power is exercised in accordance with this constitution . . .
5 then political power is exercised legitimately.

I have suggested that deliberative democracy ultimately involves (among other things) actual public or semi-public forums discussing and debating key issues. Referring to public reason seemingly *implies* a process of actual reasoning (discussing, debating, in a certain way in a variety of actual settings). But note that the location of 'public reason' in the above schema is in points 1–3, and that this is precisely where reasoning is a solitary, inward-looking, thoughtful matter; public decision making comes into the equation only in points 4–5. The affirmation or endorsement of the principles and ideals in 2 is done by individuals thinking/'reasoning' alone, not together. Affirmation is a solitary affair, even involving citizens abstracting in their minds away from the content of the 'comprehensive doctrines' they hold in their non-public lives.[20]

I pointed out above the ambiguity in the term 'reason' – an ambiguity that Rawls does little to clear up in his own use of the notion. To reason with another is to talk to them with an eye to convincing them rationally of one's viewpoint. But clearly one can also 'reason' in one's mind, perhaps by conducting an internal dialogue with imaginary others. The above comments suggest that it is the latter interpretation that most clearly captures the sense of the term in Rawls's schema.

In comments on the public's role in applying public reason to specific cases in the 1997 edition of *Political Liberalism* Rawls writes, 'For how to think about a kind of case depends not on general considerations alone but on our formulating relevant political values we may not have imagined before we reflect about particular instances.'[21] Think, imagine, reflect – these are 'internal dialogue' terms, not injunctions to real public discussion. Further, in the essay 'The idea of public reason revisited' Rawls mentions that on those occasions when they must exercise distinctively public reason citizens should 'ask themselves' what provisions it would be reasonable to enact, and, in considering 'the idea of political legitimacy based on the criterion of reciprocity' (the latter a, possibly the, crucial ingredient of public reason) Rawls writes that 'our exercise of political power is proper only when we sincerely *believe* that the reasons we *would* offer for our political actions – *were* we to state them as government officials – are sufficient, and we also reasonably *think* that other citizens *might* also reasonably accept those reasons'.[22] The added italics highlight the conditional, non-discursive – non-deliberative – character of Rawls's thinking here. One thing these comments do is drive a wedge between 'public reason' and (actual) deliberation.

It appears, then, that 'public reason' for Rawls is not an injunction *actually* to reason (deliberate, debate) in public with fellow citizens. Rather, it appears to be about content – a set of guidelines about how to think about fundamental issues in the 'public political forum'. Indeed, Rawls notes that a central part of the 'structure' of public reason is 'its content as given by a family of reasonable political conceptions of justice'.[23] So on this view public reason is a 'thing' rather than a process, something 'given' rather than created or practised. And if that is the case, no actual deliberation takes place.

We can search for the reasons for this by digging a little deeper into a related ambiguity: is the 'content' of public reason the product of the original position, or could it acceptably be derived from some other 'reasonable political conception of justice'?

On one reading of *Political Liberalism* the former answer seems correct. The basis for the content of public reason is provided by the original position:

> the guidelines of inquiry of public reason, as well as its principle of legitimacy, have the same basis as the substantive principles of justice. This means in justice as fairness that the parties in the orig-

inal position, in adopting principles of justice for the basic structure, must also adopt guidelines and criteria of public reason for applying those norms.[24]

On this interpretation the respective structures of the arguments in *A Theory of Justice* and *Political Liberalism* 'meet' in the sense that the subject of the 'overlapping consensus of reasonable comprehensive doctrines' is itself the conception of 'justice as fairness'.

However, more often Rawls notes that there may be a number of reasonable political conceptions – justice as fairness is one among various possible political conceptions of justice. Here different political conceptions of justice will contain criteria that others will reasonably be able to endorse along with us.[25] Each of these conceptions can properly be deployed in the public political forum, since (above all) each will accept reciprocity as its core principle and thereby be a reasonable focus for an overlapping consensus of reasonable comprehensive doctrines, in Rawls's terms. There are 'different liberalisms'[26] so there will be different versions; justice as fairness is 'just one' view[27] which Rawls himself prefers.[28] Clearly Rawls does not imagine these different political conceptions differing too much from each other – reciprocity qualifies each of them, and each includes a conception of rights, priorities and means directly reminiscent of the two principles of justice in justice as fairness. It does not seem unreasonable to suggest that for Rawls justice as fairness is the 'default mode' political conception for all who fail to (make the mental effort to) come up with their own.

It seems clear, then, that something *akin to* the original position is needed to provide a reasonable political conception of justice even if that conception (in line with the second interpretation, above) is not necessarily Rawls's preferred one of justice as fairness. And, of course, the original position is a purely hypothetical device: one can at any time 'simulate the deliberations of this hypothetical situation, simply by reasoning in accordance with the appropriate restrictions'.[29] It is a place in which deliberation is ideal and general and inclusive; therefore it cannot be an actual place. Recall, too, that we reach the favoured conception of the original position by a process of 'reflective equilibrium'. As discussed in *A Theory of Justice*, reflective equilibrium is a solitary thought process, engaged in (ideally) by all citizens on their own, conducted in order to reach a specific conception of an initial situation which accords with our considered convictions about the content of justice.

One strength – from Rawls's point of view, at least – of the conception of justice embodied in the specification of the original position is that each individual need not in fact engage in the process of seeking reflective equilibrium; all we need to know is that reasonable and rational people *would* reach similar conclusions, if they did so engage. So even solitary 'deliberation' is not necessary; the outcome is fixed (even given some flexibility as represented in the second interpretation), with no process of actual reasoning of any sort necessarily being involved. Again, this may be called 'public reason', but it is not open-ended, explicit reasoning or actual public deliberation. The metaphor of the original position – non-deliberative, hypothetical – runs through the structure of the argument in *Political Liberalism* and later statements on public reason too.

Despite the (inevitable, fixed) non-deliberative origins of public reason, Rawls does want citizens to engage with fundamental political questions:

> As to whom public reason applies, we say that it applies to citizens when they engage in political advocacy in the public forum, in political campaigns for example and when they vote on those fundamental questions. It always applies to public and government officers in official forums, in their debates and votes on the floor of the legislature. Public reason applies especially to the judiciary in its decisions and as the institutional exemplar of public reason.[30]

Note, first, that citizens must adopt the content of public reason in certain instances of their *voting* in particular, but it is highly ambiguous as to which instances. On fundamental political questions, citizens must vote according to canons of public reason: 'public reason with its duty of civility gives a view about voting on fundamental questions in some ways reminiscent of Rousseau's *Social Contract*. He saw voting as ideally expressing our opinion as to which of the alternatives best advances the common good'[31] . . . 'citizens and legislators may properly vote their more comprehensive views when constitutional essentials and basic justice are not at stake'.[32] But where is the neat dividing line between the fundamental political and the non-fundamental political? (Rawls implies rather than states the existence of the second category.)

So my argument is that the basis of public reason in the (purely hypothetical) original position, its related notion of the (solitary) seeking of reflective equilibrium, and the (solitary, mental) assessments by citizens as to the status of this vote (and consequently the motivation they should bring to it), render public reason a thoroughly non-deliberative notion. Or, if it chimes at all with the work of deliberative democrats, it can only be in the unhelpful sense of advocating solitary, not actual and effective, deliberation.[33] No doubt the larger Rawlsian argument welcomes citizens deliberating with each other and being attentive to the deliberations of (e.g.) representatives. The point, however, is that the status this view accords to deliberation does not match what we would need to see to regard the conception as genuinely 'deliberative'. Rawls's views, in short, provide an argument which is virtually diametrically opposed to dominant visions of deliberative democracy, each of which stresses the importance of actual deliberation whatever specific forums or sites are favoured.

The Rawlsian mirror

Arguably, the reason why Bohman and Rehg, along with Rawls himself, can readily characterize public reason as deliberative democracy has a good deal to do with the fact that Rawls's theory has changed fundamentally since *A Theory of Justice*. This, of course, is a huge topic, and not one I wish to enter into here in any detail. But in general terms public reason and the seeking of an overlapping consensus of reasonable comprehensive doctrines *sounds* like a more worldly, engaged, *political* project (and so has Rawls characterized it). In *A Theory of Justice* the device of the four-stage sequence by which the 'veils' are gradually lifted takes us through a process whereby we descend from imaginary contexts to real world politics. *Political Liberalism* by way of contrast seems to give us the real political world from the start, with irreducible pluralism of religious and other comprehensive doctrines, the possibility of different reasonable conceptions of justice, and so on. This sense is reinforced by the fact that the argumentative devices which distance the process of reaching compelling principles of justice in *A Theory of Justice* – the original position above all – are downgraded in the later work, though their presence in it is a haunting one, as I have tried too briefly to indicate above.

I want to suggest, however, that *the arguments of* Political Liberalism *can properly be interpreted as the mirror image of those of* A Theory of Justice. The architectural structure of the early work operates as a metaphor for the structure of the later work and the elements which comprise it. This conjecture in itself, if accurate, cannot alone account for the unworldliness, especially the absence of (the need or desire for) actual deliberation, in the writings on public reason and related concepts, but surely it can go some considerable way in that direction.

By examining features of the arguments in the early and later books we can draw links between key concepts within and across the arguments of the two books. Thus we being with the *individual citizen* in Story A, who has his or her *considered convictions* and takes these into the device of representation known as the *original position*. By a process of *reflective equilibrium*, our citizen brings his or her considered convictions into line with the demands of justice as modelled by the structure of choice behind the veil of ignorance. Thus our citizen reaches agreement on *the two principles of justice* in the conception known as *justice as fairness*. In Story B the citizen is identified with his or her *comprehensive doctrine* – and hopefully a *reasonable comprehensive doctrine* – which will shape and inform most of the political arguments our citizen will make, most of the time. However, when our citizen enters the *public political forum* – or, more accurately, has to think through reasonable solutions to fundamental questions that he or she may be called to vote upon – he or she must accept the constraints of *public reason*. By deploying a *political conception of justice* which satisfies public reason guidelines, our citizen can locate grounds on a given issue that he or she could reasonably expect others to reasonably agree with – an *overlapping consensus*.

By positing the interpretive device of the mirror I am suggesting that each step in each of these 'stories' can be linked with equivalent steps in the other; that is, there are equivalent concepts in each story which, so to speak, do the same work within the respective arguments. The citizen with his or her considered convictions is the citizen enfolded in his or her (reasonable) comprehensive doctrine. The citizen in the public political forum, like the citizen in the original position, is in a context where only certain sorts of arguments about courses of action are appropriate or acceptable. Public reason is an internal, mental process of finding good and right reasons for believing in a conception of justice and its implications for given issues; reflective equilibrium is likewise. And what public reason produces is a political conception of justice which (ideally) can act as the focus for an overlapping consensus of reasonable comprehensive doctrines, just as justice as fairness as one favoured such conception would be agreed by all engaged in the relevant processes.

In short, the argument in *Political Liberalism* is, at a deeper level, the mirror image of the argument of *A Theory of Justice*.[34] We have seen already how little actual deliberation takes place within the story told in Rawls's later work. Considering how that work represents a metaphorical reconstruction of the early work reinforces our suspicions that there is nothing here that deliberative democrats can call their own.[35] It may be 'political not metaphysical' on the surface; beneath that, the metaphysical is still in the driving seat.

The more things change . . .

In his much-cited essay 'Deliberation and democratic legitimacy' Cohen[36] adopts the very same architecture I have discussed above as the template for a theory of deliberative democracy. That at least is my interpretation.[37] Cohen attempts to distance himself from the Rawlsian framework just as he deploys it. To that extent his *intention* is to construct a regulative principle or ideal of deliberation that can be approximated as far as possible in practice. His is one effort to move from a Rawlsian framework to a practical ideal of deliberative democracy; Rawls's own efforts in *Political Liberalism* and 'The idea of public reason revisited' represent another. These particular efforts do not, I argue, get us far. The non-deliberative roots of the argumentative structure get in the way; the Rawlsian metaphor prevents the argument metamorphosing into something else – like a practical conception of deliberative democracy.

Ironically enough, this point can be illustrated by focusing on *differences* (e.g. in terminology) or *adaptations* of the initial Rawlsian framework in the course of these efforts to move more squarely into the realm of *democratic* theory. Clearly, someone could protest that my discussion so far has underestimated the real changes and adaptations of the Rawlsian framework from the 1970s to the 1990s. My argument here, in short, is that to the extent that he shifts away from the framework in *A Theory of Justice* Rawls is forced to make new assumptions about citizens in particular; this is done apparently to render the conception more practical in political terms. By contrast, I would argue that it is done *in order to retain control of, or certainty about, the outcomes of 'deliberations' focused on justice* – which in turn further undermines the deliberative claims of the project. Things are changed so that they may remain the same; public reason is not the original position, but it is different in ways that ensure the ultimate product and effect is the same.

By way of illustration, consider the accounts of (1) motivation (2) the wide view of public reason (3) civility and (4) the normalizing of citizens in Rawls's discussion of public reason. Like Cohen,[38] who stipulates that citizens will be motivated to seek the common good in deliberations, the later Rawls stipulates that people must 'sincerely vote in accordance with the idea of public reason'.[39] Just as judges cannot simply give their own opinion in difficult cases, citizens must not on fundamental political questions simply invoke their comprehensive doctrine: 'From the point of view of public reason, citizens must vote for the ordering of political values they sincerely think the most reasonable. Otherwise they fail to exercise political power in ways that satisfy the criterion of reciprocity.'[40] Now, the idea in the original position that citizens (or to-be-citizens) were self-interested was surely a more practical assumption for building real-world institutions. There are dangers in letting political legitimacy rest so strongly on hopes of citizens voting with certain motivations uppermost in their minds.[41] But the fact is that, having loosened the reins on his structure to some extent, Rawls has had to tighten his motivational assumptions/stipulations in an unrealistic manner in order to continue to make justice a likely achievement in the world of *Political Liberalism*.

Similarly, in the late 1990s Rawls relented somewhat on the question of whether views from people's comprehensive doctrines could rightly be invoked in public political debate on fundamental questions. On the 'wide view of public reason', citizens can now invoke elements of their comprehensive doctrines with the proviso that backing for what they invoke from within a political conception of justice is forthcoming in due course.[42] Among other things, this shift can be interpreted as partial compensation for the loss of what in the original position was the representation of all generations behind the veil of ignorance. If, for example, the views of future generations are part of the simulated deliberations in the original position, new ideas about what justice may involve can be 'on the table'. The menu of topics and possibilities will not be restricted to what one generation alone is capable of thinking. The wide view of public reason cannot capture what is lost here, but it can go part way in that new ideas from (e.g.) newly emergent ideologies like environmentalism can more readily reach the public political forum.

The 'duty of civility' has a prominent place in later work on similar grounds, too. In the original position, civility was built into the structure – if all are effectively the same, with the same views, there is hardly anyone to be (or to imagine being) uncivil to. Having loosened his grip on the derivation (and the doing) of justice, however, Rawls needs to invoke this duty, not to add something new to the mix but to *restore what was lost* on moving to the *Political Liberalism* framework. Without a duty of civility, citizens could easily refuse to act civilly, saying 'Accept my view or be damned' rather than 'fulfil their duty of civility' by explaining their positions in the appropriate way.[43]

Finally, *Political Liberalism* still gives us a 'normalized' citizen, even if it is not the severely ironed out creature that inhabits the original position. People will be different, with different comprehensive views which together provide an irreducible plurality of reasons and ways of reasoning about issues. Rawls denies that his project of public reason 'normalizes' people so that they are effectively the same on a philosophical view. Instead, he writes, 'Accounts of human nature we put aside and rely on a political conception of persons as citizens instead.' But the trick is in the latter – 'citizens' must do and be certain things, all the same, for justice to be done in the world of *Political Liberalism*. The very next sentence in 'The idea of public reason revisited' is: 'As I have stressed throughout, it is central to political liberalism that free and equal citizens affirm both a comprehensive doctrine and a political conception.'[44]

So apparently genuine and significant changes in key assumptions from the early to the later Rawlsian frameworks are in fact better seen as *devices to retain or restore* the certainty, and control by the theorist, of his own creation. I have noted this aspect of Rawls's work in order to highlight the underlying commonality regardless of whether we consider surface continuity or change in Rawls's journey to (as he sees it) deliberative democracy.

Forward to the origins?

The 'deliberative model of democracy' is surely entering its endgame period. Fragmentation characterizes the theory, whether it be (for example) differences over whether deliberative forums ought to be governmental or non-governmental, what standards for discussion and debate are regarded as appropriate, the extent to which inclusion and consensus are central goals, etc.[45] I do not seek to unify perspectives, necessarily – to do that, for a start, we would need to address the theory of *democracy*, not deliberative democracy.[46] Rather, I ask whether taking a quite different view of the Rawlsian project and deliberative democracy can illuminate the fragmentation and confusion attending the latter.

One can understand why Rawls himself does not in the end make as many significant changes to his initial framework as is often supposed – or so I have argued. The same goes for the extent to which the Rawlsian framing of questions in political theory has, and continues to, set the agenda for others.[47] In seeking to step outside the bulk of that framework while nonetheless toying with one key element of it I am saying nothing to diminish the sheer weight of the intellectual achievement of Rawls. I am, with due modesty, suggesting that we are not forced to accept that the building blocks of theory need be assembled in the way the master has done it. And with that I proceed 'to stretch fantasy too far'.[48]

I want to ask – with conscious naivety – what it may mean to attempt to approximate the terms and features of the original position in practice. If we (1) insist on actual spoken deliberation in actual deliberative forums, (2) do not worry about keeping 'control' of processes and outcomes in the way I have suggested Rawls does, but (3) try to retain where possible some real sense of both the realistic and the positive features of the original position, can we illuminate the subject of deliberative democracy?

The central conditions and descriptive features of the original position are the assumption that all present act in their self-interest and the inducement of impartiality through the imposition of ignorance on the parties via the device of the veil of ignorance. Let us retain the self-interest assumption for what follows. The key positive features of the original position from a democratic perspective are:

1 *Generality*. The outcomes reached will have general applicability across the political community for whom the original position is acting as a device of representation.
2 *Inclusiveness*. All interests are 'there', represented in the 'deliberations', including multiple generations.
3 *Impartiality*. All can fully and equally endorse the fairness of the outcomes.
4 *Productivity*. It unfailingly produces an outcome of the above sort; stalemate is not an option.
5 The *face-to-face* character of the 'deliberations'.

We may use these features as regulative principles for the design of real world deliberative institutions or contexts. But let us be very clear on the extent to which, and the ways in which, the realization of each of these principles is rendered inaccessible by the simple transfer of focus from the hypothetical to the real deliberative context. We stand to lose *generality* to the extent that the outcomes will have applicability only to living generations and to the political community that is (in some plausible respect) present in the deliberations. We stand to lose *inclusiveness* in similar respects – the interests of future (and past) generations will not/cannot be included, a more delimited territorial community will form the basis of the deliberative group, and the possibility of including non-human interests to move towards a 'democracy of the affected'[49] greatly diminishes. And the move to actual spoken discourse with differentiated, gendered, accented (etc.) others means differentiated inclusion for different styles of discourse, appearance and so forth. *Impartiality* disappears to the same extent through the limited range of interests now effectively represented in the dialogue and the fact that the 'enforced' ignorance-based impartiality of the original position is now replaced by a partiality born of particular, incomplete knowledge of self and society. And the delightful *productivity* of the ideal dialogue, which guarantees an outcome, and a thoroughly legitimate one at that, is lost to the degree that some mechanism(s) – keep talking until you all agree; take a vote and respect simple majority views? – has to be imported, and no decision mechanism exists which is universally acceptable on all grounds that count.

I have suggested that Rawls himself reinstates the features and outcomes of the lost hypothetical dialogue by restating the hypothetical in the guise of the real. This is not an option for us. Keeping an eye on the regulative principles arising from the original position, what institutional and contextual features for a democratic structure built around actual, spoken deliberation could we propose?

I will begin with inclusiveness, as this helps to establish the context for key features under other headings. Clearly everyone cannot be included in a face-to-face fashion in one deliberative forum. So the device of representation becomes critical. Arguably the best way to ensure a fair 'presence' for all in an indirect way is through the use of random sampling of the population to produce a representative body to do the deliberating on behalf of all. In this respect, something like Fishkin's deliberative polls suggests itself.[50] Any delineated population can be randomly sampled, from the local to the global, so the move from the original position's total inclusiveness to our partial exclusion need not bring in tight national or other territorial exclusions.

Now, generality too is a principle served by random sampling to produce a representative forum. If the deliberating body is (scientifically) drawn from the whole (relevant) population, we can have some confidence in its outcomes reflecting general concerns across that population. Allied to the psychological effects of having to give reasons to fellow deliberators that they can accept the premises of, if not the reasons themselves, this derivation of the forum is likely to foster generality. Clearly, we are now dealing with various forms and degrees of partiality rather than an easy impartiality. But again a forum derived in the way discussed will lessen the extent to which partial outcomes are lopsidedly or unacceptably partial.

So something like a deliberative poll *à la* Fishkin may be seen as the most defensible real-world equivalent of an original position in the sense of attempting to replicate where possible desirable and democratic features of the latter. But – and this is where the speculations start to get more interesting – there are other, additional institutional devices which we can link with the deliberative poll in order to attempt to pick up further features in line with the regulative principles identified. In particular, a dynamic civil society characterized by a strong culture of freedom of movement and expression is absolutely crucial to this skeletal vision. Primarily this is because in the original position there is no problem of agenda-setting: because all people of all generations are 'there', all issues and all ways of looking at issues are there too. A real deliberative poll, by contrast (to say the least), must have its agenda set for it. A continuous one, like that envisaged here and unlike that deployed by Fishkin and colleagues, requires continuous agenda-setting and continuous pressure to look at new issues, and at old issues in new ways (impartiality and generality too are fostered: impartiality through ignorance can be replaced by a 'higher' (or 'reflective') partiality born of knowledge of many and varied partial perspectives). This might broadly be achieved by civil society as I have very broadly characterized its ideal features, with the important addition of formal means of agenda-setting stipulating appropriate use of a device such as the citizens' initiative. Even the interests of future generations might then feature in real-world debates; if organized interests in civil society press the case for considering the future in present decisions, some small but significant part of that effect of the veil of ignorance might be recaptured.

The possibility of stalemate rears its head, of course, in reality. Here we need further, familiar devices in order to hold on to something of the substance of the relevant regulative principle. Voting according to rules that are broadly acceptable – itself a topic akin to a can of worms, but I say no more on it here – is vital if the real-world equivalent of the ideal deliberative forum is to be reasonably productive in the sense I use the term here. I refer here to voting in the deliberative-representative forum itself; but, much more broadly than that, we need citizens who have the right to vote for *further* representative bodies which can in a more formal way play an agenda-setting and implementational role. The latter are required because of the danger of randomly selected representatives being insulated from popular pressures in ways that undermine key regulative principles in practice.

This sketch is all too brief – barely a beginning, let alone an end. It is not meant to be more than suggestive. What it does suggest is that, if one were minded to replicate as far as possible the assumptions and features of the original position in the real world, one would have to produce a vision that, in terms of institutions at least, provided for a mix of mechanisms of agenda setting, deliberation and decision making, variously broad and narrow and formal and informal. More specifically, as I have hinted, a literally representative deliberative forum with real decision-making authority would need to be located in a larger matrix of institutions including elected assemblies, a free and open civil society, the device of the initiative, and so on. On one side this begins to look like a list of (mostly) familiar democratic institutions. On another, it looks like a radical re-visioning of democracy. Either way, it is a democratic vision, subject to change and uncertain outcomes. And it is arguably its democratic character that differentiates it from the contrasting vision in Rawls's *Political Liberalism* of how his early theory could be transformed into a vision of 'deliberative democracy'.

Notes

1 J. Rawls, '"The idea of public reason" revisited', *University of Chicago Law Review*, 64: 3 (1997), p. 772.

2 Arguably, political theory as a discipline pays insufficient attention to the path-dependence of theorizing; in the current era it is adaptations of the dominant dialogical metaphor – the Kuhnian paradigm of the times? – that have driven our conceptions of both justice and democracy.

3 J. Cohen, 'Deliberation and democratic legitimacy', in A. Hamlin and P. Pettit (eds), *The Good Polity* (Oxford: Blackwell, 1989).

4 S. Benhabib, 'Toward a deliberative model of democratic legitimacy', in S. Benhabib (ed.), *Democracy and Difference* (Princeton NJ: Princeton University Press, 1996), pp. 74–5.

5 J. Bohman and W. Rehg, 'Introduction', in J. Bohman and W. Rehg (eds), *Deliberative Democracy* (Cambridge MA and London: MIT Press, 1997), p. xv.

6 Rawls, '"The idea of public reason" revisited', p. 772.

7 A. Gutmann and D. Thompson, *Democracy and Disagreement* (Cambridge MA and London: Belknap Press, 1996); J. Dryzek, *Deliberative Democracy and Beyond* (Oxford: Oxford University Press, 2000); Cohen, 'Deliberation and democratic legitimacy'; J. S. Fishkin, *Democracy and Deliberation* (New Haven CT and London: Yale University Press, 1991).

8 Cohen, 'Deliberation and democratic legitimacy'.

9 Dryzek, *Deliberative Democracy and Beyond*.

10 Gutmann and Thompson, *Democracy and Disagreement*.

11 Fishkin, *Democracy and Deliberation*.

12 R. A. Dahl, *Democracy and its Critics* (New Haven CT: Yale University Press, 1989).

13 Only Dryzek's 'discursive' variant of deliberative democracy goes so far as to suggest that discursive contestation can be the basis of 'a logically complete deliberative alternative to the aggregative idea that public opinion is transmitted to government through voting that registers preferences'. (Dryzek, *Deliberative Democracy and Beyond*, p. 50.)

14 I set to one side efforts to distinguish deliberative democracy according to its ability to realize independent standards (e.g. D. Estlund, 'Who's afraid of deliberative democracy? On the strategic/deliberative divide in recent constitutional jurisprudence', *Texas Law Review*, 71 (1993). These are peripheral to a debate which accepts – indeed, often starts with – the fact of moral pluralism and the fact that political decisions inevitably include contestable moral choices.

15 J. Rawls, *Political Liberalism* (New York: Columbia University Press, 1993), p. 213.

16 J. Rawls, '"The idea of public reason" revisited', p. 767.

17 Rawls, *Political Liberalism*, p. 213.

18 *Ibid.*, p. 216.

19 *Ibid.*, p. 217.

20 J. Rawls, '"The idea of public reason": postscript', in Bohman and Rehg, *Deliberative Democracy*, pp. 97–8.

21 *Ibid.*, p. 136.

22 Rawls, '"The idea of public reason" revisited', p. 771.

23 *Ibid.*, p. 767.

24 Rawls, *Political Liberalism*, p. 225.

25 *Ibid.*, p. 226.

26 Rawls, '"The idea of public reason" revisited', p. 774.

27 *Ibid.*, p. 774.

28 Rawls, *Political Liberalism*, pp. 226–7.

29 J. Rawls, *A Theory of Justice* (Oxford: Oxford University Press, 1972), p. 138.

30 Rawls, *Political Liberalism*, pp. 252–3.

31 *Ibid.*, pp. 219–20.

32 *Ibid.*, p. 215.

33 Goodin has suggested that 'internal-reflective' deliberation is an important ingredient in deliberative democracy, given the impossibility of 'external-collective' deliberation encompassing a mass community. Certainly the term 'deliberation' – like 'reasoning', discussed above – can refer to mental, reflective processes as well as spoken interaction with others. My view, implied in my arguments here, is that deliberation as actual spoken interaction is central to deliberative *democracy*, and to that extent can in no way be replaced by other, internalist, forms. See R. E. Goodin, 'Democratic deliberation within', *Philosophy and Public Affairs*, 29 (2000).

34 In an article on Rawls's *Collected Papers* (1999) Waldron writes, 'what if an economist asks a theologian to justify anti-euthanasia laws? It is no good saying, "Well, put them behind the veil of ignorance, and see what they come up with." The veil of ignorance is itself a way of modeling ideas about fairness, and the problem posed by pluralism is that fairness may be understood quite differently (or may not figure prominently at all) in various traditions. In *Political Liberalism* Rawls insists that public justifications in a well-ordered society must in some sense stand above or apart from the religious, cultural and philosophical issues that divide the citizens. A person does not show the other the requisite respect if he responds to requests for justification in terms that he knows the other cannot accept.' (J. Waldron, 'The plight of the poor in the midst of plenty', *London Review of Books*, 15 July 1999, pp. 3–6.) Waldron here feels that he is pointing out a significant difference between the two 'stories'. In fact notice the great similarities, on his description. In the second story, it is unacceptable for particularity to affect a suitably general view being adopted by citizens – which is just what the veil of ignorance models in the

first story. And in *Political Liberalism*, of course, all must have some conception of justice, similar in structure and effect to justice as fairness if not the latter exactly. I suggest that Waldron in fact underlines the metaphorical and mirroring effects I discuss.

35 Rawls, '"The idea of public reason": postscript', p. 140, writes that his project consists of two stages: the derivation of justice as fairness as a freestanding political conception of justice, and the issue of reasonable comprehensive doctrines and the overlapping consensus. The first stage is about principles, the second about stability. But this cannot be interpreted as a chronological point as opposed to a convenient way to characterize conceptually (apparently) different aspects of the argument. And at any rate, keeping these two parts separate would undermine thoroughly Rawls's claim that there will be political conceptions of justice which respect the limits of public reason other than his own preferred conception.

36 Cohen, 'Deliberation and democratic legitimacy'.

37 M. Saward, 'Less than meets the eye: democratic legitimacy and deliberative theory', in M. Saward (ed.), *Democratic Innovation* (London: Routledge, 2000).

38 Cohen, 'Deliberation and democratic legitimacy'.

39 Rawls, '"The idea of public reason": postscript', p. 138.

40 Rawls, '"The idea of public reason" revisited', p. 797.

41 J. Wolff, 'Democratic voting and the mixed motivation problem', *Analysis*, 54: 4 (1994).

42 Rawls, '"The idea of public reason": postscript', p. 135.

43 Rawls, '"The idea of public reason" revisited', pp. 768–9.

44 *Ibid.*, p. 800.

45 Fishkin, *Democracy and Deliberation*, and J. S. Fishkin and R. Luskin, 'The quest for deliberative democracy', in Saward, *Democratic Innovation*, represent a kind of semi-governmental perspective; Dryzek, *Deliberative Democracy and Beyond*, a largely anti-statist view; Benhabib, 'Toward a deliberative model of democratic legitimacy', a view of siting forums which like J. Habermas, *Between Facts and Norms* (Cambridge: Polity Press, 1996), bridges that divide to some degree; I. M. Young, 'Difference as a resource for democratic communication', in Bohman and Rehg, *Deliberative Democracy*, discusses difference and inclusion, and Cohen, 'Deliberation and democratic legitimacy', is the key source on consensus.

46 M. Saward, *The Terms of Democracy* (Cambridge: Polity Press, 1998), pp. 64–5.

47 Ronald Dworkin, for example, is quoted as saying of Rawls, 'I do not even have to think where to start; it is automatic that I start with him. My present view is opposed to his in some ways, but only from within a field defined by him' (quoted in B. Rogers, 'John Rawls', *Prospect*, June 1999, pp. 50–5).

48 Rawls, *A Theory of Justice*, p. 139.

49 R. Eckersley, 'Deliberative democracy, ecological representation and risk: towards a democracy of the affected', in Saward, *Democratic Innovation*.

50 Fishkin and Luskin, 'The quest for deliberative democracy'.

Part II

Institutional perspectives

6

Deliberation and decision making: discontinuity in the two-track model

JUDITH SQUIRES

The 'deliberative democracy' literature that has emerged during the last decade has very little to say about decision making and nothing new to offer to debates about models of representative government. What it does offer is an account of how important it is to develop inclusive and vibrant informal public spheres for deliberation, to supplement the formal institutions of representative government. It doesn't even, I suggest, offer a sustained account about how these informal public spheres are to engage with the formal public sphere of government.

In using the term 'deliberative democracy' and in contrasting it with 'aggregative models of democracy' the implication is that these are two competing models, and the former ought to replace the latter. But consideration of the detail of most arguments in favour of deliberation reveals that what is being proposed is an augmentation of aggregative democracy with deliberation. In other words, the deliberative democracy literature does not represent a direct refutation of the liberal democratic commitment to representative democracy. Rather it suggests that we could usefully supplement this practice with others, which encourage interactive debate and the transformation of preferences.

No comprehensive theory of democracy can focus on deliberation alone. There will always be a requirement for decision making. And, as Elster has noted, deliberation is never used as the only procedure for making collective decisions – it is always supplemented by voting or bargaining, or both – because of time constraints if nothing else.[1] This means, as Saward suggests, that, while deliberation may be an ideal part of democratic processes, it can only be a part, so deliberative democracy is not a proper 'model of democracy' at all but only an ingredient of one.[2] Deliberative democrats, if they are to offer a fully articulated theory of democracy, as opposed to a partial augmentation of existing theories, need to say something specific about this relation between the deliberative and the decisional moments within the democratic process. More needs to be said about the way in which deliberation is to augment and thereby improve existing institutions of aggregative democracy. For while the current institutions of representative democracy are explicitly critiqued within the deliberative democracy literature, they are also – I suggest – implicitly assumed. A more open acknowledgement of this assumption would allow greater engagement with the issue of how deliberation is to be squared with the more conventional political procedures of representation, aggregation and decision making.

In order to explore this claim I intend to focus first on that part of the literature that appears to endorse a bifurcated model of democracy, locating deliberation within an informal public sphere and decision making in the formal public sphere. I shall then consider alternative articulations of deliberative democracy, which avoid this apparent discontinuity by introducing the idea of regulated deliberation within formal institutions, in addition to the unregulated deliberation of the informal public spheres. The virtue of these renderings of deliberative democracy is that they engage with issues pertaining to both democracy and constitutionalism, considering not only preference formation and informal group deliberation but also institutional decision making and the operation of the rule of law. What they do not really provide, I suggest, is a fully integrated account of the relation between preference formation and informal group deliberation on the one hand and institutional decision making and the rule of law on the other. The cultivation of deliberation, which is both rational and inclusive, within informal public spheres is argued to generate legitimate decision making. But if there is no clear and procedurally guaranteed link between the deliberative and decisional moments the legitimacy generated by the former cannot reasonably be claimed by the latter.

Deliberative democracy: the basic model

Advocates of deliberative democracy suggest that the idea of democracy revolves around the transformation, rather than simply the aggregation, of preferences. The basic impulse behind deliberative democracy is the notion that people will modify their perceptions of what society should do in the course of discussing this with others. The point of democratic participation is to manufacture, rather than to discover and aggregate, the common good. As Ian Shapiro notes, 'The assumption is that if people talk for long enough in the right circumstances they will eventually be brought to agree, and that this is a good thing.'[3] The ideal is one of democratic decision making arising from deliberative procedures that are inclusive and rational.

Given this, David Miller suggests that there are three central conditions stipulated for the ideal of democracy: inclusivity, rationality and legitimacy.[4] Deliberative democracy is inclusive in the sense that each member of a political community takes part in decision making on an equal basis; rational in the sense that the decisions reached are determined by the reasons offered in the course of the deliberation, and not by a simple aggregation of the interests, prejudices or demands of voters; and legitimate in the sense that every participant understands how and why the outcome was reached even if he or she was not personally convinced by the argument offered in its favour. Note that the claim is that *deliberative decision making* is legitimate because it is rational and inclusive.

Deliberative democrats take their bearings from several different theoretical traditions, creating differences between them,[5] but all are concerned with developing a theory of democratic legitimacy – a project that they argue must be grounded in deliberation. All argue that deliberation must be governed by a set of basic principles woven into fair procedures in order to yield legitimate collective decisions. They all claim that the basic principles that ought to govern deliberation are the principles that ought to be used to deduce and then justify political outcomes as legitimate. Deliberation, it is argued, can move a complex, divided political community towards decisions its members, including dissenters, ought to accept as legitimate.

So theories of deliberative democracy are concerned with the problem of political justification in the face of moral disagreement, and aim to provide a solution to that problem.[6] As Joshua Cohen states, according to the ideal of deliberative democracy 'justification of the exercise of collective political power is to proceed on the basis of a free public reasoning among equals'.[7] Participants in democratic deliberation must defend their preferred understandings of the public interest on the basis of moral reasons which are acceptable to all participants, rather than on the basis of mutual advantage. As Melissa Williams notes, 'the legitimacy of political action turns not on whether it serves all citizens' interests equally well, but on whether it is grounded in reasons that all can accept as valid'.[8] Deliberative democracy also makes demands on our character in that we must enter the conversation with sufficient open-mindedness that we can be persuaded by the arguments of others.

People advocate deliberation for different reasons: some think it inherently worthwhile; others value it for instrumental reasons. Those who think it inherently worthwhile accept a neo-Hegelian philosophical psychology according to which intersubjective recognition is the highest stage of being: we become truly human only in justifying ourselves to one another.[9] More commonly deliberation is valued for instrumental reasons: achieving consensus, discovering truth, and consciousness raising are among the most usual values.[10] For these theorists deliberation is proposed in response to various maladies that are perceived as pervading contemporary democracy. These include poor decision making, soundbite politics, low levels of participation, declining legitimacy of government, and ignorant citizens.

Most deliberative democrats locate themselves in the tradition of radical democrats who have criticized 'thin' aggregative models of democracy but reject the assumption, common among radical democrats, that complex plural society is an impediment to democracy. Rather than indulging in nostalgic longing for a simpler society, they suggest that pluralism and social complexity may promote 'free, equal, and rational deliberation in vibrant and cosmopolitan public spheres'.[11] Public deliberation, they suggest, is uniquely suited to generating legitimate political decisions out of a social situation in which no point of view commands clear allegiance. Part of the project of deliberative democrats is to convince us that current political institutions and informal political structures are fairly friendly environments for democratic decision making. The optimism is based on the idea that cultural pluralism can improve the public use of reason, rather than act as an obstacle to its operation.

Deliberation and decision making: a two-track model?

Deliberative democrats are frequently held to offer a conception of impartiality that is dialogical rather than monological. Advocates claim this to be a more acceptable conception of impartiality, which redeems the concept in the face of the charges made against the purely monological conception of impartiality proposed by liberal theorists and criticized by difference theorists.[12] This is an interesting attempt to move towards a dialogical conception of impartiality, focusing attention of the crucial link between democratic inclusion and just moral reasoning.

Deliberative democrats suggest that if the conditions of deliberation are met fully the decision we arrive at will have greater legitimacy than it could have had through any other method of decision making. The decision is impartial in the sense of being inclusive and lacking bias. It will, says Williams, have taken all relevant evidence, perspectives and persons into account, and will not favour some over others on morally arbitrary grounds.[13] Legitimacy here requires not only lack of bias but also inclusivity. As John Dryzek says, 'No concerned individuals should be excluded . . .'[14] Given that impartiality is held to entail both lack of bias and inclusivity, deliberative democrats are concerned – as Iris Marion Young states – with 'the conditions of *inclusive decision making* that might help bring about more just and wise political judgements'.[15] Yet what this means in practice is unclear, as Williams acknowledges: 'Although there may be some limitations on the degree to which this aspiration can be met,' she says, 'it remains the regulative goal of deliberative democracy'.[16]

As a regulative goal this conception of impartiality has great merit. But there is a problem in the institutional working out of the ideal within the models of deliberative democracy currently on offer. There is, I think, an unfortunate tendency to accept the practical bifurcation of 'lack of bias' and 'inclusivity' when considering the actual location and manifestation of deliberation within democratic regimes. If you look at the institutional arrangements proposed by deliberative democrats they appear to embody not simply the dialogical conception of impartiality, but rather a two-track model in which the monological and the dialogical have distinct roles, located within clearly demarcated political practices. If this is so, it alters the nature of the theoretical critique deliberative democrats are issuing in relation to liberal theories of justice as impartiality. Rather than offering a different vision, deliberative democrats may simply be offering an augmented vision: just decision making and inclusive deliberation. What they are not offering, I suggest, is a theory of deliberative decision making.

For example, Habermas suggests that legitimacy is based on 'rationally motivated agreement' that is produced in 'undeformed public spheres' through actual processes of deliberation.[17] The general public sphere is not a mere 'back room' of democratic politics, but rather an 'impulse-generating periphery that surrounds the political centre: in cultivating normative reasons, it affects all parts of the political system without intending to conquer it'.[18] Note here that there is a clear distinction between 'undeformed', informal or weak public spheres where public opinion may be formed and the strong, 'arranged', formal sites of institutionalized dialogue, which must be open to influence from the weak public spheres turning influence into a 'jurisgenerative communicative power.'[19]

In other words, laws and political decisions in complex and plural societies can be rational and hence legitimate in a deliberative democratic sense – that is, rationally authored by the citizens to whom they are addressed – if institutionalized decision-making procedures follow two tracks. As Habermas states, 'the normative expectation of rational outcomes is grounded ultimately in the interplay between institutionally structured political will-formation and spontaneous, unsubverted circuits of communication in a public sphere that is not programmed to reach decisions and thus is not organised'.[20] Political decisions must be both open to inputs from an informal, vibrant public sphere (contexts of discovery) and appropriately structured to support the rationality of the relevant types of discourse and to ensure implementation (contexts of justification).[21] This is a two-track model in which the informal, public spheres are 'contexts of discovery' and the formal, public spheres are 'contexts of justification'.

This two-track model of deliberative democracy distinguishes between communication oriented to mutual understanding, on the one hand, and instrumental action and politics on the other. Because it remains largely within the realms of ideal theory and entails very little institutional design, the distinction is decidedly unhelpful in offering any real guidance as to how to establish, monitor or measure the relation between these two types of public sphere. This is a crucial weakness for operationalizing theories of deliberative democracy, for, if deliberative democracy is primarily about re-establishing legitimacy, and if this legitimacy requires lack of bias and inclusivity, we will clearly need some means of evaluating the degree of inclusivity attained. Yet, if we are unable to clearly demarcate the public spheres in which we should be measuring inclusion, any attempt to base legitimacy upon inclusivity will necessary fail.

So, it would appear that that within deliberative democracy impartiality, and thus legitimacy, entails both inclusiveness (of persons and issues) and absence of bias (institutional structures, reasons and participants). It also appears that these are located – in certain accounts if not all – within the informal and the formal public spheres respectively. In other words the 'context of discovery' appeals to the ideal of impartiality as inclusiveness (of persons and issues) and the 'context of justification' appeals to the ideal of impartiality as absence of bias. The formal public sphere adopts a norm of impartiality that is the liberal norm of generality, while the informal public spheres adopt the more participatory and dialogic norm of democratic inclusion.

If this is the intention the deliberative model is actually liberal-democratic in a rather clear-cut way: liberal in the context of justification and democratic in the context of discovery. Whether these two different manifestations of impartiality cohere into a single vision of deliberative democracy hinges on the issue of the relation of influence between the two, yet this is frequently left unspecified. Where it is specified, the discontinuity proposed by two-track model would seem to be vindicated.

For example, Jack Knight and James Johnson offer a model of the relation between deliberation and decision making in which first democratic deliberation takes place, encouraging the transformation of preferences, and then aggregative procedures are introduced, converting the resultant preferences into an outcome.[22] This model offers a clear understanding of the relation between deliberation and decision making: deliberation must cease and aggregation must be introduced if a decision is to be reached. Democratic deliberation is, on this account, the search for truth, and majority voting a process that interrupts this search in order to reach a decision. The stages of deliberation and of closure are, as Henry Richardson points out, viewed here as 'conceptually discontinuous'.[23]

Implicitly accepting this conceptual discontinuity, Habermas seeks to play down its significance, stating, 'Majority rule retains an internal relation to the search for truth inasmuch as the decision reached by the majority only represents a caesura in an ongoing discussion; the decision records, so to speak, the interim result of a discursive opinion-forming process.'[24] But the discontinuity is nonetheless a worry for Richardson, who argues that there are both motivational and normative problems embedded within the discontinuity between deliberation and decision making at the heart of so many accounts of deliberative democracy. The motivational problem is that there is little incentive to find a reasonable compromise between preferences if the decision is understood as an aggregative polling of private preferences. The normative problem is that there is no mechanism for the decision to be recognized as a reasonable compromise if there is no formal connection between the two stages.[25]

These are, I think, serious problems for any account of deliberative democracy that claims to be offering a comprehensive model of democracy. As Richardson says, 'the challenge is to conceive the process of deliberation and the mechanism of its closure in an integrated way, so that the work of giving and accepting reasons that is done in the deliberative stage is not washed out by the way in which the decision is made'.[26] This strikes me as a crucial point, and one too rarely addressed by deliberative democrats. For if deliberative democracy is to offer a coherent model of democracy in all its aspects it must surely develop an integrated account of these two moments. It must say more about the institutional relation between deliberation and decision making than that the latter will 'interrupt' the former.

This apparent discontinuity between the context of discovery, which houses deliberation and generates dialogical impartiality, and the context of justification, which houses decision making and generates monological impartiality, matters: it matters I suggest, because unless one clearly articulates, both in ideal theory and in institutional practice, what the relation is between monological and dialogical impartiality, the danger that the latter will get subsumed or marginalized by the former will be ever present. This possibility would undermine the legitimation claims made for deliberation, based as they are on the dialogical rather than the monological moment.

For example, Williams has suggested that dialogical impartiality is a superior basis for legitimacy claims than monological impartiality, because it entails both lack of bias and inclusivity. Yet she states that: 'Deliberative democracy takes as both its premise and its conclusion that political decisions should not systematically favour some persons or interests over others. This is not to say that deliberative decisions will not sometimes require the unequal distribution of benefits and burdens, but that whenever such inequalities exist they will be justifiable through reasons which all could accept.'[27] Note two things here: firstly, the impartiality has become monological rather than dialogical when we turn our attention to the actual decisions (that is, 'all could accept' rather than 'all did accept when they engaged in actual dialogue about this'). As such it looks rather more like the Rawlsian monological form of internal deliberative justification than the actual dialogical form of deliberation implied thus far in Williams's account. Secondly, note that Williams nonetheless speaks of 'deliberative decisions'. But were the decisions deliberative, or were they perhaps merely influenced by a deliberative process? There is, in Williams's rendering of the deliberative project at least, a lack of specificity on this issue.

The issue is important, I suggest, because the assumption of discontinuity within the model of deliberative democracy undermines its claims to legitimacy, claims that are after all based upon the rationality and inclusivity of the deliberative and not the decisional moment. The three central conditions stipulated for the ideal of deliberative democracy – inclusivity, rationality and legitimacy – look decidedly problematic in the light of this endorsement of discontinuity. Recall that Miller suggests that deliberative democracy is inclusive:

> in the sense that each member of a political community takes part in *decision making* on an equal basis; rational in the sense that the *decisions* reached are determined by the reasons offered in the course of the deliberation, and not by a simple aggregation of the interests, prejudices or demands of voters; and legitimate in the sense that every participant understands how and why the *outcome* was reached even if he or she was not personally convinced by the argument offered in its favour.[28]

If, as it now appears, decisions simply interrupt the deliberative process rather than emerging out of it, each of Miller's claims is radically destabilized: members of the political community may conceivably all take part in deliberation on an equal basis, but elected representatives and judges will make the decisions;

decisions may be influenced by deliberation, but will be determined by aggregation; and finally citizens may understand how deliberation proceeded and how aggregation took place, but they are unlikely to understand the structural relation between the two if it is left unspecified as influence. Each of the inclusivity, rationality and legitimacy claims looks vulnerable.

Bridging the apparent discontinuity

Much of the deliberative democracy literature suggests this two-track model of democracy, where deliberation and decision making are located within two distinct spheres. Deliberation is largely located within informal, public spheres (or 'contexts of discovery') and decision making within the formal, public spheres (or 'contexts of justification'). This two-track model of deliberative democracy distinguishes between communication oriented to mutual understanding, on the one hand, and instrumental action and politics, on the other. It is a model based on discontinuity, which potentially undermines the claims to the legitimacy-generating functions of deliberative democracy, claims that are based on the rationality and inclusivity of the deliberative and not the decisional moment. Yet unless a direct link can be established and maintained between informal deliberation and formal decision making the decisions made cannot realistically benefit from the legitimacy generated by the deliberation alone.

The literature on deliberative democracy is, however, diverse. Its various articulations are not all equally subject to this charge of the discontinuity between deliberation and decision making. So it is only right that one considers other accounts. Within the literature there is a significant difference of opinion as to where the deliberation that is to generate political legitimacy is to be located – ranging from citizens' juries, churches, workplaces and consciousness-raising groups to political parties, Parliament and the Supreme Court. The absence of consensus on this issue is significant, not least because it has implications for the proposed relation between the deliberative and the decisional aspects of democratic government.

A brief survey of the models proposed by Fishkin, Cohen, Habermas and Young indicates that deliberative democrats are not all in agreement about the relation between decision making and deliberation, such that the institutional implications of endorsing a theory of deliberative democracy are far from clear-cut. There are, I suggest, certain articulations of deliberative democracy that introduce the idea of regulated deliberation within the formal institutions in addition to the unregulated deliberation of the informal public spheres, which may offer a resolution to the problem of discontinuity. But they also introduce problems of their own – in relation to the role of representatives as both delegates and deliberators – that are worthy of further consideration.

Fishkin's model of deliberative polls offers, for example, one fairly clear, if modest, account of this possible relation. The model entails taking a random sample of some relevant population, interviewing them, and inviting them to a single site for a deliberative weekend (all expenses paid). Participants are sent carefully balanced briefing materials examining the main policy options and the arguments for and against them. They are then set deliberating in small-group discussions led by trained moderators and in plenary sessions where they can put questions to panels of competing politicians and policy experts.[29] Fishkin's latest deliberative project is the promotion of 'Deliberation Day', to be held a week before national elections, in which everyone would be paid $150 to show up at their local school or community centre to deliberate.[30]

These deliberative polls, which are designed primarily to help participants inform and clarify their own thinking, are nonetheless thought to have a role in influencing government policy. Fishkin, for example, claims some prescriptive weight for this deliberation. 'Its results,' he says, 'have prescriptive force because they are the voice of the people under special conditions where the people have had a chance to think about the issues and hence should have a voice worth listening to'.[31] In other words, the recommendations stemming from deliberative polls should inform policy-making, in the same way that a Royal Commission informs government policy.

The location of deliberation within a clearly delimited polling process has the obvious advantage of random selection of a small number of people who are engaged in face-to-face dialogue and who do not need to come to a consensus. They are encouraged to deliberate free from the requirement of reaching a decision. There is some evidence that in these circumstances people are more likely to transform their beliefs and accept those of others. It is only in these small-scale experimental deliberative arenas that it is even remotely possible to imagine a situation free from relations of power, which inhibit open and undistorted communication. But such deliberative polls are clearly marginal to the main forms of political participation and decision making. If the entire body of deliberative democratic theory results in nothing more than the introduction of a few of these polls its contribution will have been limited indeed. It is clear, however, that within other articulations of deliberative democratic theory something altogether more profound is being suggested.

One such wide-ranging interpretation is to be found in Cohen's 'model for deliberative institutions', which highlights 'the properties that democratic institutions should embody'.[32] Rather than separating the context of discovery from the context of justification, Cohen suggests, the two are integral, requiring deliberation to lead to decision making within a single institutional structure. Ideal deliberation, he says, 'aims to arrive at a rationally motivated consensus' and where it cannot deliberation must conclude with voting, 'subject to some form of majority rule'.[33] The institutions making such decisions are not the formal institutions of representative democracy: Cohen equates institutions with 'associations' that are regulated by deliberation aimed at the common good and that respect the autonomy of their members.[34] These associations are 'arenas in which citizens can propose issues for the political agenda and participate in debate about those issues'.[35] Because they are a public good, they ought to be supported by public money. In fact, because associations organized on local, sectional or issue-specific lines are unlikely to produce open-ended deliberation, Cohen suggests that associations are best conceived as political parties.[36] So Cohen focuses on political parties as the site for deliberation. Though he does not reduce the political community to members of political parties (he recognizes, for instance, the role of other, local associations), he does argue parties to be the best institutions for deliberation.

In contrast to Fishkin's model, then, Cohen locates deliberation much more firmly within established political institutions. The pressure to reach consensus is therefore greater than in Fishkin's model, and the need to introduce voting and or bargaining is acknowledged accordingly. By locating deliberation within political parties and associations Cohen gives it a closer structural role to political decision making, but does so at the cost of lessening its claim to inclusivity. So, whereas Fishkin locates deliberation outside the formal institutions of representative democracy in autonomous public spheres, Cohen locates deliberation within state-funded political parties. Fishkin wants autonomous and informal deliberation to influence decision making; Cohen wants state-funded and formal deliberation to determine decision making.

Cohen offers a proceduralist argument for the legitimacy of deliberative democracy. He suggests that democratic decisions are legitimate in so far as they are produced by inclusive and rational deliberation.[37] The only criteria for assessing the quality of the results of deliberation are the formal, procedural conditions of inclusivity and rationality.[38] But is it realistic to demand that the inclusivity and the rationality of the deliberative procedures should occur at the same moment? Is it not actually the case that inclusive deliberation is the ideal for the informal public spheres of civil society (as with Fishkin) and rational deliberation the ideal for the formal public spheres of parties and Parliament (as with Cohen)? If so, and if legitimacy is dependent upon the existence of both inclusive and rational procedures, it becomes vital to specify the institutional mechanisms for bridging the gap between these two deliberative moments.

For a more detailed analysis of this relation one needs to turn to the work of Habermas. The basic two-track model outlined earlier implied that the monological and the dialogical have distinct roles and are located within clearly demarcated political practices – a formal decision-making sphere versus an informal opinion formation sphere. Although there is much within Habermas's work that appears to vindicate this model, a closer reading reveals that deliberation is intended to occur within both spheres, the only difference being that in the former it is procedurally regulated while in the latter it is procedurally unregulated.

Habermas argues that deliberation should take place both in formal institutions of deliberation and decision making (parliaments and courts) and in informal public spheres located in civil society.[39] As Maeve Cooke notes, 'On his view, public deliberation is important both in the formally organized processes of political decision making and legislation, and in the "anarchic" processes of will-formation in the public sphere.'[40] He cannot then be accused of locating deliberation outside the formal institutions of representative democracy in autonomous public spheres. Rather, the formal institutions act as a legitimation filter for the 'messages' they pick up from the public sphere. They also provide the setting in which our political representatives engage in deliberation, aiming to reach interim discursive conclusions about matters of public concern.[41]

In other words, Habermas's articulation of a discourse theory of democracy contains more continuity between the dialogical and the monological across the informal and formal divide than the two-track model of deliberative democracy suggests. The workings of the democratic procedures of law making allow various discourses to be fed into the decision-making process by re-enacting the deliberative process and bringing it to a temporary conclusion. The unregulated deliberation of the informal public spheres is echoed in the regulated deliberation of elected representatives (who are given more space for deliberative manoeuvre than simple delegates would be allowed). The regulation of the formal institutional setting ensures that the deliberation is always delimited by the need to reach a decision.

On this reading there is less of a discontinuity between the informal and the formal in terms of the location of deliberation: deliberation is not confined to the context of discovery, but also occurs – in regulated fashion – within the context of justification. The formal institutions are not, on this account, accurately depicted as simply the domain of instrumental action, to be contrasted with the informal spheres in which communicative reason is manifest. Rather, the formal institutions transform communicative power into administrative power: filtering unregulated deliberation into regulated deliberation, transforming this into decision-making moments and so then to the implementation of policy. The discontinuity between dialogical and monological reason remains, but it does not map neatly on to the informal and formal spheres. Instead, the discontinuity is bridged by transformative processes within the formal institutions themselves.

Yet the tension that emerged in the basic two-track model is not eradicated, it is simply relocated. If regulated deliberation is to take place among representatives within the formal institutions of the public sphere, it must be squared with the requirement that elected representatives speak on behalf of their electorate, and with the requirement that they make conclusive decisions, justify and implement these. The second tension could be resolved if the regulated deliberation were limited to Parliament whilst the executive and judiciary adopted the decision-making and implementation roles. This is a feasible solution, but one that replicates the discontinuity between deliberation and decision making within the formal public sphere rather than eroding the discontinuity altogether. Discontinuity between the context of discovery and the context of justification is still a feature of the model, but it is now located in the separation between the legislature on the one hand and the executive and judiciary on the other.

This has the effect of making the move from deliberation to decision making more gradual, because it becomes a three-stage process – moving from unregulated, inclusive deliberation to regulated, rational (but perhaps not inclusive?) deliberation and then to (purely aggregative?) decision making. But it also intensifies the significance of the first tension: namely the model of political representation assumed within the model. For representatives are given a demanding role here: they are required both to echo the unregulated deliberation of the informal public sphere and to engage in regulated deliberation themselves. There will clearly be moments when the two functions stand in tension one to the other, when – for example – the regulated deliberation among the representatives leads them to depart from, rather than 'filter', the unregulated deliberation of the informal public spheres. This will inevitably undermine the perceived legitimacy of the elected representatives in the eyes of their electors.

Habermas says, on this issue, that:

> Discourses conducted by representatives can meet the condition of equal participation on the part of all members only if they remain porous, sensitive, and receptive to the suggestions, issues and contributions, information and arguments that flow in from a discursively structured public sphere, that is, one that is pluralistic, close to the grass roots, and relatively undisturbed by the effects of power.[42]

There is here a basis of a model for determining which political decisions have emerged through imposition and which through genuinely open processes of dialogue, but it is a rather vague one. And the distinction is made to carry a heavy burden.

At this point it is probably worth noting that Habermas doesn't choose to label his theory 'deliberative democracy' at all: instead he calls his approach a 'discourse' theory of law and democracy. The significance of this lies, perhaps, in the fact that he recognizes that under the conditions of modern complexity the aspiration to realize one single shared common political will is no longer viable. In these circumstances the role of procedural will-formation becomes essential. Citizens who engage in public deliberation cannot expect this deliberation to lead directly to a single shared consensual decision: they must accept the need for procedural institutions, the function of which is to transform the political wills emerging from diverse deliberative spheres into uniform legislative decisions.[43] This recognition helps us to square the ideal of deliberative democracy with the reality of complex modern society. It also makes clear, I would suggest, the extent to which an adequate theory of deliberative democracy needs an account of representation.

In this context it is interesting to consider the work of Iris Young, who suggests that: 'Increasing opportunities for serious and plural public debate that both holds powerful actors accountable and *is connected to institutional or policy outcomes* . . . may be a means by which democratic processes in a society with structural social and economic inequalities can address some of their injustices.'[44] She is, in other words, aware of the importance of connecting the deliberation of informal public spheres with institutional or policy outcomes. Emphasizing the context of 'large-scale mass society', she argues that the

> challenge for a theory of discussion-based democracy is to explain how its norms and values can apply to mass polities where the relations among members are complexly mediated rather than direct and face to face. This requires, among other things, a political theory of representation consistent with those norms.[45]

This is an important insight, and one that highlights a serious absence within most other articulations of deliberative democracy. In opposition to those who would reject representative democracy altogether, Young argues that 'the anti-representation position . . . refuses to face complex realities of democratic process, and wrongly opposes representation to participation'.[46] This position is untenable, she suggests, because the decision-making bodies that affect one's life are so numerous and so dispersed that it is impossible to propose that one be present in them all. Moreover, even when one is present in decision-making bodies, the pressures of time and the dynamics of social interaction are likely to lead to *de facto* representation which – unlike formal representation – lacks mechanisms of accountability. On this basis Young develops an account of representation, which she suggests is consistent with the norms of deliberative democracy.

This is a positive move, which goes some way towards developing an integrated account of deliberation and decision making, but it remains frustratingly vague on detail. Like Habermas, Young suggests that the representative's responsibility entails more than simply expressing a mandate: representatives should also engage in regulated deliberation, 'participate in discussion and debate with other representatives, listen to their questions, appeals, stories and arguments, and with them try to arrive at wise and just decisions'.[47] Yet, again like Habermas, she suggests that representatives – whilst not mandated – should nonetheless act as filters for the deliberation of the informal public spheres: 'During these sustained moments of independent action and judgement, however, the representative ought to recollect the discussion process that led to his authorization and anticipate a moment of being accountable to those he claims to represent.'[48]

The 'theory of representation' that Young is proposing as compatible with deliberative democracy is one that requires both regulated deliberation among the representatives themselves and also that this deliberation 'bears the traces of the discussion that led to authorization or in other ways persuasively justifies itself in a public accounting'.[49] As with Habermas, we find a model of democracy based on two distinct forms of deliberation: unregulated deliberation within informal public spheres and regulated deliberation among elected representatives. In addition, we again find that the procedures for specifying the relation between the unregulated and the regulated deliberation are left incredibly vague.

Within the deliberative democratic literature there is then a significant difference of opinion as to where the deliberation that is to generate political legitimacy is to be located: ranging from representative to unrepresentative bodies, from formal to informal. Current examples of deliberative moments within democratic systems are commonly assumed to include deliberative forums, town meetings, designated deliberation times, citizen juries and deliberative polls: small groups of randomly chosen citizens brought together to debate issues of current concern, with a view to influencing government policy.[50] But it appears that one should perhaps also consider parliaments, executives and judiciaries as sites for deliberation. This would require, however, greater specificity about the procedures for ensuring that both the unregulated deliberation of the informal spheres and the regulated deliberation of these formal spheres are rational, inclusive and therefore legitimate – and that the former filters directly into the latter. One would expect more to be said about how the deliberative ideal relates to the practices of political representation.

In order to realize the deliberative ideal one would need to address two questions. What is the likelihood that informal public spheres will be genuinely inclusive without resorting to some structural mechanisms of inclusion? And what is the likelihood that the deliberation within these informal spheres will 'influence' the representatives in the formal public spheres? How, in other words, are deliberative democrats to ensure both 'pluralistic' informal public spheres and 'porous' formal public spheres? There is a reasonably robust literature on the problems of securing pluralistic public spheres, but it largely ignores the distinction between the informal and formal, resulting in an impoverished literature on the second question. This leads to a frustrating lack of specificity about which sites of participation are actually being discussed. It also results in silence on the issue of the porosity of formal public spheres.

Augmenting motivational concerns with institutional ones

Theories of deliberative democracy have provoked a wealth of diverse criticism to date. The critical literature falls into three broad kinds, emerging from social choice theorists, realists and difference theorists.[51] This issue of the discontinuity between deliberation and decision making – apparent in so many articulations of deliberative democratic theory – relates to this existing critical literature in several distinct ways, but it also shifts the terrain of debate away from motivational and epistemological issues towards institutional considerations.

In order to grasp the nature of this shift, it is helpful to recall the two separate ways in which Elster locates the distinctiveness of deliberative democracy. Firstly, he suggests, where there is no consensus a group can make a decision in one of three ways: arguing, bargaining or voting (where arguing and bargaining require communication but voting does not). Secondly, participants in the decision-making process may be motivated by reason, interest or passion (where arguing is connected with reason, while bargaining and voting may be motivated by any one of the three).[52] Theories of deliberative democracy are characterized by their commitment to the importance of arguing in the face of a democratic system largely based on bargaining and voting, and to reason in the face of a society largely motivated by interest and passion.

The suggestion here is that academic debates about the merits of deliberative democratic theories have tended to focus on the motivational rather than the decision-making issue. Specifically, realists have argued about the feasibility of privileging reason over interests, and difference theorists have insisted on the importance of acknowledging passion as well as reason. For example, realists suggest that the ideal of deliberative democracy is too nostalgic and that large complex societies simply cannot depend on small slow-moving bodies; that most political decisions are taken at a speed which doesn't allow popular consultation, let alone deliberation; that even if deliberative forums are introduced participants are likely to manipulate the institution to their own advantage; and that the model assumes too great a degree of social responsibility on the part of citizens, which isn't borne out by experience. They suggest that a credible defence of deliberative democracy would have to show how its institutions would be any less corrupted by those with the resources to control agendas and bias decision making than existing institutions are. They are sceptical about the likelihood of such a defence, arguing that the ideal does not take on board the fact that the modern state is inevitably structurally hierarchical, secretive and unequal in the resources it grants to participants in and against its processes.[53]

This last criticism echoes the normative concerns of difference theorists, who argue that deliberative democracy is biased against groups that have historically been disadvantaged such as the poor, women and ethnic minorities. Difference theorists argue that deliberation is not a neutral procedure but one that works in favour of people with certain cultural attributes. The decisions reached via deliberation are no more just than those reached in existing liberal democracies. The claims to inclusivity and legitimacy are therefore rejected because of scepticism about the role of rationality in the model. If the rationality claims falls, so does the legitimacy claim. It is argued that, in its current formulations, deliberative theories of democracy exclude too many kinds of communication and are too preoccupied with reaching general agreement to be satisfying accounts of recognizing difference.[54] Agonistic democrats argue that deliberative democrats are too wedded to rationalistic, rule-governed order and ignore the extent to which modern democracy itself constitutes a system of power relations.[55]

The critical debate about deliberative democracy has, in other words, focused on the issue of whether participants in the decision-making process are, and ought to be, motivated by reason, interest or passion. Theories of deliberative democracy are characterized by their commitment to reason in the face of a society largely motivated by interest and passion. Realists and difference theorists have responded to this commitment by asserting the relative merits of interest and passion respectively.

In contrast, I have here focused on the fact that theories of deliberative democracy are characterized by their commitment to the importance of arguing in the face of a democratic system largely based on bargaining and voting. Critics have had relatively little to say about this commitment, offering few alternative proposals as to the relative merits of bargaining and voting as a means to reach a decision.

Conclusion

The desire to develop a deliberative model of democracy, in contrast to the dominant aggregative model, has been propelled by a sense that the aggregative model lacks, in Young's words, 'any distinct idea of a public formed from the interaction of democratic citizens and their motivation to reach some decision. Thus there is no account of the possibility of political co-ordination and co-operation.'[56] Deliberative democrats have attempted to address this lack by focusing attention on precisely these motivational issues, located within civil society. This has the positive effect of placing the issues of preference formation and informal group deliberation on the political agenda. What still remains is the task of relating this new agenda to the more orthodox, but nonetheless important, agenda of institutional decision making and the operation of the rule of law.

One of the real strengths of the deliberative democracy literature is extent to which it demands that constitutionalism and democracy should be viewed as equiprimordial, or equally basic. If constitutionalism comes to predominate, it is suggested, politics is reduced to 'juridification'; if democracy comes to dominate, politics is reduced to the tyranny of the majority. Deliberative democracy is offered as a means of realizing the equiprimordial status of each.[57] As such one would expect advocates of deliberative democracy to offer sustained accounts of the range of issues pertaining to both democracy and constitutionalism: the appropriate relation between preference formation, informal group deliberation, institutional decision making and the rule of law. Yet such a sustained account demands more attention to the issue of institutional decision making than has yet emerged in the literature on deliberative democracy.

The claims to rationality and inclusivity, and thus legitimacy, made by deliberative democrats look decidedly weak in the face of the apparent discontinuity that is assumed to exist between deliberation and decision making. If decisions simply interrupt the deliberative process rather than emerging out of it, as I have suggested on the basis of existing normative theory, each of the claims to inclusivity, rationality and legitimacy appears vulnerable as a result. Unless this issue is addressed deliberative democrats cannot claim to offer a comprehensive or coherent account of democracy.

Perhaps deliberative democrats don't think that deliberation will occur within the 'context of justification' or the 'decision-making assemblies' at all. If such is the case, the existence of deliberative decision making, and thus the principle of equal access to decision-making bodies, is simply not an issue for their model, as long as these assemblies can claim to be porous in some sense. If this isn't the case, deliberative democrats have a lot of work to do specifying the mechanisms for inclusion in the formal public sphere of decision making.

In any event, it remains unclear what mechanisms for fostering and evaluating degrees of porosity are envisaged. How is one to cultivate channels of influence between informal and formal public spheres and how would one evaluate the extent to which decisions had been influenced by the deliberation of these spheres? These are fairly conventional questions relating to the institutional design of the mechanisms of representative democracy. But they are important questions and ones to which deliberative democrats have, as yet, offered few interesting answers. Instead they have focused their attention on the more expansive issue of social and cultural inclusion in informal publics. But even here, the material reality of strategies for ensuring equal access to the 'context of discovery' has been largely overlooked. Given all this, I suggest that deliberative democrats need to move from the realms of ideal theory and on to the task of institutional design.

Notes

Sincere thanks to Shane O'Neill, Michael Saward and Maurizio Passerin d'Entrèves, who offered such helpful comments on a draft of this chapter.

1 Jon Elster, 'Introduction', in Jon Elster (ed.), *Deliberative Democracy* (Cambridge: Cambridge University Press, 1998), p. 5.

2 Michael Saward, 'Less than meets the eye: democratic legitimacy and deliberative theory', in Michael Saward (ed.), *Democratic Innovation: Deliberation, Representation, Association* (London: Routledge, 2000).

3 Ian Shapiro, 'Optimal Democracy', unpublished paper (2000), p. 5.

4 David Miller, Chapter 9 in this volume.

5 One of the main points of disagreement is what is to count as deliberation. Rawls offers a framework within which public reason operates, while Habermas claims to adopt a strictly proceduralist approach to the scope and content of deliberation. Accordingly, Habermasians criticize Rawlsians for having too rigid an understanding of the procedures and principles that ought to guide deliberation, while Rawlsians criticize Habermasians for understanding them too loosely.

6 Melissa Williams, 'The uneasy alliance of group representation and deliberative democracy', in Will Kymlicka and Wayne Norman (eds), *Citizenship in Diverse Societies* (Oxford: Oxford University Press, 2000), p. 127.

7 Joshua Cohen, 'Procedure and substance in deliberative democracy', in James Bohman and William Rehg (eds), *Deliberative Democracy* (Cambridge MA: MIT Press, 1997), p. 412.

8 Melissa Williams, 'The uneasy alliance of group representation and deliberative democracy', p. 127.

9 See Charles Taylor, 'The politics of recognition', in Amy Gutmann (ed.), *Multiculturalism: Examining the Politics of Recognition* (Princeton NJ: Princeton University Press, 1994).

10 Amy Gutmann and Dennis Thompson, *Democracy and Disagreement* (Cambridge MA: Harvard University Press, 1996); James Bohman, *Public Deliberation: Pluralism, Complexity and Democracy* (Cambridge MA: MIT Press, 1996); Seyla Benhabib (ed.), *Democracy and Difference: Contesting the Boundaries of the Political* (Princeton NJ: Princeton University Press, 1996); Bruce Ackerman and James Fishkin, 'Deliberation Day', paper delivered at the conference 'Deliberating on Deliberative Democracy', Austin TX: University of Texas, 4–6 February 2000.

11 Bohman, *Public Deliberation*, p. 21.

12 See particularly Shane O'Neill, *Impartiality in Context* (New York: State University of New York Press, 1997).

13 Williams, 'The uneasy alliance of group representation and deliberative democracy', p. 129.

14 John Dryzek, *Discursive Democracy* (Cambridge: Cambridge University Press, 1990), p. 43.

15 Iris Marion Young, *Inclusion and Democracy* (Oxford: Oxford University Press, 2000), p. 31.

16 Williams, 'The uneasy alliance of group representation and deliberative democracy', p. 129.

17 Jürgen Habermas, *Between Facts and Norms* (Cambridge MA: MIT Press, 1996), p. 14.

18 *Ibid.*, p. 442.

19 *Ibid.*, p. 147.

20 Jürgen Habermas, 'Popular sovereignty as procedure', in Bohman and Rehg, *Deliberative Democracy*, p. 57.

21 James Bohman, 'Complexity, pluralism, and the constitutional state: on Habermas's *Faktizität und Geltung*', *Law and Society Review*, 28: 4 (1994), p. 914.

22 Jack Knight and James Johnson, 'Aggregation and deliberation: on the possibility of democratic legitimacy', *Political Theory*, 22: 2 (1994), p. 286.

23 Henry Richardson 'Democratic intentions', in Bohman and Rehg, *Deliberative Democracy*, p. 356.

24 Habermas, *Between Facts and Norms*, p. 179.

25 Richardson, 'Democratic intentions', pp. 356–7.

26 *Ibid.*, p. 356.

27 Williams, 'The uneasy alliance of group representation and deliberative democracy', p. 131.

28 Miller, in this volume, Chapter 9 (emphasis added).

29 This experiment has been tried out in Britain in the form of five national deliberative polls which were conducted in collaboration with Channel Four: crime (1994), Britain's future in Europe (1995), the monarchy (1996), economic issues in the general election (1997) and the future of the National Health Service (1998).

30 Bruce Ackerman and James Fishkin, 'Deliberation Day', paper delivered at the conference 'Deliberating on Deliberative Democracy', Austin TX: University of Texas, 4–6 February 2000.

31 James Fishkin, *Democracy and Deliberation: New Directions for Democratic Reform* (New Haven CT: Yale University Press, 1991), p. 4.

32 Joshua Cohen, 'Deliberation and democratic legitimacy', in Bohman and Rehg, *Deliberative Democracy*, pp. 72–3.

33 *Ibid.*, p. 75.

34 *Ibid.*, pp. 78–9.

35 *Ibid.*, p. 85.

36 *Ibid.*, p. 85.

37 *Ibid.*, p. 73; Benhabib, *Democracy and Difference*, pp. 70–2.

38 See Maeve Cooke, in this volume, Chapter 3.

39 Habermas *Between Facts and Norms*, pp. 418–27.

40 Maeve Cooke, Chapter 3 in this volume, pp. 69–70.

41 O'Neill, *Impartiality in Context*, chapter 6.

42 Habermas, *Between Facts and Norms*, p. 182.

43 Thanks to Shane O'Neill for this point.

44 Young, *Inclusion and Democracy*, p. 36 (emphasis added).

45 *Ibid.*, p. 45.

46 *Ibid.*, p. 124.

47 *Ibid.*, p. 131.

48 *Ibid.*

49 *Ibid.*

50 Anna Coote and Jo Lenaghan, *Citizens' Juries: Theory into Practice* (London: Institute of Public Policy Research, 1997).

51 See David Miller, Chapter 9 in this volume.

52 Elster, *Deliberative Democracy*, pp. 5–7.

53 Michael Saward, 'The oldest innovation: from deliberative to direct democracy', in Saward, *Democratic Innovation*.

54 Iris Marion Young, 'Difference as a resource for democratic communication', in Bohman and Rehg, *Deliberative Democracy*, pp. 383–406.

55 Chantal Mouffe, 'For an agonistic model of democracy', in Noel O'Sullivan (ed.), *Political Theory in Transition* (London: Routledge, 2000), pp. 113–30.

56 Young, *Inclusion and Democracy*, p. 20.

57 James Tully, unpublished paper given at the colloquium on 'Constitutionalism, Democracy and Citizenship', University of Exeter, 24–5 November 2000.

7

Citizens' juries and deliberative democracy

GRAHAM SMITH AND CORINNE WALES

The growing interest in forms of deliberative democracy indicates, on the one hand, widespread dissatisfaction with aspects of our contemporary political practices and, on the other hand, a reflective awareness that alternative practices are plausible options for us. Within contemporary democratic theory, there is an emerging concern with the growing difference and distance between the subjectivity, motives and intentions of citizens and the political decisions made in their name.[1] The activities, backgrounds and interests of political representatives are seen as far removed from the lives and perspectives of citizens. Although periodic elections act as 'a continuous discipline on the elected to take constant notice of public opinion',[2] the mandate that representatives enjoy extends over a period within which citizens have very little impact on decisions made in their name. The principal–agent form of representation, so dominant within liberal democracies, rests on the fact that the political representative is able to deliberate and decide *for* others.[3] But, critics contend, the lack of presence or 'voice' of the politically marginalized, such as women and ethnic minorities, in political decision-making processes means that their interests and perspectives are systematically excluded or at least not adequately addressed. As Phillips argues, 'when policies are worked out *for* rather than *with* a politically excluded constituency, they are unlikely to engage all relevant concerns'.[4]

Clearly political activity and influence extend beyond voting, and contemporary society is marked by a plurality of interest groups and associations. However, such pluralism is undermined by the social and economic imbalances inherent within society. Expressions of economic power and social influence undermine, to a large extent, the assumption of political equality on which representative forms are frequently defended.[5] As Beetham argues, 'The freedoms of speech and association not only provide the guarantee of a more extensive political activity than the vote; they are also the means whereby the inequalities of civil society are transmitted to the political domain.'[6]

The inequality inherent within civil society and political institutions is taken to undermine the apparent neutrality of widely used social choice mechanisms, such as voting, opinion polling and the market, which embody the liberal principle that the role of democracy is to aggregate individuals' pre-given preferences into a collective choice.[7] Not only are such social choice mechanisms subject to strategic manipulation,[8] but by taking preferences as given and incorrigible, aggregation processes fail to recognize that preferences, interests and values are shaped and constrained by the political, social and economic context in which individuals find themselves – numerous social forces shape an individual's sense of what is possible. Preferences are not exogenous to institutional settings. As Sunstein argues, 'preferences are not fixed and stable, but are instead adaptive to a wide range of factors . . . The phenomenon of endogenous preferences casts doubt on the notion that a democratic government ought to respect private desires and beliefs in all or almost all contexts.'[9] Hence decision-making procedures should be concerned not only with aggregating preferences but also with the nature of the processes through which they are *formed*. All institutions 'shape' how judgements are made. But liberal institutions are not designed to encourage engagement and the testing of preferences and value orientations – citizenship is a passive affair which, it is argued, leads to 'a moral and political "de-skilling" of the electorate and the spread of cynical attitudes about public affairs and the notion of a public good'.[10]

In such a climate, the very legitimacy of liberal forms of political authority, grounded on the neutrality of procedures, is challenged. As Warren argues:

> rules and procedures always have normative purposes, and the authority they carry depends on these. They are never neutral, and our decision to abide by them cannot be neutral. We hold rules as authoritative (or lacking in authority) because of the normatively significant work they do. If the rules and procedures produce normatively questionable outcomes, then they tend to lose their authority.[11]

Deliberative democratic theory has evolved in response to the perceived weaknesses of liberal democratic theory and practice and offers a challenge to, and a critical perspective from which to judge, contemporary liberal representative institutions.[12] Although there is recognition that a division of political labour is necessary, given the complexity of contemporary political, economic and social conditions,[13] deliberative democracy offers the possibility of a different *form* of that division; one in which increased opportunities for citizen participation are taken to be both feasible and desirable and where citizen engagement forms part of an on-going critical dialogue upon which more legitimate forms of political authority can be grounded. As Benhabib argues:

> According to the deliberative model of democracy, it is a necessary condition for attaining legitimacy and rationality with regard to collective decision-making processes in a polity, that the institutions in this polity are so arranged that what is considered in the common interest of all results from processes of collective deliberation conducted rationally and fairly among free and equal individuals.[14]

Deliberative democracy particularly concerns itself with the *process* through which political decisions are made. As with liberal theories, deliberative democrats are interested in creating institutions that will resolve conflict but recognize that, in the process of engagement, preferences and value orientations can be transformed.[15] At its heart a deliberative polity promotes political dialogue aimed at mutual understanding, which 'does not mean that people will agree, but rather that they are motivated to resolve conflicts by argument rather than other means'.[16] Hence what is fundamental to democratic dialogue is 'deliberative' as opposed to 'strategic' or 'instrumental' rationality. In contrast to the strategic manipulation and manoeuvring that is often characteristic of contemporary politics, we can describe a collective as *deliberatively* rational 'to the extent that its interactions are egalitarian, uncoerced, competent, and free from delusion, deception, power and strategy'.[17]

Why then should we value deliberative democracy? Deliberative democracy promises more trustworthy and legitimate forms of political authority, more informed decisions and a more active account of citizenship. Legitimate forms of authority and decision making rest on two aspects of deliberative democratic theory: inclusivity and the nature of democratic dialogue. Inclusivity relates to both presence and voice:

in principle all citizens are entitled to participate in the process of political dialogue and have an equal right to introduce and question claims, to put forward reasons, to express and challenge needs, values and interests.[18] Voices should not be excluded; parties have an equal right to be heard.

Democratic deliberation encourages mutual recognition and respect and is orientated to the public negotiation of the common good. Miller stresses the 'moralising effect of public discussion': the requirement to put forward reasons and to respond to challenges will tend to eliminate irrational preferences based on false empirical beliefs, morally repugnant preferences that no one is willing to advance in the public arena, and narrowly self-regarding preferences.[19] Participants orientate themselves towards the common good and preferences held on purely self-interested grounds become difficult to defend in a deliberative context: 'we have good reason to expect the deliberative process to transform initial policy preferences (which may be based on private interest, sectional interest, prejudice and so on) into ethical judgements on the matter in hand'.[20]

Taken together, inclusivity and the nature of democratic dialogue offer the basis of more legitimate and trustworthy forms of political authority. As Manin contends, it is 'necessary to alter radically the perspective common to both liberal theories and democratic thought: the source of legitimacy is not the predetermined will of individuals, but rather the process of its formation, that is deliberation itself'.[21] Along similar lines, Gutmann argues: 'the legitimate exercise of political authority requires justification to those people who are bound by it, and decision making by deliberation among free and equal citizens is the most defensible justification anyone has to offer for provisionally settling controversial issues'.[22] Democratic legitimacy and trust in authority are generated by an on-going context of critical scrutiny and opportunities for discursive challenge.[23]

Democratic deliberation not only has the potential for institutionalizing more legitimate and trustworthy forms of political authority but also promises more informed judgements. Deliberation has the ability to lessen 'bounded rationality': 'the fact that our imaginations and calculating abilities are limited and fallible'.[24] Deliberation offers the conditions whereby actors can widen their own limited and fallible perspectives by drawing on each other's knowledge, experience and capabilities.

Fearon argues that this increases the odds on good judgements emerging, for two reasons: it may be 'additively' valuable in the sense that one actor is able to offer an analysis or solutions that had not occurred to others; or it may be 'multiplicatively' valuable in that deliberation can lead to solutions that would not have occurred to the participants individually.[25]

Finally, deliberative democracy offers a more active account of citizenship, one that recognizes that political engagement has the potential to transform the values and preferences of citizens in response to encounters with others.[26] There is a long tradition in democratic theory in which emphasis is placed on the 'educative' potential of participation and deliberation which 'broaden the viewpoints of citizens beyond the limited outlook of their private affairs'.[27] Implicit within deliberative democracy is a commitment to a particular sort of disposition of citizens towards other perspectives, one of mutual respect.[28] As Warren argues:

> democracy works poorly when individuals hold preferences and make judgements in isolation from one another, as they often do in today's liberal democracies. When individuals lack the opportunities, incentives, and necessities to test, articulate, defend, and ultimately act on their judgements, they will also be lacking in empathy for others, poor in information, and unlikely to have the critical skills necessary to articulate, defend, and revise their views.[29]

Thus we have three emergent criteria from deliberative democratic theory with which to judge political arrangements: inclusivity, deliberation and citizenship.[30]

Towards deliberative institutions

The question remains for deliberative democrats as to how democratic dialogue can be institutionalized. In turn this raises questions about whether deliberative democracy should be seen as an alternative to liberal representative democracy, based on a complete restructuring of liberal political institutions, or whether it points to the reform and supplementation of representative structures. It is a fair criticism that writing on deliberative democracy generally remains highly abstract and theoretical – that it fails to engage in the more 'messy' task of institutional design. For example, much of the work in this area concentrates on the 'constitution' of deliberative democracy –

the rights and principles that are the necessary conditions for the emergence and sustenance of democratic dialogue and judgement.[31]

Beyond the discussion of constitutional rights and principles, a variety of approaches to the 'institutionalization' of democratic deliberation can be distinguished. The first is largely sceptical toward the institutions of the state, celebrating the public sphere of civil society as the natural location of deliberative politics.[32] Dryzek is representative of a number of deliberative theorists who are concerned that deliberative democratic institutions attached to the state would be systematically undermined or subverted by powerful actors, 'undertaken with co-optation of potential troublemakers in mind, or as a veneer for decisions reached independently by conventional political means'.[33] In the face of such manipulation, Dryzek argues, incipient designs ought to be developed in the public sphere, independent from, and in confrontation with, state power. That a rejuvenated civil society and reinvigorated public spheres are a necessary component of deliberative politics is unquestionable, especially with respect to the development of democratic citizenship. However, the institutions of the state cannot simply be sidestepped.

Where theorists have reflected on the possible structure of deliberative decision-making institutions, a number of different approaches can be discerned. For example, Cohen and others have suggested the supplementation of representative government with secondary associations – the establishment of a deliberative associative democracy.[34] Other recommendations include the institutionalization of group representation[35] and the need for processes of deliberation to legitimize majoritarian decision rules.[36] However, such work will be of limited value unless practical examples of deliberative arrangements can be institutionalized and assessed. As Bohman argues in a survey article on deliberative democracy, 'there is still a surprising lack of empirical case studies of democratic deliberation at the appropriate level and scale'.[37]

A small number of such empirical case studies have begun to emerge, typically assessments of mainstream institutions. So, for example, Mansbridge develops an analysis of town meetings and workplace democracy,[38] both Hunold and Young, and Forester have developed deliberative criteria to judge different aspects of the planning process,[39] Elster has made an historical comparison of the deliberative settings of constitution-making processes,[40] and Chambers has revisited the language-rights politics of Quebec.[41] Such studies are illuminating, but perhaps more valuable insights are to be gained from investigating the development of innovative democratic institutions such as citizens' juries, deliberative opinion polling, mediation and consensus conferencing.[42] It is from the analysis of such innovative democratic designs that we are likely to learn more about the feasibility of institutionalizing opportunities for democratic deliberation and the strengths and weakness of deliberative theory. Certainly the rhetoric of advocates of citizens' juries resonates with the insights of deliberative democrats. It is commonly argued that citizens' juries afford the opportunity for informed deliberation and active citizenship and are a potential mechanism for overcoming the growing cleavage between 'the privileged "decision makers" and the "administrees", the majority of the population'.[43]

Citizens' juries: innovative deliberative institution?

A citizens' jury brings together a group of randomly chosen citizens to deliberate on a particular issue, whether it is the setting of a policy agenda or the choice of particular policy options. Over a number of days participants are exposed to information about an issue and hear a wide range of views from witnesses, who are selected on the basis of their expertise or on the grounds that they represent affected interests. With trained moderators ensuring fair proceedings, the jurors are given the opportunity to cross-examine the witnesses and, on occasion, call for additional information and witnesses. Following a process of deliberation among themselves, the jurors produce a decision or make recommendations in the form of a citizens' report. Typically, the sponsoring body (a government department, a local authority or other agency) is required to respond, either by acting on the report or explaining why it disagrees with it. Although there are obvious differences, analogies are often drawn with legal juries: 'in common with the legal jury, the citizens' jury assumes that a small group of ordinary people, without special training, is willing and able to take important decisions in the public interest'.[44]

Citizens' juries have been promoted and run since the 1970s

in both the United States by Ned Crosby at the independent Jefferson Institute[45] and in Germany by Professor Peter Dienel at the Research Institute for Citizen Participation, University of Wuppertal. Such juries in the United States have attracted media attention, but as yet appear to have had little direct influence on the political decision-making process.[46] In Germany, where the juries are known as 'planning cells' (*Planungzellen*), government bodies and agencies have commissioned the Research Institute to run planning cells, providing financial support and agreeing to take into account their recommendations and judgements in future decision-making processes.[47] Whereas Crosby tends to promote single juries of between twelve and twenty-four people, Dienel often runs a number of planning cells, each containing twenty-five citizens, concurrently and/or in series. To date, the largest project involved 500 citizens from all over Germany.

Inspired by such innovative democratic practice, the Institute of Public Policy Research (IPPR), the King's Fund Policy Institute and the Local Government Management Board (LGMB) have advocated the use of citizens' juries in the United Kingdom, each independently sponsoring a series of pilot projects typically in conjunction with health authorities and local government.[48] The pilot juries have all consisted of between twelve and sixteen citizens. The New Labour administration has shown some interest in these pilot projects, initiating a series of women's juries[49] and offering the process as a potential mechanism for reinvigorating interest in local politics and overcoming cynicism towards, and distrust of, local authorities.[50]

Inclusivity

Ideally, deliberative democratic arrangements entitle each citizen to participate in decision-making processes. Citizens' juries cannot fulfil this ideal and it is difficult to envisage an institutional design which could practically instantiate such a principle. However, citizens' juries approximate the ideal by aiming for a broadly representative jury selection which is able to draw on a wide range of experiences and backgrounds.

The idea of 'inclusivity' rather than 'representativeness' is used here as a criterion of analysis to avoid conceptual and practical confusion. We have already seen that deliberative democrats often point to the principal–agent nature of representation in liberal democracies as a source of political alienation and democratic deficit. It is often argued, in contrast, that citizens' juries aim to realize the 'microcosm' model of representation.[51] The logic of this form of representation is proportionality: a decision-making institution 'should be an exact portrait, in miniature, of the people at large, as it should think, feel, reason, and act like them'.[52] However, there are both conceptual and practical problems with this account of representation. First, no selected jury can accurately mirror all the standpoints and views present in the wider community.[53] Secondly, there is a danger of creating false essentialisms. Are, for example, women jurors expected to represent all women in the wider community; elderly jurors, all other elderly citizens?[54] Thirdly, this could entail that individual citizens are unable to represent the interests of others who do not share the same characteristics; an 'assumption that people cannot empathise across lines of difference'.[55] Finally, it raises a question as to whether jurors are chosen as representatives of others with similar characteristics, interests and values or as citizens who, whilst reflecting on their own values and experience, are also open to the possibility of transformation in the light of their reflections and deliberations with other participants.

Such problems emerge in Burnheim's conception of 'statistical representation' where the individuals chosen within a representative sample are taken to be representatives of particular interests.[56] This emphasis on representation may undermine the democratic ideal of the inclusive jury. As Abramson argues in a discussion of legal juries, 'In the end, what is at stake is whether we want jurors to understand their task primarily in terms of deliberation or representation.'[57]

> We do not want to encourage jurors to see themselves as irreconcilably divided by race, selected only to fill a particular racial or gender slot on the jury. Yet we do want to encourage jurors to draw upon and combine their individual experiences and group backgrounds in the joint search for the most reliable and accurate verdict. The difference is subtle but real.[58]

The use of stratified random sampling in the United Kingdom and United States is thus controversial, but seems to be necessary where the jury process involves so few individuals (between twelve and twenty-four). Such small numbers of citizens will also likely have a negative impact on the variety of backgrounds and experiences that jurors are able to draw on. In contrast, in Germany, Dienel uses a simple random selection process for his planning cells – each citizen has an equal chance of being selected for the jury. Because of the higher number of citizens involved – planning cells are run concurrently and/or in series – no voice or perspective can claim to be *systematically* excluded from the process.[59] However, there remain problems for the inclusion of small minority populations which may require mechanisms to ensure their presence, otherwise deliberations will not be able to draw on their particular experiences and knowledge. This caveat aside, Dienel's approach, understood as equality of opportunity to participate and deliberate, avoids many of the tensions within the smaller jury processes developed in the United Kingdom and US and, in many ways, transcends the issue of representation defined in terms of either the principal–agent or the microcosm model.

The composition of the jury is not the only important issue with regard to inclusiveness. Two further problems arise. First, before any citizens are actually selected, there is a prior problem of deciding upon the appropriate population from which the jury is to be drawn. The relevant constituency entitled to participate is not always obvious and the impact of this on deliberations is far from clear.[60] The logic of citizen juries is such that the population from which citizens are to be drawn should be appropriate to the nature and scale of the issue in question. This corresponds with the deliberative insight that the legitimate constituency of deliberation may cut across existing boundaries of political authority,[61] which in itself may cause some problems for potential sponsors such as local authorities.

Second, questions of presence and voice also extend to the selection of witnesses. We shall have more to say about this in the next section on deliberation, but procedures need to be in place such that all groups potentially affected by the decision have the opportunity to present evidence for the jury's consideration.

Deliberation

Do citizens' juries create conditions which promote unconstrained, open and reasoned dialogue? Organizers of citizens' juries are well aware that any accusation of bias and manipulation is one of the most damaging criticisms that can be made of the process. Concern about the affects of bias do not centre only on the process of deliberation between citizens. Well before citizens have been selected, decisions have been taken on the subject of discussion: a 'charge' (or question) has been framed and relevant information and witnesses have been selected. There is a danger that, even before citizens are directly involved, issues, information and witnesses may be mobilized out of the process. Such a problem is recognized by Crosby, who argues that 'the aim of the staff in setting the charge is to frame a question which is satisfactory to the sponsors of the project, fair to the parties affected by the issue, and which will provide a framework within which jurors can make good judgements. These goals are not easy to meet simultaneously.'[62]

The stage *prior* to any jury deliberations is thus fundamental to the overall fairness of the process. Experiments with *complete* juror control of the process have found that participants, in the initial stages, do not have enough of an overview of a subject to deal competently with setting the charge, agenda organization or witness selection.[63] In practice, advocates of the jury process recommend that a steering group consisting of 'stakeholders' should be established to develop the question, select witnesses and set the agenda. This may be time-consuming, yet the very integrity of the whole citizens' jury process is dependent on decisions made at this point. However, the composition of the stakeholder group itself creates a series of problems to which there are no easy and obvious answers. Stakeholders are likely to be 'self-selecting' – where organizations lack resources, or where affected interests have not been able to organize, the likelihood of access to this initial stage of the process is minimal. Imbalances of power and resources in society will be replicated in the initial decision-making process which may lead to the exclusion and marginalization of certain types of knowledge and experience.[64]

In the United Kingdom this problem has been partially addressed by bringing together lay people to look at the charge in pre-jury focus groups: 'the presence of a wider range of people than just members of the organising authority can bring a degree of independent scrutiny to the planning process'.[65] Also, rather than complete control, juries are instead given the power to alter the charge and call new witnesses *as* they deliberate and learn about the issues under consideration – usually up to half a day's space is allocated towards the end of the process.[66]

Once the jurors have come together, there are a number of

features of the process which appear to foster democratic deliberation and an orientation towards the common good. To fulfil the ideals of deliberative democracy, citizens should develop a disposition of mutual respect toward the perspectives of other participants. In many of the juries run in the United Kingdom, time is set aside at the beginning to draw up 'rules of conduct' which typically emphasize the need to respect and listen to the arguments of others. The worth of this exercise was noted by the organizers of the Association of British Insurers' jury on genetic testing, who stated in their debriefing session that the jurors 'produced some excellent rules, and felt a clear sense of ownership often referring each other back to them throughout the four days'.[67] Davies and Sang, who have facilitated juries for the King's Fund, also use this technique to create 'a jury culture of mutual respect for the individuals present, encouraging an appreciation of difference for everyone involved'.[68]

Although publicity is fundamental to citizens' juries – the citizens' report is designed to explain the jury's judgements and recommendations and is publicized widely[69] – only a small number of observers (including media representatives) are present during plenary sessions when witnesses provide evidence and are questioned, and when jurors deliberate among themselves. Thus publicity is limited and some deliberation in small groups occurs entirely away from the public gaze. This is particularly important if jurors are not to be seen as 'representatives' of particular interests or groups and are to be encouraged to alter their positions in the light of new evidence and reasoned arguments.[70]

We have already raised the concern that the small size of one-off juries (as in the United States and United Kingdom) limits the range of different perspectives and experiences that citizens can draw on. However, the small size of the jury and the time that jurors spend together both appear important for enhancing the deliberative quality of the process. An environment is created where stable expectations and relations of trust can be fostered between participants, so essential for mutual understanding.[71] Dynamics of large assemblies tend to differ markedly. As Elster argues, 'In a large assembly, it is not possible to pursue an argument in a coherent and systematic fashion. The debates tend to be dominated by a small number of skilled and charismatic speakers . . . who count on rhetoric rather than argument'. In comparison, in a small jury setting, 'one is more likely to observe the substance and not only the form of deliberation. The small size reduces the scope for demagogy and allows all speakers to be heard'.[72] Suspicion of strategic action on the part of citizens is also lessened, given that the jury process 'does not represent an opportunity for advancement, promotion or re-election' for those involved.[73]

This 'face to face' interaction of jurors, made possible by the small number of participants, is often celebrated: 'The face-to-face nature of debates is seen as a way of drawing people into the political process, enabling them to think not as isolated, anonymous individuals, but as citizens, working together via dialogue and consensus for the "common good" of society.'[74] However it is important to remember Mansbridge's warning: 'In moments of genuine conflict, face-to-face contact among citizens encourages suppression of that conflict.' There may well be 'face-to-face temptations to false unanimity'[75] but, unlike the small-town meetings that Mansbridge has analysed, in juries there are marked differences between participants which lessen 'the pressure to conform that spontaneously arises between individuals when a group is constituted'.[76]

Quite clearly there is an important role here for the moderator in facilitating the discussions, encouraging an ethos of mutual respect and guiding decision-making processes. Questions have been raised by some jurors as to whether, on occasion, moderators push for consensus among the jurors at the expense of allowing participants to understand and work through their differences.[77] There must be space for disagreement built into the process: even though juries accommodate majority/minority decisions, an expectation of consensus can create a barrier to critical dialogue, with particular perspectives dominating the agenda and defining the consensus.[78] Most moderators are alert to the manner in which deliberations can be dominated by confident and outspoken individuals and to the fact that, for some citizens, speaking in front of between twelve and fifteen fellow citizens is intimidating. Dialogue occurs not only in full jury sessions but also in smaller group settings.

Importantly, there is growing empirical evidence emerging that the deliberative process has a significant effect on both the citizens involved and the decisions and judgements made by the jury. We shall discuss some of these findings below, but it is clear that there is a marked difference between the pre-deliberative preferences of citizens which would have been aggregated within existing social choice mechanisms and their preferences and judgements after the process of deliberation. The detailed and informed nature of the conclusions and recommendations of many of the pilot juries in the United Kingdom differed from the results of non-deliberative consultation mechanisms and, on a number of occasions, appear to have affected the sponsors' policies and spending priorities.[79]

Citizenship

In contrast to a passive understanding of citizenship that is dominant within contemporary democracies, it is argued that citizens' juries reassert the importance of a more active form of citizenship. As the Institute of Public Policy Research argues, citizens' juries could have an important part to play in the 'development of democratic practice built on active citizenship. They offer the opportunity to bring into the public domain experience and judgement too often excluded from it, and to enhance the quality of deliberation.'[80] Do the actions and attitudes of participants offer support to this idea of active citizenship?

Given that citizens spend around four days in the company of others from different social backgrounds, reflecting on a variety of evidence and experiences, it should not be a surprise that this affects the preferences and values of participants. Crosby has collected empirical data to support the belief that 'jurors almost always change their minds during the sessions, as they become more involved with the issues'.[81] The UK experience supports these findings: questionnaires before and after juries highlight changes in jurors' attitudes. There is also emerging evidence that some jurors are more civically active long after the jury process has ended.[82] Dienel frequently argues that citizens tend to develop a different attitude to the world after participating in a process of reflection on their own and others' values and experiences. 'Surveys of those who have taken part in completing a [planning cell] all show that participation in this kind of process does have an effect on the individual's sense of purpose.'[83] Both the changes in preferences and attitudes during and beyond the jury process are important, since this offers empirical backing for the theoretical claims made for the transformative power of democratic deliberation.

One of the important factors that facilitates attitudinal change is likely to be political efficacy – the extent to which

citizens feel confident in their ability to participate and to influence decision-making processes and policies.[84] Moderators are
key figures in building up this confidence, although perhaps
most important is the practice of drawing up a pre-jury contract
between the independent facilitating organization, the commissioning body and the jurors. Under the conditions of this contract, the commissioning body is bound either to act on the
jury's recommendations or to give reasons why it has decided
not to.[85] This not only increases the democratic legitimacy of
the decision-making process but also gives jurors the sense that
their deliberations will be taken seriously.

Those who have witnessed citizens' juries are frequently
impressed by the commitment shown by participants. As
Lenaghan and Coote stress, 'right from the start . . . we were
deeply impressed – as were most other observers – with the level
of competence with which jurors tackled their task'.[86] A South
Somerset councillor affirms this positive judgement: 'the jurors
have spent more time considering this issue in an unbiased and
deliberative way than most councillors have'.[87] Such impres-
sions can only encourage confidence and trust in the decision-
making capacity of ordinary citizens.

Lessons from citizens' juries?

How does the practice of citizens' juries stand up to deliberative
democratic ideals? What can we learn about the institutionalization of democratic deliberation from the small number of
pilots and experiments? Institutional design is a developmental
process and reflections on these experiments may offer insights
into alternative arrangements for engaging citizens in decision-
making processes.

It is difficult to imagine a fully inclusive institutional design
wherein all citizens have the right to engage in political decision-making processes. Citizens' juries offer one approximation
of that ideal and aim to achieve a broadly representative jury
through a random sampling procedure. However, as we have
argued, there is a tension between representation and democratic deliberation. It is important that those chosen are not
seen simply as representatives of their social groups, rather that
deliberation should progress with participants able to reflect
and draw on a diversity of backgrounds and experiences.

Moreover, it is clear that the process of deliberation itself can also be subverted by prior decisions on the choice of charge, relevant information and witnesses. It is thus essential that the facilitators and organizers of juries are seen to be independent. Where biases can be minimized, juries offer a conducive environment for deliberation and the development of a more active ethos of citizenship.

So what role for citizens' juries and other innovative democratic designs? At one extreme we may imagine a 'jury democracy', at the other juries are seen as an expensive irrelevance. In many ways Burnheim's vision of 'demarchy' can be seen as a logical progression from innovations such as citizens' juries, with positions of authority decided through random sampling procedures.[88] However, as we argued earlier, there are problems with his conception of statistical representation. At the other extreme, critics have contended that citizens' juries are a charade – decision makers will simply cherry-pick decisions, use juries to validate unpopular judgements, selectively fulfil recommendations or ignore findings completely when the judgement is unfavourable. The practice of drawing up a pre-jury contract partially counters such objections. Where a citizens' jury has been constituted and the relevant institutions respond to recommendations (whether positively or negatively), the democratic legitimacy of the decision-making process is increased. Citizens' juries may then be understood as part of a democratic, critical authorisation process that enhances the legitimacy of political decision making.

The recognition that citizens' juries should be judged not simply in isolation but as part of a wider democratic process is important. Citizens' juries are not a panacea for all contemporary democracies' ills and need to be understood in a wider institutional and political context. At a minimum, citizens' juries should be seen as a potential supplement to representative institutions, a way of bringing informed citizens' perspectives into the decision-making process. However, there is need for imaginative and creative thinking about possible relations with both existing institutional forms and other innovative democratic designs such as referendums, deliberative opinion polls and mediation. At the very least citizens' juries offer valuable insights for deliberative democrats into how citizens may be afforded meaningful deliberative opportunities to engage with decision-making processes.

Notes

We would like to thank Susan Stephenson, David Owen and James Connelly for their comments and suggestions, as well as participants at the MANCEPT and ECPR conferences where a version of this chapter was presented.

1 See, for instance, C. Offe and U. Preuss, 'Democratic institutions and moral resources', in D. Held (ed.), *Political Theory Today* (Cambridge: Polity Press, 1991); B. Barber, *Strong Democracy* (Berkeley CA: University of California Press, 1984); A. Philips, *The Politics of Presence* (Oxford: Oxford University Press, 1995).

2 D. Beetham, 'Liberal democracy and the limits of democratisation', *Prospects for Democracy*, special issue of *Political Studies*, 40 (1992), p. 47. See also B. Manin, *The Principles of Representative Government* (Cambridge: Cambridge University Press, 1997).

3 H. Pitkin, *The Concept of Representation* (Berkeley CA: University of California Press, 1967), pp. 42–3.

4 Phillips, *The Politics of Presence*, p. 13. See also J. Squires, 'Rethinking Representation: Between Liberalism and the Cultural Politics of Difference', paper presented at the Political Studies Association annual conference, University of York (1995), p. 12.

5 A. Arblaster, *Democracy* (Buckingham: Open University Press, 1987), p. 76.

6 Beetham, 'Liberal democracy and the limits of democratisation', p. 48.

7 Phillips, *The Politics of Presence*, p. 149; D. Miller, 'Deliberative democracy and social choice', *Prospects for Democracy*, special issue of *Political Studies*, 40 (1992), p. 54.

8 Miller, 'Deliberative democracy and social choice', p. 59.

9 C. Sunstein, 'Preferences and politics', *Philosophy and Public Affairs*, 20 (1991), p. 5.

10 Offe and Preuss, 'Democratic institutions and moral resources', p. 165.

11 M. Warren, 'Deliberative democracy and authority', *American Political Science Review*, 90 (1996), p. 55.

12 Deliberative democracy has also been termed discursive and communicative democracy. However, there is no consistent usage of the terms which would suggest that they represent distinct positions. The account offered here is a general 'characterization' of the main elements of deliberative democratic theory. For a useful typology see R. Blaug, 'New theories of discursive democracy: a user's guide', *Philosophy and Social Criticism*, 22 (1996), pp. 49–80.

13 D. Held, 'Democracy: from city state to a cosmopolitan order?', *Prospects for Democracy*, special issue of *Political Studies*, 40 (1992), pp. 10–39; Beetham, 'Liberal democracy and the limits of democratisation'. The recognition that a division of political labour is necessary separates deliberative democracy from some conceptions of direct democracy.

14 S. Benhabib, 'Toward a deliberative model of democratic legitimacy', in S. Benhabib (ed.), *Democracy and Difference* (Princeton NJ: Princeton University Press, 1996), p. 69.

15 Miller, 'Deliberative democracy and social choice'; Phillips, *The Politics of Presence*.

16 M. Warren, 'The self in discursive democracy', in S. White (ed.), *The Cambridge Companion to Habermas* (Cambridge: Cambridge University Press, 1995), p. 181. There is some disagreement within deliberative democratic theory as to the status of consensus: for some it acts as a regulative ideal of deliberation; for others the

stress on this ideal can act as a barrier to critical dialogue – more powerful interests are liable to dominate the agenda and the definition of consensus.

17 J. Dryzek, 'Green reason: communicative ethics and the biosphere', *Environmental Ethics*, 12 (1990), p. 202. Habermas captures the concept of an understanding-oriented deliberative or 'communicative' action by setting it against strategic action. Both types of action are social action characterized by meanings 'as intended by the actor or actors' which are 'orientated' in that they take 'account of the behaviour of others'. The orientation of strategic action is towards success, that is, 'the appearance in the world of a desired state, which can, in a given situation, be causally produced through goal-oriented action or omission'. As such, strategic action follows the rules of rational choice, and impacts on the decisions of rational 'opponents'. Habermas argues that competent speakers can themselves tell when they strategically attempt to influence causally a hearer's action, when they use means such as deceit, manipulation and coercion to bring about compliance. Communicative action, in contrast, is defined by actors oriented 'not through egocentric calculations of success but through acts aiming towards reaching understanding'. J. Habermas, *The Theory of Communicative Action I* (Cambridge: Polity Press, 1984), pp. 279–86.

18 Benhabib terms these the principle of universal moral respect and the principle of egalitarian reciprocity. S. Benhabib, *Situating the Self* (Cambridge: Polity Press, 1992), p. 29.

19 Miller, 'Deliberative democracy and social choice', p. 61.

20 *Ibid.*, p. 62.

21 B. Manin, 'On legitimacy and political deliberation', *Political Theory*, 15 (1987), pp. 351–2.

22 A. Gutmann, 'Democracy, philosophy, and justification', in Benhabib, *Democracy and Difference*, p. 344.

23 Warren, 'Deliberative democracy and authority', p. 55.

24 J. Fearon, 'Deliberation as discussion', in J. Elster (ed.), *Deliberative Democracy* (Cambridge: Cambridge University Press, 1998), p. 49.

25 *Ibid.*, p. 50.

26 K. Baynes, 'Democracy and the *Rechtsstaat*: Habermas's *Faktizität und Geltung*', in S. White (ed.), *The Cambridge Companion to Habermas* (Cambridge: Cambridge University Press, 1995), p. 216; I. M. Young, 'Communication and the other: beyond deliberative democracy', in Benhabib, *Democracy and Difference*, pp. 126–8.

27 Manin, 'On legitimacy and political deliberation', p. 354; C. Pateman, *Participation and Democratic Theory* (Cambridge: Cambridge University Press, 1970).

28 A. Gutmann and D. Thompson, 'Moral conflict and political consensus', *Ethics*, 101 (1990), pp. 79–82; T. McCarthy, 'Kantian constructivism and reconstructivism', *Ethics*, 105 (1994), p. 62.

29 M. Warren, 'What can we expect from more democracy?', *Political Theory*, 24 (1996), p. 242.

30 For an alternative set of deliberative criteria based on the ideals of 'competence' and 'fairness' see O. Renn, T. Webler and P. Wiedemann (eds), *Fairness and Competence in Citizen Participation* (Dordecht: Kluwer, 1995).

31 For example, J. Habermas, *Between Facts and Norms* (Cambridge: Polity Press, 1996); Benhabib, *Situating the Self*; Gutmann and Thompson, *Democracy and Disagreement* (Cambridge MA: Belknap Press, 1996); J. Cohen, 'Deliberation and democratic legitimacy', in A. Hamlin and P. Pettit (eds), *The Good Polity* (Oxford: Blackwell, 1989).

32 C. Calhoun (ed.), *Habermas and the Public Sphere* (Cambridge MA: MIT Press, 1992); Habermas, *Between Facts and Norms*; Benhabib, 'Toward a deliberative model of democratic legitimacy'.

33 J. Dryzek, 'Ecology and discursive democracy: beyond liberal capitalism and the administrative state', *Capitalism, Nature, Socialism*, 3 (1992), p. 34.

34 J. Cohen and J. Rogers, 'Secondary associations and democratic governance', in J. Cohen and J. Rogers (eds), *Associations and Democracy* (London, Verso, 1995); J. Cohen and C. Sabel, 'Directly-deliberative polyarchy', *European Law Journal*, 3 (1997), pp. 313–42. For sceptical remarks on the deliberative potential of associative democracy see the responses in Cohen and Rogers, *Associations and Democracy*.

35 I. M. Young, *Justice and the Politics of Difference* (Princeton NJ: Princeton University Press, 1990); Phillips, *The Politics of Presence*.

36 Manin, 'On legitimacy and political deliberation', p. 359; Habermas, *Beyond Facts and Norms*, p. 304. For sceptical comments on the interplay of deliberation and majoritarian decision rules see S. Chambers, 'Discourse and democratic practice', in White, *The Cambridge Companion to Habermas*, p. 255.

37 J. Bohman, 'Survey article: The coming of age of deliberative democracy', *Journal of Political Philosophy*, 6: 4 (1998), p. 419.

38 J. Mansbridge, *Beyond Adversary Democracy* (Chicago: University of Chicago Press, 1983).

39 C. Hunold and I. M. Young, 'Justice, democracy and hazardous siting', *Political Studies*, 46 (1996), pp. 82–95; J. Forester (ed.), *Critical Theory and Public Life* (Cambridge MA: MIT Press, 1985).

40 J. Elster, 'Deliberation and constitution making', in J. Elster (ed.), *Deliberative Democracy* (Cambridge: Cambridge University Press, 1998).

41 S. Chambers, *Reasonable Democracy* (Ithaca NY: Cornell University Press, 1996).

42 A small number of such assessments have begun to emerge. See, for example, Renn *et al.*, *Fairness and Competence in Citizen Participation*; J. Fishkin, *Democracy and Deliberation* (New Haven CT: Yale University Press, 1991); *The Voice of the People* (New Haven CT: Yale University Press, 1995); G. Smith, 'Toward deliberative institutions', in M. Saward (ed.), *Democratic Innovation* (London, Routledge, 2000).

43 P. Dienel, 'Contributing to social decision methodology: citizen reports on technology projects', in C. Vlek and G. Cvetkovich (eds), *Social Decision Methodology for Technical Projects* (Dordecht: Kluwer, 1989), p. 133. See also J. Stewart, E. Kendall and A. Coote, *Citizens' Juries* (London: Institute of Public Policy Research, 1994); A. Coote and J. Lenaghan, *Citizens' Juries: Theory into Practice* (London: Institute of Public Policy Research, 1997).

44 A. Coote and D. Mattinson, *Twelve Good Neighbours* (London: Fabian Society, 1997), p. 4.

45 Ned Crosby has copyright of the term 'citizens' jury'.

46 N. Crosby, 'Citizens' juries: one solution for difficult environmental questions', in Renn *et al.*, *Fairness and Competence in Citizen Participation*; 'Trustworthy Democratic Facilitation', MS (Minneapolis MN: Jefferson Center, 1996); N. Crosby, 'Creating an Authentic Voice for the People', paper presented at the Midwest Political Science Association (1996); Stewart *et al.*, *Citizens' Juries*.

47 P. Dienel, 'Contributing to social decision methodology'; P. Dienel, 'Das "Burgergutachten" und seine Nebenwirkungen' (trans. Corinne Wales as 'The "citizens' report" and its wider effects'), *Forum für Interdisziplinäre Forschung*, 17 (1996), pp. 113–35; P. Dienel and O. Renn, 'Planning cells: a gate to "fractal"

mediation', in Renn *et al.*, *Fairness and Competence in Citizen Participation*; Stewart *et al.*, *Citizens' Juries*.

48 For a discussion and evaluation of some of these pilots see Coote and Lenaghan, *Citizens' Juries: Theory into Practice*; D. Hall and J. Stewart, *Citizens' Juries in Local Government: Report from the LGMB on Pilot Projects* (Luton: LGMB, 1997); S. McIver, *An Evaluation of the King's Fund Citizens' Juries Programme* (Birmingham: Health Services Management Centre, 1997); R. Kuper, 'Deliberating waste: the Hertfordshire citizens' jury', *Local Environment*, 2 (1997), pp. 139–53.

49 Speech given by Joan Ruddock at the IPPR symposium on citizens' juries and other methods of public involvement, July 1997. See C. Delap, *Making Better Decisions* (London: Institute of Public Policy Research, 1998), pp. 20–1. To date, two pilot women's juries have been run.

50 Department of the Environment Transport and the Regions, *Modernising Local Government: Local Democracy and Community Leadership* (London: DETR, 1998), p. 25.

51 Crosby, 'Citizens' juries: one solution for difficult environmental questions', p. 160.

52 John Adams, quoted in Pitkin, *The Concept of Representation*, p. 60.

53 Pitkin, *The Concept of Representation*, p. 80.

54 A. Armour, 'The citizens' jury model of public participation: a critical evaluation', in Renn *et al.*, *Fairness and Competence in Citizen Participation*, p. 180.

55 Squires, 'Rethinking representation', p. 13.

56 J. Burnheim, *Is Democracy Possible?* (Cambridge: Polity Press, 1985).

57 J. Abramson, *We, the Jury* (New York: Basic Books, 1994), p. 141.

58 Abramson, *We, the Jury*, p. 11.

59 Although Dienel does not use a quota system, random selection appears to generate a range of citizens quite similar in characteristics to those chosen by Crosby. See Stewart *et al.*, *Citizens' Juries*, pp. 23–4. On this issue, deliberative opinion polling has an advantage over juries in that around 300 citizens are brought together to deliberate. However, citizens are not engaged in collective decision making – rather their post-deliberative votes are aggregated. See Fishkin, *Democracy and Deliberation*; Fishkin, *The Voice of the People*; Smith, 'Toward deliberative institutions'.

60 Fishkin contends that 'Amazingly little serious work in political theory has been done on this problem.' See Fishkin, *Democracy and Deliberation*, p. 78.

61 Benhabib, 'Toward a deliberative model of democratic legitimacy', p. 70.

62 Crosby, 'Trustworthy democratic facilitation', p. 161. In the United Kingdom one of the major critics of citizens' juries, the Association of Community Health Councils of England and Wales, has argued that health authorities may well manipulate the process 'where questions are set and witnesses chosen . . . in order to influence the jury's decision'. See McIver, *An Evaluation of the King's Fund Citizens' Juries Programme*, p. 69.

63 Crosby, 'Trustworthy democratic facilitation', pp. 18–19.

64 B. Wynne, 'May the sheep safely graze? A reflexive view of the expert–lay knowledge divide', in S. Lash, B. Szerszynski and B. Wynne (eds), *Risk, Environment and Modernity: Towards a New Ecology* (London: Sage, 1996). See also Hunold and Young, 'Justice, democracy and hazardous siting' – they argue that such problems can be countered if the deliberative criteria of inclusiveness and equality of resources are respected.

65 McIver, *An Evaluation of the King's Fund Citizens' Juries Programme*, p. 68. In the pilots run by the King's Fund all the charges put to lay people for consideration were changed in some way.

66 This freedom can create tensions between juries, moderators and the sponsoring body. See Stewart *et al.*, *Citizens' Juries*, p. 22.

67 Noted by Jo Lenaghan after the ABI jury (14–19 November 1997). For an example of rules established by jurors see G. Smith and C. Wales, 'The theory and practice of citizens' juries', *Policy and Politics*, 27: 3 (1999), p. 303.

68 S. Davies and B. Sang, 'Perfect Strangers', MS (London: King's Fund Policy Institute, 1997), p. 15.

69 On the importance of publicity in the design of democratic institutions see D. Luban, 'The publicity principle', in R. E. Goodin (ed.), *The Theory of Institutional Design* (Cambridge: Cambridge University Press, 1996).

70 Elster, 'Deliberation and constitution making', p. 109.

71 Dienel and Renn, 'Planning cells', p. 137.

72 Elster, 'Deliberation and constitution making', p. 109.

73 Dienel, 'Das "Burgergutachten" und seine Nebenwirkungen', p. 114.

74 Stewart *et al.*, *Citizens' Juries*, p. 10. See also Fishkin, *Democracy and Deliberation*, pp. 92–3.

75 Mansbridge, *Beyond Adversary Democracy*, pp. 276–7.

76 S. Moscovici and W. Doise, *Conflict and Consensus* (London: Sage, 1994).

77 The drive towards some notion of consensus or at least a decision outcome by strong moderation was clearly evident in a jury observed by one of the authors. The subsequent evaluation report of one black juror, who throughout the proceedings had tried to express some misgivings, conveys her feelings of marginalization: 'I would have liked to hear other ethnic minorities' views in the Jury. As I am the only black female it was hard to get my views across . . . the minorities have no significant [voice] in the final decisions' (from juror evaluation form, ITC jury, 1997). In the Camden jury the evaluation reports revealed that some jurors felt they were being 'pushed towards an agreement' (Camden jury evaluation form, 1997).

78 I. M. Young, 'Communication and the other: beyond deliberative democracy', p. 126; Mansbridge, *Beyond Adversary Democracy*, p. 5.

79 McIver, *An Evaluation of the King's Fund Citizens' Jury Programme*, pp. 51–6; Coote and Lenaghan, *Citizens' Juries: Theory into Practice*, pp. 15–22.

80 Stewart *et al.*, *Citizens' Juries*, p. 5.

81 *Ibid.*, p. 25. For similar findings in deliberative opinion polling see Fishkin, *The Voice of the People*, p. 168.

82 McIver, *An Evaluation of the King's Fund Citizens' Jury Programme*, pp. 58–9; Coote and Lenaghan, *Citizens' Juries: Theory into Practice*, pp. 65 and 89–90.

83 Dienel, 'Contributing to social decision methodology', p. 10.

84 Pateman, *Participation and Democratic Theory*.

85 This practice was originally developed by Dienel. See Stewart *et al.*, *Citizens' Juries*, p. 47.

86 Coote and Lenaghan, *Citizens' Juries: Theory into Practice*, pp. 88–9.

87 Hall and Stewart, *Citizens' Juries in Local Government*, p. 14.

88 Burnheim, *Is Democracy Possible?*

8

Democratic deliberation and cultural rights: the Orange Order march at Drumcree

SHANE O'NEILL

Deliberative democracy and deep conflict

Deliberative models of democracy tie political legitimacy to the achievement of reasoned agreements.[1] Citizens bring a diversity of perspectives to public debate and in the encounter with others they seek mutual understanding so that they can think of the laws that emerge from their deliberations as shared rules they give to one another as a self-regulating legal community. One of the main advantages of deliberative models, therefore, is that legitimate decisions are conceived as the outcome of a process of open and inclusive public dialogue that takes place under conditions of fairness. Rival models of democracy that are based on bargaining, as opposed to the quest for mutual understanding, tend not to distinguish adequately between fair compromises and those bargains that reflect a relation of power. If bargaining positions are unequal, those who occupy the less advantaged positions will eventually feel forced into a compromise. Not only is the outcome unstable, since power relations can change, but it is unfair, since the interests of some citizens have been allowed to count for more than those of others. For this reason outcomes that are based on the force of argument alone as it emerges through public deliberation provide a more just and stable basis for a democratic community.

One of the main challenges that deliberative models face, however, is to show how they can address political issues of deep conflict, controversies that seem to preclude the emergence of any reasoned agreement among the parties involved.[2] There are several issues of moral conflict that would be worthy of analysis, including abortion, pornography, capital punishment, animal rights and so on. There are also a number of issues of deep cultural pluralism that seem to be fed by the clash of two or more incommensurable world views. The depth of animosity and the mistrust between the opposed groups can often be of such intensity that one or more of the parties is unwilling to engage in dialogue of any form. In such a situation of stalemate, theories of deliberation may seem to have nothing to say, since the legitimate rights of the parties can be settled only as the outcome of an inclusive dialogue. In this chapter I want to focus on one such deeply contentious issue of cultural pluralism where a beginning to the very process of dialogue, at the time of writing, remains elusive. I want to show how a normative theory associated with the demand for a deliberative form of democratic politics can be used critically to assess the competing right claims involved and to show how a dialogically impartial outcome is possible. Even when dialogue is not yet taking place among the citizens involved in such conflicts, we can use this normative perspective to work out certain legal principles that seem appropriate to the particular culturally plural context with which we will be concerned.

The conflict surrounding the marching season in Northern Ireland, and specifically the Orange Order parade from Drumcree Church in Portadown, has, each July since 1995, had a seriously destabilizing effect on the peace process there. The matter has been widely presented in the media and by political commentators as an irreconcilable conflict of two rights: the Orange Order's right to parade on its traditional route and the residents of the Garvaghy Road's right to refuse to host that parade. This dispute cannot be resolved rationally, or impartially, if we are to take as given the incommensurability of these claims. I want to apply here Jürgen Habermas's discourse theory of rights in an attempt to evaluate critically the competing claims so as to assess which, if any of them, should take priority.[3] The aim is to indicate how Habermas's theoretical framework, probably the pre-eminent source for models of democratic deliberation, can help us to clarify an appropriate basis for just resolutions of deep conflicts even when no dialogue has taken place. More specifically I hope to defend a set of principles according to which disputes about marches in Northern Ireland, particularly the one at Drumcree, can be regulated in a way that is fair to all concerned.

I first sketch the political context in which the controversy must be understood. Then I draw on Habermas's discourse theory of democratic legitimacy so as to present an account of legally enforceable rights as conditions of equal citizenship. Once this theoretical framework is in place I try to reconstruct, in a virtual dialogue, the best arguments that could be made on either side of this dispute. We can then test the rational acceptability of the rights claimed with reference to the theory. Contentious yet legally binding decisions have been required on this matter in recent years in the face of a considerable threat to the peace process. This analysis will allow us to judge whether or not the forces of the state have been used legitimately in the years since 1998 to uphold the right claimed by Portadown's nationalist community to have the parade rerouted.[4] Finally, some conclusions can be drawn as to how the legitimate rights of the two national cultures in Northern Ireland can be protected in the long term without sacrificing either the civil and religious liberties of the Loyal Orders or the equal membership status of nationalist citizens.

The threat to political accommodation

The constitutional crisis in Northern Ireland is often thought to be intractable.[5] One of the reasons given to explain this is the fact that the problem is one of a double minority.[6] While Irish nationalists have lived as a minority marginalized from the circulation of power within the Northern jurisdiction set up by the partition of Ireland in 1921, unionists who identify themselves as British have always been conscious of the fact that they remain a minority on the island of Ireland. Nationalists have found any constitutional arrangement that fails to recognize their Irish identity to be unacceptable and unionists have found it difficult to achieve a lasting accommodation with nationalists because they fear that nothing but political and cultural dominance throughout Ireland could ultimately quench the thirst of Irish republicanism. Many unionists fear that they will suffer exactly the same kind of marginalization within Ireland that members of the nationalist minority claim to have suffered in Northern Ireland since partition. So the apparent intransigence of many unionists may be explained by their insecurity within the United Kingdom. This insecurity intensifies whenever they sense that the British government is in collusion with Irish nationalists, particularly with respect to the close links established with the Irish government since the signing of the Anglo-Irish Agreement of 1985.[7] Since many unionists do not trust the British government's loyalty to them, their own loyalty to its political authority is conditional on its acting in ways that secure the Union.[8]

The constitutional arrangement proposed by the Good Friday Agreement of 1998, and endorsed by over 71 per cent of voters in the Northern referendum, is an attempt to solve this double minority problem. It seeks to protect both national communities from political domination. By setting up power-sharing, or consociational, arrangements within Northern Ireland it aims to avoid the unacceptable consequences for nationalists of a politics of internal majoritarianism.[9] At the same time, by securing the principle of consent regarding any future change in constitutional status, it reassures unionists that a united Ireland could never be forced on an unwilling Northern majority. There is recognition of the Irish identity of nationalists in the North–South Ministerial Council, and a guarantee that the British identity of unionists would be recognized through the workings of the British–Irish Council within a possible future united, though almost certainly federal, Ireland. Both national communities are protected from discrimination and both cultural traditions are to be afforded equal respect, no matter which of them is to find itself, at any particular historical juncture, in the minority.[10]

Efforts to implement this constitutional settlement have been fraught with serious difficulties, many of which have been generated by the political wrangling of those who, in effect, have been seeking to renegotiate the agreement. Our focus here is on another set of obstacles to mutual accommodation, one that reflects the continuing cultural conflict in Northern Ireland. This cultural conflict manifests itself in an alarming manner in the controversies surrounding contentious marches organized by the Loyal Orders, especially with regard to the conflict at Drumcree. With the considerable scaling down of armed conflict, this problem has in recent years provided a channel for the violent expression of sectarian hatred. In the years from 1995 it led to rioting, widespread public disorder and innumerable attacks on property and persons far beyond the Portadown area. In stoking the fires of sectarian division, it continues to constitute a serious threat to the political progress that has been made during this period and to the spirit of accommodation that is required to make the new arrangements work. Opponents of the agreement have not been slow to harness the hurt and bitterness on both sides in seeking to undermine efforts at cross-community co-operation.

Portadown Orangemen insist that it is their right, as one of their civil and religious liberties, to parade from their annual church service at Drumcree through the mainly nationalist area surrounding the Garvaghy Road. This is the traditional route they have taken in returning to the town centre. Members of the Garvaghy Road Residents' Coalition have protested against the parade, since they see it as a provocative display of triumphalism that allows the Orange Order to assert the supremacy of Britishness and Protestantism over Irishness and Catholicism. They have argued that the Orange Order must engage in direct talks with them regarding their plans for the parade. By doing so the Orange Order would recognize the coalition as representative of a significant minority group in Portadown. This would allow them to affirm positively the idea that members of that minority have an equal right to respect, despite the fact that they express different national and religious identities from those of the majority of the townspeople. In many ways the conflict brings into clear focus the drama of the past thirty years of political strife.[11] A nationalist minority demand recognition and the right to be treated as equals while the Unionist majority fear they will lose everything if they compromise on the liberties they have enjoyed through weight of numbers. Both sides are insistent that they are defending their legitimate rights and both have appeared to be deeply entrenched in their positions. Since their claims are entirely incompatible, accommodation has, not surprisingly, been remarkably elusive.

Given that our aim is to interrogate the rights claims of both parties to the dispute in a critically impartial manner, we must make a theoretical detour here so as to clarify how rights are best understood within the framework of a modern constitutional democracy. I shall be drawing on the discourse theory elaborated by Jürgen Habermas, since it offers the most sophisticated and influential theoretical grounds for a deliberative model of democracy. Habermas's account connects the process of social integration in modern, complex, plural societies with the legitimation of laws through procedures of inclusive dialogue. This emphasis on dialogue should prove to be instructive in this case, as it seems clear that the only basis on which the dispute is likely to be resolved in a manner that is fair to all concerned is through a process of inclusive dialogue. So, once the discourse-theoretical framework is in place, we can work our way back into the particular context of Drumcree in an effort to assess the merits of the arguments that could be made in support of the conflicting claims.

The fact that both sides have been careful to couch their claims in the language of rights has been a key feature of the conflict. They have done so because they want to present their claims not as the imposition of their will on their adversaries but as legitimate rights to which they are entitled as equal members of the political community. But once the participants make this appeal to legitimacy by using the language of rights they become vulnerable to the possibility of their being embroiled in the complexities of theoretical debate regarding the nature of legally enforceable rights, and the grounds of their justification. Their understanding of rights must be open to challenge, since they have to acknowledge that claiming a right is not the same thing as justifying it.

There has been some confusion among those who claim the right to march down the Garvaghy Road as to whether that right is grounded in legal discourse or in some moral, religious or traditional discourse that is prior to the law.[12] I shall be considering here only arguments that can be presented in the terms of modern legal discourse, broadly construed, since that is the only medium appropriate to the justification of legally enforceable rights in a constitutional state. As we shall discover, however, there has been a general failure, even among those who restrict themselves to legal discourse in defending the right to walk this route, to distinguish between the various levels at which legal discourse may operate. There are at least four significantly distinct levels, ranging from the abstractly universal to the contextually particular: charters of human rights; constitutionally guaranteed rights; the legal rights that citizens enjoy through the protection of legislation regulating some controversial matter of potential conflict; and finally the particular rights of parties in a specific case of conflict. Before we can sort this confusion out, we need to develop a convincing theoretical perspective on rights that would be appropriate to a deliberative model of politics.

Rights as a condition of equal citizenship

From the perspective of a discourse theory of law, legally enforceable rights are justified on the basis of inclusive and reasoned agreement among all those affected by their exercise. Rights make possible the on-going realization of a particular self-regulating legal community of free and equal citizens in its distinctive historical context. They are legitimated as the discursively agreed conditions of equal citizenship. Jürgen Habermas argues that a system of rights 'should contain precisely the basic rights that citizens must mutually grant one another if they want to legitimately regulate their life in common by means of positive law'.[13]

The medium of positive law is unavoidable for those seeking to make rights claims in a modern democracy. It presupposes the idea that citizens can think of themselves not only as subjects of the law but also as its authors.[14] A reconstruction of the basic communicative presupposition of the legal medium itself shows that both the private and public autonomy of the citizen must be given equal weight.[15] A legally institutionalized set of civil rights represents the conditions of possibility for both the protection of a private sphere of action for the individual citizen, and the exercise of political autonomy by the legal community. Individual rights and popular sovereignty are fused together as the bedrock on which democratically generated law becomes possible.[16]

This discourse theory presents rights neither as external constraints nor as an internal reflection of the will of the sovereign, but rather as the internal constraints that represent the conditions for collective self-legislation by citizens sharing equal status as members of a political community. Rights cannot be justified in a modern context as being granted to us by God or any such higher authority. Nor can their justification be contingent on the vagaries of particular cultures. They must, rather, be accounted for in relation to the core presuppositions of the very idea of a self-regulating legal community. Habermas's analysis yields a principle of democracy that states that we regulate our life in common legitimately when we confer on one another those rights 'to which all possibly affected persons could agree as participants in rational discourses'.[17]

This approach throws light on the grounds of justification for many familiar rights. There are certain basic categories of civil rights that would appear to be essential if private and political autonomy were to be secured.[18] These rights are intended to satisfy conditions of equal citizenship in guaranteeing for all basic individual liberties, membership status, legal protection and communicative freedom in the exercise of political autonomy. It is up to the citizens themselves to exercise their political autonomy by interpreting and extending these basic rights in their own particular constitutional context. They must also guarantee to one another those rights that would secure for each citizen the socio-economic means to render civil rights and individual liberties effective for all.[19]

A variety of social groups have also had to demand special rights so as to enable them to achieve equal membership status within the political community.[20] There is no competition between individual and collective rights, since the effective exercise of individual rights depends on the relative needs of social groups that provide individual citizens with their identity-forming context.[21] Women have argued that strictly equal treatment will exacerbate the dangers of their marginalization in public life if it fails to grapple with the reality of unequal circumstances for men and women in a gendered society.[22] Similarly some minority cultures have demanded special rights that would protect them in their efforts to retain their cultural distinctiveness while enjoying equal status as citizens.[23] In a deeply divided society such as Northern Ireland each national community should have a right to express its national, religious and cultural identity to an extent that is consistent with equality of membership status for all citizens.[24]

Rights, then, are conferred by citizens on one another through an on-going discursive process that allows them to exercise their political autonomy in an inclusive and non-oppressive manner. We justify a claim to a right if we convince others that all citizens could, as participants in rational discourses, agree to that right as a legally enforceable norm. Rights are generated as responses to problems that citizens encounter in their everyday lives and they are justified when citizens with a diversity of perspectives can achieve agreement based on collective insight.[25] It is in this sense that legitimate rights make possible the realization in a particular constitutional state of a self-regulating legal community of free and equal citizens. The use of the state's coercive authority is legitimated by the discursive justification of whatever rights are necessary to this collective achievement.[26]

We must recall now the fact that legally enforceable rights operate at various institutional levels. Charters of human rights explicitly invoke general norms that claim universal validity. These rights are justified as the moral-political norms that all human beings, regardless of their context, could agree to as participants in rational discourses. They should be legitimated through an on-going global discourse that is both universally inclusive and non-oppressive. At the constitutional level, citizens of particular legal communities interpret these general norms in a way that is sensitive to their own context. Of course, they also affirm certain constitutional rights that are uniquely particular to their context in dealing with specific problems.[27] In Northern Ireland some such rights are specified in the constitutional arrangements outlined in the Good Friday Agreement, such as the guarantee that executive power will be shared across national communities.

Laws are generated in a politically autonomous manner within a constitutional regime if the formal legislative authority is genuinely responsive and open to the needs and interests of all citizens as they are articulated in a vibrant and vigilant public sphere.[28] While legitimate laws must be consistent with human rights and constitutional principles in seeking to guarantee conditions of equal citizenship, they must be generated on the basis of an inclusive dialogical process so that the differing perspectives of all citizens can be filtered through to the formal, representative, legislative procedures. The inclusion of all relevant perspectives is a necessary condition of a process that is to be sensitive to the actual contexts in which the potential for conflict can arise. Furthermore, if all citizens are to think of themselves as authors as well as subjects of the law, each citizen must have some good reason to affirm that law. All representative parties must, therefore, seek to propose norms that all others can agree to for good reason. This means that they themselves must be willing to revise their goals, aims and aspirations if these turn out to conflict with the peaceful coexistence of each group under conditions of equal citizenship.

Laws specify the rights that citizens have in relation to potential conflicts that may arise regarding, say, the institutionalization of a procedure, the distribution of a material resource, the regulation of a specific practice such as ceremonial marching, or whatever. Once a law has been generated legitimately through formal democratic procedures, it is the role of the judiciary to protect and uphold the rights of citizens by adjudicating in particular cases. Of course, one hopes that citizens can resolve their differences without resort to the courts but when necessary judges must apply the law in both an impartial and a contextually sensitive manner by basing their judgement on an objective reading of all relevant facts.[29]

I will return, in the concluding section, to the question of how appropriate rights guaranteeing equal citizenship in relation to the parades controversy might be legitimated and institutionalized in Northern Ireland. But, now, in order to throw light on the possibility of a just resolution to the conflict at Drumcree, we need to examine the arguments that could be put forward by those directly affected.[30] There are two main points to bear in mind from the theoretical perspective outlined here in testing the rational acceptability of the competing claims. First, an impartial judgement has to be based on an objective account of the empirical reality, one that is sensitive to the context in reflecting the perspectives of all affected. Second, the only just resolution will be one based on an impartial norm, one that all affected would have good reason to affirm as being appropriate to this context. In evaluating the claims we must ask, therefore, which, if any, of the positions expresses an impartially grounded norm that is sensitive to the actual context of the dispute. Which, in other words, can take on board the legitimate concerns of the other, by making possible a resolution based on normative principles that all could affirm with good reasons?

Since members of the Orange Order have refused, consistently over the years, to engage, unconditionally, in direct dialogue with residents, we may be tempted to dismiss their claim altogether. But to do so would deprive us of the opportunity to take the rationale behind their position adequately into account in seeking a just resolution. We can anticipate the better arguments that may be made on both sides by presenting here a virtual dialogue in which imaginary representatives can articulate their concerns in a direct encounter.[31] In this virtual dialogue a variety of familiar constitutional rights are invoked by Joan, who insists that local members of the Orange Order have a legitimate right to march down the Garvaghy Road. Martha counters each of his arguments in turn by defending the right of the residents to refuse to host the parade.[32]

A virtual dialogue

Joan. What I can't understand, Martha, is why the residents can't accept this as the Orange Order's traditional route. The Order has made many compromises over the years, but if it were to give up on this route it would be giving up on the traditions that its members hold dear. This is a very sensitive matter, since the parade commemorates the ultimate sacrifice made by those many Ulstermen who died defending the British interest in the battle of the Somme of 1916. Surely the residents can show some tolerance on this matter?

Martha. Of course it is vital that we should all be allowed to honour the dignity of such tragic losses but that in itself does not legitimate any right to walk this particular route. Nor does the claim that it is part of a tradition. Tradition, as you should know Joan, validates nothing. Women would still not have the vote if we were to be loyal to the traditions that many men held dear until earlier this century. An appeal to tradition cannot, therefore, be the *primary* basis of rights in a modern democracy. The whole thrust of rights-discourse, beginning historically with the development of European liberalism, has always been to challenge those traditions that cannot stand up to rational scrutiny. This dispute, therefore, will have to be worked through not in terms of the traditions that we have but rather in relation to a set of principles, or rights, that can help us to discern which of our traditions are compatible with just and peaceful coexistence in a plural democracy. Which traditions, in other words, can we afford to tolerate?

Joan. If we want to talk in those terms, I have to say that in a plural democracy we have to protect the *right to religious liberty* for all. If members of the Orange Order are to be treated as equals they should be allowed to walk home from a church service without harassment from those who are intolerant of their religion. We cannot resolve this dispute if we do not respect religious freedom.

Martha. I agree with you, Joan, that in a plural society, the right to religious liberty is a vital aspect of equal citizenship. Members of the Orange Order certainly do have a right to practise their religion freely and to walk to and from their church on uncontentious routes without harassment. Of course, we must remember that this right has been denied over sustained periods in the recent past to Catholics attending Saturday evening mass in Harryville.[33] But that is not the main issue regarding the ceremonial parade from Drumcree. What *is* at stake is another vital aspect of equal citizenship related to the question of religious freedom in a deeply divided society like ours. Here mutual accommodation depends on our challenging all forms of sectarianism, and this means that religious minorities should not be subjected to practices that systematically devalue their beliefs. In an area populated almost exclusively by Catholics and nationalists, residents have a right, in this political context, to withhold their consent to host a ceremonial parade by an exclusively Protestant organization that has always viewed Catholicism with suspicion and hostility.

Joan. But the *right to freedom of expression*, Martha, is, surely, vital to the life of an egalitarian democratic society. All groups in society should be allowed to express their values and their opinions publicly without obstruction from citizens who do not share their perspective. And this includes the right to hold this march. The price of living in a tolerant society is that we sometimes have to put up with the expression of values and opinions we consider offensive.

Martha. It is true that the right to freedom of expression is an important condition of political autonomy here as elsewhere and it means that we do, sometimes, have to tolerate certain views that may offend us. But you are forgetting, Joan, that there are always limits on the exercise of the right to freedom of expression. It has to be considered, for example, whether or not particular forms of expression can be justified if they lead to the humiliation or intimidation of others, or to the incitement of violence against them.[34] Certainly, in a bi-national context like ours, we need to assure all citizens of their equal membership status within the political community by guaranteeing that their national and religious identities are to be afforded due recognition and respect. This means that if we are to heal the wounds of political division we should limit those forms of free expression that fail to respect others in their national, cultural and religious difference. For the Orange Order to force this march through without seeking to engage with residents in dialogue would seem to fall beyond that limit of toleration. Of course, in other contexts different limits may apply but, given the history of this parade, no enforced march can be compatible with equal citizenship.[35] It's not that the residents are particularly sensitive or easily offended but rather that the Drumcree conflict now has symbolic importance for the relationship between the two national groups throughout Northern Ireland.

Joan. Whatever may be said about the significance of the history of this particular parade, the *rights to free assembly and freedom of movement* are aspects of individual liberty that we simply cannot afford to curtail lightly. People should be allowed to assemble freely for properly organized religious, cultural or political events, and no group should be allowed to control exclusively a main arterial route of a town, or any stretch of the 'Queen's highway'. Mutual accommodation surely demands that much.

Martha. Yes, Joan, the rights to free assembly and freedom of movement, like the right to freedom of expression, are important conditions of political autonomy. But no organization can simply stop the traffic whenever it likes without legitimate authority and this can be granted only if the needs and concerns of those affected are given due consideration. Surely, this is best achieved through direct, inclusive and unconditional dialogue among all concerned at local level. An abstract right to free assembly should not be asserted against the will of a group directly affected by its exercise in a particular context, especially given the sensitivity of the divisions here. The Orange Order cannot justify the claim that it seeks accommodation if it refuses to engage in such an open dialogue. This refusal is most plausibly interpreted as a failure on the Order's part to acknowledge the legitimate rights of the residents, or to acknowledge that they should have an appropriate say in how the parade should be organized. It seems as if the nub of the problem is the Orange Order's inability to recognize the residents as their equals.

Joan. What you don't seem to appreciate, Martha, is the fact that this parade represents a stand against the ghettoization of Portadown along national and religious lines. The Orange Order seeks 'accommodation not segregation'. By using this slogan they are seeking to contrast their willingness to conduct the parade in a dignified manner as a contribution to the creation of a tolerant society, with the nationalist residents' exclusive territorial claim, a claim that is supported implicitly by a threat of violence. The residents' protest is designed to create a no-go area for Protestants and this is something we have to resist.

Martha. The question of segregation is certainly of great significance to the overall problems of sectarian division in

Portadown. But the main reason for this segregation, as in many other places in Northern Ireland, is the sectarian tension and violence associated with the political conflict. The segregation certainly has not been to the advantage of the nationalist population that is concentrated in the most socio-economically deprived area of the town. Of course, one consequence of this segregation is that is restricts freedom of movement for all the town's inhabitants but the restriction has been felt most acutely, in relation both to parades and to the activities of everyday life, by the intimidated nationalist minority. The town centre is, for residents of the Garvaghy Road, virtually a no-go area all year round, especially at night, and the threat of sectarian violence from loyalists has intensified because of the residents' efforts to stand up for their rights in relation to this parade. Furthermore, it is the residents who are prisoners in their own area for the duration of the stand-offs associated with the parade. If we want to deal with the problems associated with restrictions on our freedom of movement, perhaps we should begin by presenting an accurate account of the actual restrictions that are currently at work.

Joan. You are speaking as if the nationalist residents were the ones under threat. For me the real issue here is the survival of Protestant culture against the threat of an arrogant Irish nationalism. All over the world we are learning that the demands of justice and of peaceful coexistence would seem to require us to protect cultural identities from the hostile threats of others.[36] This means that we have to guarantee *protective rights for cultures* under such threat. The route of the parade is an important aspect of the Protestant British tradition in Portadown, represented by the Orange Order. The route itself expresses the cultural identity of its members and so it is vital to the survival of their culture that they continue to use it. Those who wish to deny them access to the route are intent on destroying that culture and forcing on them an alien identity.

Martha. Once again, Joan, I can agree with the norm you invoke, but not with the way in which you seek to apply it in this context. In a plural democracy, cultures that are under threat from hostile others should certainly be protected from prejudice, harassment, discrimination or violence whether the injustices are rooted in racism, sectarianism, homophobia or any form of ethnocentric or nationalistic xenophobia. But the only rights a group can have to express its culture are those that are compatible with an inclusive political community. For an exclusively Protestant organization to force a march through a Catholic area, without reference to the legitimate concerns of the residents, is to express an aspect of their culture that is not compatible with an inclusive political community that treats all its citizens as equals. There can be no right to protect this aspect of the Protestant British culture of the Orange Order. Rather, the creation of an inclusive political community depends on that aspect of culture being abandoned.

This aspect of British culture is, in any case, highly unrepresentative of many Ulster Protestant citizens, not to mention the people of England, Scotland or Wales. The insistence of the Orange Order on marching down the Garvaghy Road, regardless of the views of the residents, misrepresents the identity of those many unionists who do not view the use of this particular route as a vital aspect of their culture. Many unionists will accept that the right to parade must be exercised with due respect to the equal status of nationalist citizens. Both nationalist and unionist cultures should be afforded the right to public expression of their identity so long as it does not undermine the basis of equal citizenship. At present there are far more restrictions on the public celebration of the minority nationalist culture. It would be simply unthinkable, for example, for a nationalist parade to be forced through an almost exclusively Protestant area. Of course, that would be just as unacceptable as forcing this march through, but the fact that it would be unthinkable should remind us that it is the nationalist community who bear the brunt of any current inequality of cultural expression. If we have to celebrate and express our cultural identities in public, and it might be better if we didn't, then we must do so in a way that is sensitive to the concerns of others. If we do not succeed in finding ways of doing this, and direct dialogue is surely the best way to do it, then we cannot have equality of status for all citizens.

Joan. You continue to stress the need for dialogue, but what reasons do we have to believe that the residents will ever consent to allow a parade to go through? If the legitimacy of the route is to be dependent on the consent of the residents, the Order can just forget it. Can you really say that such an outcome would be fair?

Martha. Your claim has still to be tested empirically. What is of the utmost importance here is the recognition we give one another when we agree to engage in dialogue. The Order must engage with representatives the residents choose for themselves. Once that happens the onus is shared equally to work towards an accommodation that can be agreed freely under conditions of fairness. We can only hope that this may be possible but if dialogue fails we need to have laws in place that can allow transparently impartial judgements to be made on the matter.

Assessing the competing claims

Our aim in seeking to reconstruct the best arguments on either side of the dispute has been to assess the state of play in the discourse about this issue in the broader public sphere. We must now evaluate the arguments so as to make an intervention that aims to further the cause of a dialogical resolution to the problem. Which of the positions adopted here comes closer to realizing conditions of equal citizenship? Which can take on board the legitimate concerns of all as a basis for reasoned agreement? There is no question but that all the rights invoked by Joan, those associated with religious liberty, freedom of expression, assembly and movement, and the protection of cultures from hostile forces, have an important role to play in securing equality of citizenship in a plural democracy like Northern Ireland. In fact it is the concern for equality in securing both private and political autonomy that is the grounds for the justification of these rights at a relatively abstract level. The vital issue here, however, is how legitimate rights are to be applied in this context in a way that guarantees equal membership status to all citizens.

Martha's arguments emphasize the need to set limits to the exercise of certain constitutionally valid rights in particular contexts. While she acknowledges that all the rights invoked by Joan are indeed conditions of equal citizenship that all could agree to, none should be exercised in a way that undermines the very grounds of its own justification. If the exercise of a right is incompatible with the equal membership status of other citizens it cannot be legitimate in that context. In such a case, the right of other citizens to be treated as equals constrains, or in Dworkin's terms 'trumps', our liberty.[37] By providing a more contextually sensitive account of the reality of the conflict Martha is implicitly challenging Joan to broaden her perspective. She invites her to imagine herself to be in the position of the residents. In other words, she encourages Joan to think of the matter dialogically, to think in a way that is sensitive to the differing concerns of all those affected by the issue. By doing this she believes that she can convince Joan that the restrictions on our rights are impartially grounded in that they are based on principles that could be affirmed by all. The restrictions generate another set of rights that will, in some circumstances, take priority.

It seems, then, that the position adopted by the Orange Order, and defended by Joan, does not provide us with a basis for reasoned agreement. *Neither* national community in Northern Ireland could agree to the unrestricted exercise of the rights Joan invokes. *Both*, however, would have reason to affirm those rights as constitutionally valid once we acknowledge the need for them to be qualified by restrictions protecting the equal membership status of all citizens regardless of their national and religious identity. Joan's argument is insufficiently contextualized in relation to the reality of deep sectarian division in Portadown. The restrictive rights that Martha appeals to are needed to protect the equal status of the nationalist minority there, just as the same should hold for a small unionist minority ghettoized into one area of a predominantly nationalist town. We cannot simply assert abstract constitutional rights while turning a blind eye to the empirical reality in which they are to apply.

In the light of this analysis, how are we to judge the actions of the state's coercive forces in relation to the controversy at Drumcree in recent years? It is, I hope, clear that we are not facing a tragic conflict of incommensurable claims here. It is not the case that there are two dark cultural forces opposing one another with no hope of a rationally acceptable solution to their quarrel. It is not the case that the coercive forces are doomed to act in a way that is oppressive of one group or the other. There are criteria available according to which a reasoned judgement can be made on the matter, and those criteria are concerned with the sensitivity that is shown to the legitimate concerns of others in the reasoning of the competing parties. It would appear to be the case that, in the absence of an agreed accommodation among the parties, the weight of reason supports the claim of the residents. Their position, with its insistence on dialogue, is the one that all parties have good reasons to accept. The coercive powers of the state were, therefore, used illegitimately in previous years when the march was forced through. Since 1998, by upholding the right of residents to refuse to host the parade, the parades commission has got it right.

Political legitimacy and cultural expression

The Good Friday Agreement recognizes that in Northern Ireland each national culture is to enjoy equal respect no matter which of them is to find itself, at a particular historical juncture, in the minority. This means that the only public expressions of culture that can be tolerated are those that do not undermine the equal respect on which the political arrangements must be built. Political progress depends on the critical appropriation of all cultures and not on the continuing expression of exclusivist aspects of cultural traditions that are blind to the rights of others. Following on from our exploration of the arguments that may be used to defend the conflicting rights claims at Drumcree, we can now draw out certain normative conclusions regarding the on-going marching controversies. In relation to ceremonial parades that are expressive of particular religious, cultural or national identities, the following principles should apply as conditions of equal citizenship in Northern Ireland:

1 While the right to religious freedom must be protected, it is legitimate to restrict the right in cases where the religious beliefs of others are systematically and publicly devalued.
2 While the right to freedom of expression must be protected, it is legitimate to restrict this right in cases where the equal political status of members of one national community is undermined.
3 While the rights to freedom of assembly and freedom of movement must be protected, it is legitimate to restrict those rights in cases of national and religious sensitivity where those directly affected have not been given due consideration.
4 While national cultures should enjoy rights that protect them from harassment, discrimination and violence, only those aspects of culture that are compatible with an inclusive political culture can be protected.

This normative framework is informed by certain key ideas that were raised by Martha in the virtual dialogue. The importance of dialogue in a context in which mutual accommodation

depends on learning to treat others as equal citizens in their religious and national differences is underscored here. Dialogue is the
best protection against the danger that the parades issue will be
used as an excuse for sectarian intimidation or violence.
Furthermore, the present efforts to overcome the restrictions on
freedom of movement should focus on the political and socio-
economic problems that are the root causes of segregation, and
not on enforcing contentious marches through areas where they
are not welcome. Finally, the best way to challenge sectarian prejudice is to grasp the political, economic and socio-psychological
roots of the problem by seeking to secure for all citizens the political and social bases of self-respect.

These principles can provide a basis for some future legislation designed to ensure that the problem of contentious
marches can be dealt with in a clear and impartial manner.[38] All
citizens have good reasons to accept the proposed limits on their
constitutional rights, at least until a politics of mutual accommodation can be fully secured. This is because all will seek
these forms of protection should they find themselves in the
same situation as the residents of the Garvaghy Road. In a
deeply divided society like Northern Ireland, these principles
should generate legal rights that would represent conditions of
equal citizenship. While the vast majority of the more than
3,000 parades organized by the Loyal Orders each summer
would be unaffected, those that are most contentious would be
regulated fairly by such legislation. The freedom to engage in
the practice of marching, as a form of cultural expression, would
also be guaranteed, subject to these principles of restriction,
should the constitutional status of Northern Ireland change in
the future, leaving unionists as a minority in some form of
United Ireland.

This principled legislation could overcome the current problems encountered by the Parades Commission.[39] The commission has been seen by both sides as insufficiently accountable in
its determinations on contentious marches that have not been
resolved through local dialogue. It has also been accused of
engaging in trade-offs, of making judgements that are insufficiently clear or consistent, and of caving in to the greater threat
of violence. Some of the criteria according to which the law
empowers the commission to reach its determinations reflect
the government's response to the report of the Independent
Review on Parades and Marches by including a concern for

mutual respect and wider community relations.[40] But these concerns sit uneasily alongside certain other criteria that can influence the determinations. These are factors that respond to the threat of violence such as 'possible disruption of everyday life', 'law and order' and the 'protection of property'. There are at least two problems with the commission's approach.

The first problem is that the criteria, taken as a whole, are too vague to allow for transparently impartial and consistently principled judgements on these matters. The normative framework presented here takes us further by emphasizing the responsibility to engage in dialogue and by insisting clearly that determinations should seek to guarantee equality of status for members of both national communities. Secondly, by allowing considerations that are responsive to the greater threat of violence to impinge on their deliberations, the criteria lack a critically normative edge, since they will reflect and reproduce the balance of illegitimate power in society. One of the requirements of transparent impartiality is that these controversies are regulated in a way that is effectively critical of illegitimate power. Judicial decisions, in cases where they are needed, can be neither consistent nor impartial unless some such clear and critical normative perspective informs them.

While the Belfast Agreement provides the beginnings of a workable constitutional framework for Northern Ireland, it leaves much work to be done in institutionalizing the rights that could secure equal citizenship status for all. I have been focusing on one area where legislative progress must be made if we are to ensure that both national cultures are to be afforded equal respect. The aim of such legislation would be to make possible the contextually sensitive application of an impartially grounded set of rights that would be appropriate to controversies such as the one at Drumcree. Whether or not there is the will to produce such legislation is a question that is likely to be asked for some time yet.

Notes

An earlier version of this chapter appeared as 'Liberty, equality and the rights of cultures: the marching controversy at Drumcree', *British Journal of Politics and International Relations*, 2: 1 (2000), pp. 26–45.

1 See J. Bohman and W. Rehg (eds), *Deliberative Democracy: Essays on Reason and Politics* (Cambridge MA: MIT Press, 1997); J. Elster (ed.), *Deliberative Democracy*

(Cambridge: Cambridge University Press, 1998); and the other contributions to this volume.

2 See also W. Rehg, 'Intractable conflicts and moral objectivity: a dialogical problem-based approach', *Inquiry*, 42: 2 (1999), pp. 229–57.

3 See especially J. Habermas, *Between Facts and Norms: Contributions to a Discourse Theory of Law and Democracy*, trans. W. Rehg (Cambridge: Polity Press, 1996).

4 In 1996 and 1997 protesting residents were forcibly removed from the road by the security forces so as to make way for the march. In 1996 (Drumcree II) this was due to a reversal of an initial decision to have the march blocked. The state capitulated that year to the systematic civil disorder and violence of the loyalist reaction to the stand-off across Northern Ireland.

5 J. Whyte, *Interpreting Northern Ireland* (Oxford: Clarendon Press, 1991), pp. 234–5.

6 J. McGarry and B. O'Leary, *Explaining Northern Ireland* (Oxford: Blackwell, 1995).

7 J. Ruane and J. Todd, *The Dynamics of Conflict in Northern Ireland: Power, Conflict and Emancipation* (Cambridge: Cambridge University Press, 1996), pp. 113–15.

8 N. Porter, *Rethinking Unionism: An Alternative Vision for Northern Ireland* (Belfast: Blackstaff Press, 1996), pp. 109–25.

9 *Agreement Reached in the Multiparty Negotiations*, unspecified publisher, 1998. See also B. O'Leary, 'The nature of the agreement', *Fordham International Law Journal*, 22: 4 (1999), pp. 1628–67.

10 *Agreement*, 'Constitutional issues', section 1 (v), p. 2.

11 While Northern Ireland in general has seen some progress on the achievement of mutual accommodation at the constitutional level, there has been a noticeable absence of such a spirit of accommodation in Portadown.

12 R. D. Jones, J. S. Kane, R. Wallace, D. Sloan and B. Courtney, *The Orange Citadel: A History of Orangeism in the Portadown District* (Portadown: Portadown Cultural Heritage Committee, 1996).

13 Habermas, *Between Facts and Norms*, p. 118.

14 *Ibid.*, p. 33.

15 J. Habermas, 'On the internal relation between the rule of law and democracy', *European Journal of Philosophy*, 3: 1 (1995), pp. 12–20, 17–18.

16 Habermas, *Between Facts and Norms*, pp. 84–104, 447–62.

17 *Ibid.*, p. 107.

18 *Ibid.*, pp. 122–3.

19 J. Bohman, 'Deliberative democracy and effective social freedom: capabilities, resources and opportunities' in J. Bohman and W. Rehg (eds), *Deliberative Democracy: Essays on Reason and Politics* (Cambridge MA: MIT Press, 1997), pp. 321–48.

20 W. Kymlicka, *Multicultural Citizenship: A Liberal Theory of Minority Rights* (Oxford: Oxford University Press, 1995).

21 J. Habermas, 'Struggles for recognition in the democratic constitutional state', in A. Gutmann (ed.), *Multiculturalism: Examining the Politics of Recognition* (Princeton NJ: Princeton University Press, 1994), pp. 107–48.

22 D. L. Rhode, *Justice and Gender: Sex Discrimination and the Law* (Cambridge MA: Harvard University Press, 1989); M. Minow, *Making all the Difference: Inclusion, Exclusion and American Law* (Ithaca NY: Cornell University Press, 1990); I. M. Young, *Intersecting Voices: Dilemmas of Gender, Political Philosophy and Policy* (Princeton: Princeton University Press, 1997).

23 W. Kymlicka (ed.), *The Rights of Minority Cultures* (Oxford: Oxford University Press, 1995); W. Kymlicka and W. Norman (eds), *Citizenship in Diverse Societies* (Oxford: Oxford University Press, 2000); A-G. Gagnon and J. Tully (eds), *Struggles for Recognition in Multinational Democracies* (Cambridge: Cambridge University Press, 2001).

24 S. O'Neill, 'The idea of an overlapping consensus in Northern Ireland: stretching the limits of liberalism', *Irish Political Studies* 11 (1996), pp. 83–102.

25 W. Rehg, *Insight and Solidarity: The Discourse Ethics of Jürgen Habermas* (Berkeley CA: University of California Press, 1994).

26 Habermas, *Between Facts and Norms*, pp. 142–3.

27 S. O'Neill, *Impartiality in Context: Grounding Justice in a Pluralist World* (Albany NY: State University of New York Press, 1997), pp. 169–73.

28 Habermas, *Between Facts and Norms*, pp. 359–87.

29 *Ibid.*, chapters 5–6.

30 In the reconstruction that follows I draw on many newspaper and other media reports on the views of actual participants to this dispute. I have also referred to the submission of the Garvaghy Road Residents' Coalition to the Independent Review on Parades and Marches, *Public Attitudes to Parades and Marches in Northern Ireland (Garvaghy Road)* (Belfast: Stationery Office, 1997). The Orange Order did not make any submission to this review, which was set up after the violence of Drumcree II in July 1996. The outcome was the Independent Review of Parades and Marches, *Report* (the 'North Report', Belfast: Stationery Office, 1997). This report, in turn, was the main inspiration for the establishment of the Parades Commission in the Public Processions (Northern Ireland) Act 1998 (Belfast: Stationery Office, 1998). I will present a critique of the guidelines used by the Parades Commission in the concluding section. On the Orange Order's position see Jones *et al.*, *The Orange Citadel*, and the contributions to G. Lucy and E. McClure (eds), *The Twelfth: What it Means to Me* (Lurgan: Ulster Society, 1997).

31 The role of this virtual dialogue is to give a clear grasp of the best arguments on both sides of the conflict. Of course, in reality much of the real dispute has centred on accusations from one side that the other is insincere in making its claims. It is my contention that the best way to assess whether the competing claims can be made with sincerity is to expose them to rational scrutiny according to the theoretical perspective outlined here. As we shall see, our virtual participants are both sincere and reasonable in the sense that they are willing to support their position with reasoned argument.

32 It is the Orange Order's intended action, to parade on this particular route, that is to be justified to all affected. It is for this reason that the dialogue follows a structure in which Joan first claims certain rights to justify the action while Martha seeks to criticize the claims in turn by encouraging Joan to adopt a more inclusive perspective.

33 The Harryville protest was initiated as a loyalist response to a dispute about an Orange Order march in the nearby village of Dunloy.

34 What Martha has in mind here, perhaps, is an application of the harm principle in restricting freedom of expression, as defended by John Stuart Mill in the opening paragraph of the third chapter of *On Liberty*. See J. S. Mill, *Utilitarianism, On Liberty and Considerations on Representative Government*, ed. H. B. Acton (London: Dent, 1972), pp. 123–4; also M. Midgley, 'Drumcree and freedom', *Guardian*, 10 July 1998.

35 The limits of toleration *may* be quite different in polyethnic societies than in the bi-national context of Northern Ireland. The distinction is introduced by Will Kymlicka in *Multicultural Citizenship*.

36 See especially the influential essay by Charles Taylor, 'The politics of recognition', in A. Gutmann (ed.), *Multiculturalism: Examining the Politics of Recognition*, Princeton University Press, 1994, pp. 25–73, and the responses of his critics in the same volume.

37 R. Dworkin, *Taking Rights Seriously*, second edition, with a Reply to Critics (London: Duckworth, 1978), pp. 277–8.

38 Once again, recall the four institutional levels at which legally enforceable rights may operate. Abstract human rights (1) are embedded in a particular constitutional framework (2) which in the case of Northern Ireland's Good Friday Agreement insists that both national communities are to be protected from political domination. The proposed legislation (3) I discuss here is intended to regulate conflict concerning the parades issue by specifying the conditions under which restrictions may be placed on general norms so as to satisfy constitutional demands. These rights would then be upheld in particular cases through the adjudication of the judiciary (4).

39 It should, I hope, be clear that my main aim in this chapter has been to clarify what the normative principles are according to which a just resolution of the conflict could be achieved. The focus has not been on the way in which the law has sought to deal with the problem up to now, through the establishment of the Parades Commission and so on. In this conclusion, however, I want to highlight the crucial lessons that may be learned from this normative analysis so that the problems can be dealt with in a more effectively impartial manner in the future.

40 See the Public Processions (Northern Ireland) Act 1998, section 8 (6), and the Independent Review on Parades and Marches, *Report*.

9

Is deliberative democracy unfair to disadvantaged groups?

DAVID MILLER

Over the last ten years or so, many democratic theorists have been drawn to the idea of deliberative democracy. This is not because they believe that existing liberal democracies already conform to their conceptions of how an ideal deliberative democracy would work: no one could sensibly maintain that. But there appears now to be something of a consensus that if we want the real-world systems that we call democracies to become more truly democratic, we should be looking for ways of propelling them towards the deliberative ideal.[1] What, then, is that ideal? A democratic system is deliberative when the decisions it takes are arrived at through a process of open discussion to which each participant is able to contribute freely but is equally willing to listen to and consider opposing views; as a result, the decisions reached reflect not simply the prior interests or prior opinions of the participants but the judgements they make after reflecting on the arguments made on each side, and the principles or procedures that should be used to resolve disagreements.[2] Such an ideal democracy promises to meet at least the following three conditions: it is *inclusive*, in the sense that each member of the political community in question takes part in decision making on an equal basis; it is *rational*, in the sense that the decisions reached are determined by the reasons offered in the course of deliberation, and/or the procedures used to resolve disagreement in the event that no consensus can be found; and it is *legitimate*, in the sense that every participant can understand how and why the outcome was reached even if he or she was not personally convinced by the arguments in its favour.

Critiques of deliberative democracy

These are bold promises to make, and we need to put deliberative democracy under the microscope to see whether it can really live up to the claims that have been made on its behalf. Moreover, although deliberative democracy has won favour among many democratic theorists, it has not escaped powerful criticism. I shall just mention two kinds of criticism before coming to a third kind that forms the main subject of this chapter. The first set of critics are realists who point to the huge and seemingly unbridgeable gap between the deliberative ideal and the practice of existing democracies.[3] How is it possible for large and complex societies to be governed by deliberative assemblies which in their nature must be small, slow-moving bodies? Deliberative democracy may have suited the ancient Athenians, who could listen to and reflect upon the orations of Pericles, Alcibiades and the rest before deciding whether to send a fleet to attack the Peloponnese, but how could it function in a world in which not only military but many other decisions – financial decisions, for example – have to be made in minutes rather than days, leaving no time for popular consultation, let alone deliberation? Furthermore, even where deliberative assemblies might have a feasible role to play in decision making, why should we believe that the participants will adhere to the norms of deliberation sketched above, and not merely manipulate the institution to their own advantage? Deliberative democracy requires a high degree of social responsibility on the part of each participant, yet everything we know about politics suggests that it attracts people with Machiavellian dispositions and rewards those who act on them to greatest effect.

The second critical assault on deliberative democracy comes from social choice theory. Here it is said that whereas deliberative democracy assumes that something like a general will can emerge from the deliberative process, social choice theory tells us that this must be an illusion.[4] Arrow's 'impossibility theorem' and its descendants prove that there is no method of reaching a collective decision from an array of individual preferences that conforms to a set of conditions that we would expect a democratic procedure to respect. Since we cannot assume that public discussion will always result in unanimity, deliberative democracy must finally employ a decision procedure which may, for instance, be majority voting among the body in question. But social choice theory reveals the indeterminacy and arbitrariness of procedures such as majority voting, and so undermines both the rationality and the legitimacy claims of deliberative democracy. If the decision made depends upon arbitrary features of the procedure used to reach it (such as the order in which alternatives are put to the vote) its success is not simply a reflection of the weight of the reasons offered to support it, and equally there seems to be no strong reason why those who end up on the losing side should regard the decision as a legitimate one.

So deliberative democracy has to withstand both the empirical criticism of the realists and the formal criticism of the social choice theorists. Now I believe that on both fronts good defences can be offered, but I don't propose to offer them here.[5] I have introduced these critiques mainly to distinguish and contrast them with a third critique that has emerged more recently and from a quite different quarter. This third critique challenges deliberative democracy's credentials as a fair method of reaching collective decisions in a plural society; it claims that deliberative democracy is biased against groups that historically have been disadvantaged – the poor, ethnic minorities, women, and so forth. Deliberation is not a neutral procedure but one that works in favour of people with certain cultural attributes, especially white middle-class males. This is a serious challenge because it directly contests one of the main claims advanced in support of deliberative democracy, namely that it is capable of reaching decisions that are more socially just than those reached in existing liberal democracies, where the distribution of political power tends to reflect the distribution of wealth and other forms of social advantage. According to deliberative democrats, what should count in deliberative settings are reasons and arguments, not the colour of one's skin or the size of one's bank balance. This ideal may never be fully realized, but, to the extent that it is, democratic procedures can serve as a counterweight to the inequalities generated in a society in which capitalists dominate workers, men dominate women, and whites dominate blacks and other ethnic groups. But the critics dispute this, or at least wish to qualify it severely. And in so doing they also put in question the claims about inclusion, rationality and legitimacy that I sketched earlier. Deliberative democracy may be formally inclusive, in the sense that everyone is permitted to enter and speak in democratic forums, but if the debate by its very nature favours some groups at the expense of others it is not inclusive in a substantive sense. Similarly if the reasons that prove to count in deliberative settings are not reasons for everyone, but reasons only for particular groups or coalitions of groups, the outcome cannot be described as rational in a sense that transcends group membership. If the rationality claim falls, so does the legitimacy claim, for why should the disadvantaged groups accept as legitimate a procedure that relies upon methods of argument and reasons they cannot share?

So there is much at stake here, and we must look more closely at the substance of the third critique, as it has been articulated by authors such as Lynn Sanders and Iris Young.[6] I distinguish two aspects of this critique, the second raising deeper and more difficult issues than the first.

Inequality in deliberative institutions

Sanders and Young both argue that there is inequality within deliberative institutions between advantaged and disadvantaged groups. This goes beyond the problem of access to such institutions. Currently, as we well know, disadvantaged groups tend to be underrepresented in political forums – they vote less often, play a smaller role in most pressure groups, have fewer elected representatives, and so forth. From the standpoint of deliberative democracy this is unacceptable, since deliberation cannot be inclusive, and therefore cannot be expected to produce fair outcomes, unless the composition of the deliberating body reflects with reasonable accuracy the composition of the whole body of citizens to whom its decisions will apply. How this state of affairs is to be rectified is the subject of ongoing debate: in particular there is disagreement about whether in the case of representative institutions there should be quotas to ensure proportional representation of women and ethnic minorities.[7] This controversy about the best policy to ensure inclusion should nevertheless not obscure the underlying agreement between deliberative democrats and their critics about the need for disadvantaged groups to have access to democratic institutions on an equal footing with other citizens. According to Young and Sanders, however, equal access is not sufficient, because it provides no guarantee that members of disadvantaged groups will be treated as equals once they are inside the institutions. They may, for instance, be reluctant to engage in political argument, feeling that they have no right to speak or that others will not take their interventions seriously. Sanders cites evidence about the behaviour of men and women on juries, and about school groups made up of whites and blacks, which suggests that men in one case and white students in the other contribute disproportionately to group discussion.[8] Assuming, as seems reasonable, that there is a connection between the volume of argument behind a position and the likelihood of its prevailing, the implication is that, in cases where men and women or whites and ethnic minorities had different concerns and interests in a deliberative forum, the disadvantaged groups would tend to lose out because of their reluctance to state their case in public.

Even Sanders concedes, however, that the position is more complex than my brief summary has suggested. As she says 'it appears that some styles of group discussion are more likely to elicit the views of all group members than are others'.[9] In the case of juries, she makes use of a contrast between 'verdict-driven deliberation' and 'evidence-driven deliberation' which was first introduced in an empirical study of jury behaviour.[10] The evidence-driven style of deliberation encourages a wide range of views to be expressed, and therefore tends to draw more of the participants into the discussion; it also favours open-mindedness, in the sense of willingness to change position when fresh evidence is produced. It has been found that women tend to favour this style of deliberation more than men, and in particular that all-female groups are characterized by active attempts to draw the more silent members into discussion.[11] The lesson for deliberative democrats, therefore, is not that they should throw up their hands in dismay when it is pointed out that members of disadvantaged groups tend to participate less in collective deliberation, but that they should look for ways of ensuring that deliberation takes a form that corresponds to an evidence-driven jury, which means that instead of trying to move quickly to a yes/no decision, the arguments for and against different options should be explored without individual participants having to declare which they support. This, it seems to me, is what good political deliberation would in any case require. Where a decision has to be reached on an issue of some complexity, it is better for discussion to be open and exploratory at first, and it would be a mistake to require participants to signal at an early point which option they support, because the effect of doing so would be to encourage the deliberators simply to marshal the arguments that support their initial view, rather than to listen to and engage with all the perspectives put forward.

A similar point can be made about Iris Young's remarks about parliamentary debates and adversarial court procedures in which as she puts it: 'Deliberation is competition. Parties to [the] dispute aim to win the argument, not to achieve mutual understanding.'[12] It may indeed follow that such contexts 'privilege those who like contests and know the rules of the game. Speech that is assertive and confrontational is here more valued than speech that is tentative, exploratory, or conciliatory' and that 'this privileges male speaking styles over female'. But this shows that parliamentary debates and adversarial courts, whatever their other virtues, are not good examples of deliberative democracy at work, and it is hard to imagine deliberative theorists saying otherwise. Deliberative democracy requires that political debate should be structured in such a way that, first, as wide a range of relevant views and arguments as possible should enter the debate, so that the ensuing discussion should genuinely reflect the concerns, interests and convictions of the members of the deliberating body; and, second, that as the body attempts to move towards a solution to the issue that they confront, it should be the weight of the reasons offered in support of the different positions that counts. This means that participants, rather than trying to win, in the sense of ensuring that their initial preferences prevail, should be listening to and weighing up what others are saying, searching for the solution that has the strongest reasons behind it. That, of course, is an ideal description. But it can be approximated more or less exactly, depending partly on the structure and partly on the ethos of the deliberating body. To give one example, studies of citizens' juries – small groups of randomly chosen citizens brought together to debate issues of current concern such as health policy – emphasize the importance of having moderators whose job it is to ensure that everyone has a chance to contribute to the discussion, and that different points of view get properly explored and critically scrutinized.[13] Now, in so far as these conditions for good deliberation correspond to forms of speech and argument that Young characterizes as typically female

rather than typically male – speech that is 'tentative, exploratory, or conciliatory', speech used 'to give information and ask
questions rather than state opinions or initiate controversy' – a
deliberative form of democracy should serve women far better
than the institutions that she castigates for their male bias.[14]

Is deliberation biased against disadvantaged groups?

So far I have been addressing the claim that deliberative settings
will inevitably be dominated by privileged groups at the expense
of women and disadvantaged minorities because the former will
dominate the discussion; my reply is that there are ample
reasons stemming from the deliberative ideal itself to favour
forms of debate in which this does not happen. But I said there
was also a deeper issue here, and that is the issue whether the
very idea of deliberation – the idea that decisions should be
made through a process of reasoned argument in which the
weightier arguments finally prevail – is not biased against disadvantaged groups. This indeed is Young's claim when she says
that deliberation privileges speech that is 'formal and general',
speech that is 'dispassionate and disembodied' and speech that
'proceeds from premise to conclusion in an orderly fashion that
clearly lays out its inference structure'.[15] Sanders, likewise,
asserts that deliberation requires talk that is 'rational, con-
tained, and oriented to a shared problem' as opposed to talk that
is 'impassioned, extreme, and the product of particular interests'.[16] Both maintain that these norms of acceptable speech discriminate against women and ethnic minorities, whose
perspectives and demands need to be presented in other ways. It
is not simply that the speech of members of the disadvantaged
groups tends to be more 'excited and embodied', using physical
gestures and forms of emotional expression that are lacking in
the speech of white middle-class men, but that prevailing norms
of deliberation are inherently unsuited to the presentation of
their concerns. According to Young and Sanders, what disadvantaged groups need is not deliberation at all, but other forms of
political interaction in which their distinct perspectives and
distinct concerns can emerge more clearly.

What, then, are these alternative modes of political communication? Young mentions three – greeting, rhetoric and storytelling – and Sanders mentions one – testimony – which

corresponds roughly to what Young means by storytelling.[17] Greeting refers to the various formal and informal ways in which parties to political discussion recognize one another prior to and during the discussion. Rhetoric refers to forms of speech and argument that identify the speaker with a particular audience, and which evoke particular symbols or cultural values that resonate with this audience; rhetoric also serves to engage and motivate the audience not merely to think but also to act in certain ways. Storytelling, finally, refers to speech in which someone presents a personal narrative – their life story, so to speak – as a way of explaining what it means to occupy a certain place in society and/or to dramatize the injustice suffered by a certain group. Young gives the example of wheelchair users describing the obstacles they have faced in getting around, and Sanders suggests that the position of American blacks may remain incomprehensible to the white majority unless blacks can describe their historical experience through forms of personal testimony.

Now it would be very easy – too easy – to respond to these proposals by saying that greeting, rhetoric and storytelling can all be added to the deliberative pot by treating them as additional forms of dialogue that deliberative democrats have no reason to reject. That response is too easy because it overlooks the fact that deliberation is one method of reaching political decisions among others, with particular virtues that distinguish it from its rivals and that are unlikely to be preserved if all forms of political interaction are allowed to count indiscriminately as 'deliberation'. For instance, deliberation must exclude forms of bargaining where groups capitalize on the advantages they enjoy along particular dimensions to secure outcomes that lean as far as possible in their direction. Bargaining certainly involves political communication, and even one could say forms of argument – along the lines 'If you opt for X, then I'm sorry to say that I'll have to do Y' – but this is quite different from the kind of argument required by deliberation.[18] But we have not yet established precisely which forms of communication and reasoning are consistent with the deliberative ideal, and so we cannot yet say whether greeting, rhetoric and storytelling should be included as legitimate elements in deliberation. Nor can we say whether these alternative forms of communication are likely to serve the interests of disadvantaged groups better than familiar styles of deliberation. We need first to establish how deliberation proper is supposed to proceed, and then ask whether there is any reason to think that this method of reaching political decisions is biased against disadvantaged groups.

Unfortunately supporters of deliberative democracy have given rather different accounts of the modes of reasoning required by the deliberative ideal. One view, inspired by the work of John Rawls, and presented most eloquently in a series of essays by Joshua Cohen, describes the ideal deliberative procedure as involving 'public reasoning'.[19] This requires participants in deliberation to confine themselves to arguing for the proposals they favour in a certain way: they must put forward reasons that they believe others must accept, their differing personal commitments notwithstanding. As Cohen puts it:

> it will not do simply to advance reasons that one takes to be true or compelling: such considerations may be rejected by others who are themselves reasonable. One must instead find reasons that are compelling to others, acknowledging those others as equals, aware that they have alternative reasonable commitments, and knowing something about the kinds of commitments that they are likely to have – for example, that they may have moral or political commitments that impose what they take to be overriding obligations.[20]

According to this view, then, deliberation must proceed by presenting arguments that everyone has reason to accept, arguments in other words that appeal to common ground – to shared principles of justice, or to ideas of the common good. Equally there must be a high probability of arriving at a consensus – if everyone appeals only to reasons that everyone else can accept, it is hard to see how there can be substantive disagreement about what should be done. Cohen escapes this conclusion by pointing out that there could be disagreement about the relative *weight* of considerations that passed the public reason test, and so there may still have to be a majority vote at the end of deliberation. But still, on this view, everyone would endorse the reasons that lay behind the decision reached; it's just that some would have weighted them differently, and come to a different practical conclusion.

Clearly the Rawls–Cohen view passes with flying colours the tests of rationality and legitimacy that I referred to at the beginning of the chapter. Deliberative decisions will be rational in the sense that they are justified by reasons that everyone in the relevant community has in common, and their legitimacy flows directly from the same source. But at the same time it seems highly vulnerable to the critique launched by authors such as Sanders and Young. For it requires disadvantaged groups in putting forward their case to restrict themselves to arguments that are also compelling to advantaged groups. Or, to be more precise, although they are not formally barred from presenting arguments that make sense only from their particular perspective, they have to be prepared to switch to public reasoning if they are to count as reasonable, and therefore as people who meet the conditions for inclusion in the deliberation.

I believe, however, that this view of deliberation is too restrictive: it offers too monolithic an account of the type of reasoning that must lie behind a decision if it is to pass the test of democratic legitimacy. To begin with, unless we are going to confine deliberative democracy to a small sub-set of the decisions that a democratic political community may have to take, deliberative procedures have to be flexible enough to cope with many different kinds of issues. In the case of some issues, the scope for reason-giving in the Rawls–Cohen sense is very limited. Some questions, for instance, require first of all that people should simply state their preferences.[21] Suppose that as members of a local community we have to choose between various possible sites for our new public library: here the main role for democratic deliberation will be to discover who mainly uses the library and then which location they will find most convenient. We may also believe, of course, that we should pay special attention to the needs of certain groups, say the elderly or the disabled, in which case we will need to give extra weight to the preferences expressed by members of these groups. In that sense our final decision will be informed by a principle as well as by expressed preferences. But the primary information that we need in reaching a decision in a case such as this is information about what most people prefer, at that point consulting only their own convenience. It may be that one site is so overwhelmingly preferred that there is no need for further deliberation. If, on the other hand, there is substantial disagreement, we may need to settle on a procedure to resolve it (for instance, we might ask participants to rank the sites in numerical order and then use a Borda count to select a preferred site). In that case, there would have to be a reasoned argument as to why *that* procedure is the appropriate one to use for *this* issue. But the point is that participants do not have to offer substantive reasons in support of the site they favour in a case like this; it may be enough that they state their preferences and agree on a fair procedure for reaching a decision. There is no need for people to move to the moral high ground and present only reasons that pass the Rawls–Cohen test.

In other cases the problem may be that people move on to the moral high ground too quickly, in the sense that they find themselves arguing from incompatible moral premises that they nevertheless take to be fundamental. The debate over the legalization of abortion is often taken as an example here. The difficulty is that, if we apply the Rawls–Cohen test, then both sides are reduced to silence because they know that the arguments they want to make will not be compelling to those who disagree. Thus pro-life advocates will typically rest their arguments on religious assumptions about the sanctity of life that they cannot reasonably expect their secular opponents to share. If deliberation is to proceed here, it must take the form of looking for solutions that neither side finds completely abhorrent. In an illuminating discussion of the issue Gutmann and Thompson speak of 'an economy of moral disagreement'.[22] This involves first of all showing that you respect the reasons advanced by your opponents even though you do not share them – you recognize the depth and the sincerity of their commitment. Then it involves finding practical solutions that do not blatantly offend that commitment.[23]

Sometimes deliberation will indeed involve appealing to substantive principles that everyone (or almost everyone) in the political community holds in common. Thus in a debate about educational policy it may turn out that a principle of equal opportunity is universally endorsed – everyone agrees that children should have the same opportunities to learn no matter what their sex, class or ethnic background. But rather than this principle being invoked because it passes the reasonable rejection test, it may be applied simply because it turns out in the course of discussion that this is indeed a principle that everyone endorses. In other words, people begin by arguing about education from a variety of perspectives, some tightly bound up with their personal values or religious beliefs, but they realize as discussion progresses that the arguments they are making have little appeal to others. Thus a Muslim might argue in favour of state-supported Muslim schools by claiming that it is vitally important for a child's religious background to be reinforced by his or her school, but quickly discover that this view was not shared by others, indeed that many people held precisely the opposite opinion. But this line of argument having run into the sand, he might argue instead that Muslim children would in many cases not flourish academically unless they were sent to a school where the teaching reflected their cultural values, and this argument invokes a principle of equal opportunity that can appeal to many others in the deliberating body – not because it reflects some universal standard of rationality, but simply because as a matter of fact it forms part of the underlying ethos of the community in question. Rather than deliberation being legitimate only when the deliberators confine themselves to public reasoning in the Rawls–Cohen sense, the suggestion here is that the search for agreement will itself act as a filter on the kinds of reasons that prevail in the discussion, sectarian reasons being weeded out precisely because it becomes apparent to their supporters that they are not going to command wide assent. It is unnecessary to specify in advance what kinds of reasons will be permitted to determine policy; we should rely instead on the process of deliberation to select reasons that are generally accepted.[24]

It may be said by way of criticism here that deliberative democracy requires only that a *majority* should be convinced of the rightness of a certain policy: unanimity may be the ideal, but we know that in most cases it is unrealizable, so decisions will have to be made by majority vote. By the same token, the principles that survive the deliberative filter need only be principles that attract majority support – if I can see that most of my audience are nodding in agreement when I invoke principle P, I need not be concerned by the fact that others are rolling their eyes and grinding their teeth, so long as my concern is just that my arguments should prevail in the debate. If we apply the Rawls–Cohen criterion, by contrast, I am obliged to find reasons that are compelling to everyone, and this is a stronger constraint on deliberation than the one I am offering.

Well, I agree that democratic deliberation must include more than just searching for whatever arguments will bring a majority of your fellow deliberators on to your side. The deliberative process must aim to discover the policy outcome that enjoys the widest possible support, even though it is unrealistic to suppose that strict unanimity will ever be achieved. Thus if it turns out that 51 per cent of the deliberating body will support outcome O, but that 80 per cent will support outcome O', which is not radically different from O but omits elements that many of the 29 per cent find quite objectionable, then good deliberation should culminate in choosing O'. What motivates this choice is first of all respect for one's fellow deliberators. They have sincerely held reasons for rejecting O, reasons which I do not share, but which I can recognize as reasons for them. If there is an alternative such as O' which accommodates these reasons without requiring me to give up a great deal, I should favour that. Moreover I should do so not only out of respect for those I disagree with, but in order to promote a general atmosphere of trust inside the deliberating body. Next time round I may turn out to be in the minority which has strong and sincere reasons for objecting to the policy that commands majority support, and I will want my reasons listened to and if possible accommodated.[25]

My proposal, then, is that we should understand deliberation not as requiring us to restrict ourselves to offering reasons and arguments that must commend themselves to all members of the deliberating body, but as requiring only that we should seek agreement on terms that respect our fellow deliberators and their convictions.[26] This requirement, I have suggested, will itself serve as a filter that eliminates certain arguments in the course of the debate without disqualifying them *a priori*. Armed now with this more accommodating understanding of how deliberation is supposed to work, let's return to the challenge posed by Young and Sanders, which as you will recall holds that deliberation is inherently biased against disadvantaged groups, who must use other forms of communication – greeting, rhetoric and testimony/storytelling – if their perspectives and concerns are to receive proper attention. And let's consider the charges against deliberation first, and then the merits of the proposed alternatives.

Among the charges levelled at deliberation by Young and Sanders are that it privileges speech that is rational and dispassionate at the expense of speech that is emotional and passionate; that it privileges formal and abstract reasoning at the expense of the concrete concerns of particular groups; and that it privileges speech that is 'moderate' at the expense of speech that is 'extreme'. Consider the first charge. To me it seems to rely on a false dichotomy between reason and emotion, false in the sense that all political speech and argument must convey the feelings and commitments of the speaker but also give reasons either positively for some proposal, or negatively against some alternative (which may just be the *status quo*). A cry of pain is not a political intervention, unless it is implicitly or explicitly linked with some proposal for relieving the pain. It's true that speakers sometimes say, in effect, 'This state of affairs is intolerable,' and show why it is intolerable, but this makes sense only in a context in which other speakers have remedies to suggest. As we move from protest or outrage towards solutions, standard canons of rationality must apply – it would clearly be unreasonable to propose as a solution a policy that actually made matters worse for the affected group, or that subjected some other group to precisely the kinds of suffering or deprivation that inspired the original protest. Emotional speech is important because it demonstrates to others how strongly the group in question feel about the situation they find themselves in, but rational speech is important too, because of the need to convince others that the remedy you propose is indeed a remedy.[27] It seems to me, in fact, rather insulting to disadvantaged groups to suggest that norms of argumentative rationality are loaded against them, because it implies that they cannot give coherent arguments for the changes they want to bring about.

Next we have the charge that deliberation favours 'speech that is formal and general' and in that way discriminates against speakers who want to draw attention to some concrete injustice or the concerns of a particular group. Once again I believe this creates a false dichotomy. Very often political argument takes the form of connecting the situation in which a particular group finds itself with some general principle that has been applied in the past to other groups and that now commands widespread assent. Thus wheelchair users may want to describe in some detail the way their mobility opportunities are reduced by thoughtless town planning or building design. But the relevance of these descriptions is that they bring the group under the rubric of a more general principle, namely the principle that those with special needs should be granted the resources that allow them to enjoy the same set of basic opportunities as other citizens. It is true that in moving from the particular case to the more general principle we lose something of the specificity of the particular – by classifying wheelchair users as people with special needs we are putting them into the same general category as blind people, people suffering from certain diseases and so on – but this may not be to their disadvantage. They may attract more sympathy and support precisely because we now see them alongside others whose needs may be seen as more urgent still. The claim 'We are like the Xs, who everyone agrees should be given special treatment' is a powerful claim to make in political argument, but its logic is to advance a particular claim under the umbrella of a general principle.

Finally, we have the charge that deliberation favours moderate speech over extreme speech, which I am taking here to be an observation not about the *manner* of speech that is favoured but about its *substance*; the charge, in other words, is that radical demands and proposals are disfavoured, and middle-of-the-road, compromise proposals favoured. In one way, I believe, this charge is indeed true. Take an issue like affirmative action on which people hold a wide spectrum of views – at one extreme there is the view that employers should be totally free to employ whomever they like, even if they are sexually or racially prejudiced; at the other extreme there is the view that justice requires us to apply strict ethnic, racial and sexual quotas to ensure that in every branch of employment each group is represented in exact proportion to its size; in between there are a number of positions that we could describe as moderate. Suppose the members of our political community hold views that are evenly distributed across this spectrum. The outcome of (good) deliberation is likely to be one of the moderate views, for reasons that should be clear from my earlier account of the deliberative process – people will abandon arguments that they find command little general support, they will search for a solution that does not blatantly offend the commitment of others, and so forth. But then it may be said that this is exactly what democracy requires in such a case. To complain that one of the extreme views – say the strong quotas view, which may indeed attract the support of some members of disadvantaged racial groups – has not been adopted is to complain about democracy itself, and not about deliberation as a procedure. Sanders says, at one point, 'In settings where there are gross inequities in power and status, calling for compromise may be perilously close to suppressing the challenging perspectives of marginalized groups. Such suppression, when it occurs, is not democratic.'[28] But there is a crucial difference here between *suppressing* a perspective – not allowing it to enter the democratic debate, or ignoring it when it is introduced – which is indeed undemocratic, and *not following* it when a final decision is reached. Except in cases where everyone has the same preferences, or can be brought to concur with the same set of judgements, democracy cannot help but be a process of compromise in which participants give up some part of their initial demands for the sake of reaching agreement. The claim made on behalf of deliberative democracy is that it allows each perspective to be considered and weighed in the course of deliberation, without of course being able to guarantee that any particular perspective will prevail in the final outcome.[29]

Alternatives to deliberation

Let me turn now from the critical charges levelled against deliberation to the alternatives proposed by Young and Sanders. I do not propose to spend much time either on greeting or on rhetoric. I think that Young is perfectly right to say that greeting rituals may perform a significant function within political communities, particularly perhaps when the community is being enlarged to include new members. But the role of greeting here is only to create an atmosphere in which deliberation or other forms of politics can proceed, making people feel at home, and giving them some confidence that their arguments will be listened to. Indeed one might say that greeting may be impossible unless there is already some degree of sympathetic recognition between the parties concerned – witness the difficulties encountered in getting hardened enemies to shake hands or sit down at the same table. Greeting is as much symptomatic of trust as it is generative. But the main point here is that greeting surely cannot substitute for deliberative or other procedures that move a political body towards a collective decision.

As to rhetoric, while one can say that it is a powerful motivating force when people are united in their aims, it is equally clearly a divisive force in situations of conflict, because the rhetoric used by one group may be more alienating to the others than the concrete policies it is used to support. In 1968 the proposal that some restrictions should be put on immigration into Britain would have commanded widespread assent, even among ethnic groups who were themselves recent immigrants, but when Enoch Powell justified it by saying that he saw 'the river Tiber foaming with much blood' if (non-white) immigration were allowed to continue, the effect of his rhetoric was severely to inflame relations between whites and ethnic immigrants. This also underlines the point that no group has a monopoly of rhetoric. Indeed, in so far as historically advantaged groups are better placed than disadvantaged groups to engage in political *argument*, one would also expect them to be better placed to produce political *rhetoric*, having at their disposal the resources of the established culture to draw upon for their symbols and analogies (in Powell's case, a classical education gone to waste). So when rhetoric enters political discourse there is no reason to think that disadvantaged groups will benefit, and one might go further and say with Benhabib that Young's proposal 'would limit rather than enhance social justice because rhetoric moves people and achieves results without having to render an account of the bases on which it induces people to engage in certain courses of action rather than others'.[30] In other words, because rhetoric conceals rather than reveals the grounds on which decisions are taken, it is less likely than reasoned argument to produce socially just policies.

A better case, I believe, can be made on behalf of 'testimony' or 'storytelling'. It may be difficult for people who have not experienced certain kinds of oppression or deprivation to understand the predicament of those who have without it being brought to life by personal testimony. So it has a legitimate role to play in the process of deliberation. Yet as a mode of political communication it suffers from two limitations.[31] First, it is difficult to know how reliable or how representative one person's life story is unless it is being used to corroborate and illuminate a more impersonal (for instance, sociological) account of the general position of the group he or she belongs to. Young says 'because everyone has stories to tell . . . and because each can tell her story with equal authority, the stories have equal value in the communicative situation'.[32] But this is surely false. Stories can be treated merely as expressions of personal feeling, but if they are supposed to be more than that, their value depends first on their veracity and second on their capacity to capture the experience and the perspective of a wider group. In a later paper Young acknowledges this: 'valid generalities about people and groups of course must be supported by well known methods of inductive inference, including relying on many cases'.[33]

Second, it is unfortunately not the case that by adding together the testimony of many different individuals we can arrive at an overall perspective which provides a solution to the problems that the various stories are highlighting.[34] A multiplicity of perspectives is just that: a multiplicity. Young sometimes speaks as though the perspectives of the various groups were complementary, so that we can get an accurate overall picture of how our society looks by allowing each group to fill in one part of the canvas from its own perspective. She speaks of 'comprehensive social knowledge' emerging from interaction between groups with different stories to tell about the social world.[35] But the perspectives may give rise to *conflicting* accounts, in which case the only way to get at the truth will be to bracket off all perspectives and call in the social scientists. For example: it is well known that rich people and poor people tend to have conflicting perceptions of the opportunity structure of liberal societies – the rich seeing these societies as meritocratic (where people end up on the social ladder depends largely on their own talents and efforts), the poor seeing them as unmeritocratic (where people end up depends largely on factors outside their control, such as family background and connections). Juxtaposing these two perspectives doesn't tell us much except perhaps that people are always inclined to rationalize their own position. To discover which perception is nearer to the truth – and therefore what we need to do assuming that we value equality of opportunity as an ideal – we have to go beyond subjective experience and begin looking systematically at the evidence about relative rates of social mobility and the factors that may explain them.[36]

I am also very doubtful about Young's claim that the effect of introducing competing perspectives into political discussion is to encourage the participants 'to express their proposals as appeals to justice rather than expressions of mere self-interest or preference'.[37] It is common ground between us that political discussion can proceed to a legitimate conclusion only if this process occurs – if discussants present reasons for their proposals that go beyond narrow self-interest and sectarian conceptions of value and appeal to conceptions of justice and other principles that others may share or at least find acceptable. The question is whether introducing new perspectives through personal testimony and the like will have such an effect. Young's idea, I think, is that being confronted with a new and radically different perspective on some issue will force participants to question the assumptions from which they have been arguing up to now. Suppose there is some convenient way of selecting people to hold special offices that most of us have up to now regarded as uncontentious (a seniority rule, for instance). When the effects of this practice on a particular minority group are pointed out, we are forced to ask whether the rule we have been using is really fair, or whether it has not served merely to perpetuate the position of well-established groups. So far, so good: we can imagine this happening in certain cases. But now consider another possible effect of introducing unfamiliar perspectives into democratic debate: by widening the perceived social distance between groups, it may weaken each group's commitment to deal justly with the others.

In suggesting this I am relying on research undertaken by social psychologists which shows that the boundaries of the moral community within which people are willing to apply principles of justice to fellow members are affected by perceptions of similarity and common identity. In these studies, each subject's degree of identification with a range of social groups is measured, and then the subject is asked whether he or she is willing to extend justice to the group in the form, for example, of respecting its members' civil rights, or providing resources to support its activities.[38] It turns out that there is a strong correlation between identification and justice, even among subjects whose political attitudes are generally liberal. Other studies have shown that people who identify exclusively with their ethnic sub-group as opposed to embracing a more inclusive identity alongside it are less willing to accept the authority of procedures that may be used to resolve disputes or allocate resources, and become more concerned about how well or how badly they have fared personally in the outcome – in other words their thinking tends to be instrumental rather than justice-driven.[39] Now deliberative legitimacy depends upon participants being motivated to find principles of justice that can be shared by all members of the political community in question, and being willing to accept the outcome of deliberative procedures as fair even if they are required to give up a substantial part of what they had initially demanded, or initially enjoyed. Highlighting radical differences between groups within the community may erode these motivational conditions.

In consequence, as I have argued elsewhere, democratic deliberation that serves the cause of social justice is most likely to occur in a community whose members share a common identity that transcends their group-specific identities – which in practice means a shared national identity.[40] My focus here, however, is on how to proceed in democratic deliberation if you want your fellow deliberators to deal with you fairly – to assess and act on your claims in terms of principles of justice that command wide support in the deliberating body. The answer, I think, is that you must strike a fine balance between emphasizing what you have in common with other members of your audience, so as to win their sympathy and motivate them to see you as someone to whom justice is owed, and emphasizing the ways in which you are different, and which mean that you have special needs or suffer special disadvantages.[41] So, returning now to the question of testimony, this may form an effective mode of communication so long as the content of the testimony, and the form in which it is presented, are not so alien to the audience as to raise barriers between the group the testifier is trying to represent and the rest of the community, so inducing hostility rather than a concern for justice. When Sanders, for example, cites approvingly the claim that rap music may be an effective form of testimony for young blacks she seems to see the testimony only through the eyes of the blacks themselves; it is difficult to envisage this being a persuasive means of communication with citizens generally. But perhaps that does not concern her. She says, 'There's no assumption in testimony of finding a common aim, no expectation of a discussion oriented to the resolution of a community problem.'[42]

This statement may serve to highlight a difference in perspective between deliberative democrats and their critics in the third camp, a difference which is concealed within the title of this chapter. If we ask, 'Is deliberative democracy unfair to disadvantaged groups?' we may be asking, 'Is deliberative democracy *materially* fair?', meaning 'Does it give minority groups a fair chance to influence the outcome, thereby also delivering policies that address their needs and interests in a fair way?' This is how I would understand the question, and also I believe how other deliberative democrats such as Cohen would understand it. But the critics may understand it differently, as the question 'Does deliberative democracy give adequate recognition to the perspectives of disadvantaged groups?', a question that places the emphasis on giving everyone a chance to speak politically in their own authentic voice. As we have seen, the assumption here is that every story is of equal value. As Sanders puts it, 'testimony is also radically egalitarian: the standard for whether a view is worthy of public attention is simply that everyone should have a voice, a chance to tell her story'.[43] By contrast, the deliberative ideal requires that we should endeavour to put forward views and arguments that commend themselves to our fellow deliberators, on grounds of their intrinsic cogency, or because they invoke reasons and principles that are widely shared – a standard that involves discrimination between expressed views, and that is therefore not egalitarian in Sanders's sense.

What concerns me, however, is that fairness in this expressive sense may come at the expense of fairness in the material sense. Consider the position of disadvantaged groups in contemporary liberal democracies, especially ethnic minorities with a history of material and cultural disadvantage. Their members typically have fewer resources and fewer opportunities than people in the mainstream. They have comparatively little economic bargaining power, nor do they have much political clout if they form conventional pressure groups and engage in lobbying. Threats to engage in political disruption or violence are largely empty: when minority groups take to the streets they usually inflict more harm on their own community than on outsiders. For groups in this position, democracy on the deliberative model seems to provide the best chance of using political power to counteract social disadvantage. Yet even here their only real resource is their capacity to invoke the sense of justice of their fellow citizens, and use it to win policies that work in their favour. If a democratic forum is reduced to a talking shop in which each person has their own story to tell, but discussion is not constrained by the need to find practical solutions that are acceptable to all, the strongest weapon a disadvantaged minority has – indeed, almost its only weapon – is blunted. Individuals may have the satisfaction of hearing their stories voiced on a public stage, but nothing is done to compensate for the huge inequalities of wealth and power that disfigure liberal democracies.

Notes

Earlier versions of this chapter were read to audiences at York University, Bristol University and Manchester University, and to the Nuffield Political Theory Workshop. I am very grateful for the many suggestions made on those occasions, and especially to John Dryzek, Cécile Fabre and Amy Gutmann for their written comments on the penultimate draft.

1 The literature on deliberative democracy is now too extensive to be cited in full. Among book-length discussions see especially J. Dryzek, *Discursive Democracy* (Cambridge: Cambridge University Press, 1990); J. Fishkin, *Democracy and Deliberation* (New Haven CT and London: Yale University Press, 1991); S. Chambers, *Reasonable Democracy* (Ithaca NY and London: Cornell University Press, 1996); A. Gutmann and D. Thompson, *Democracy and Disagreement* (Cambridge MA: Harvard University Press, 1996); J. Bohman, *Public Deliberation: Pluralism, Complexity and Democracy* (Cambridge MA: MIT Press, 1996); J. Dryzek, *Deliberative Democracy and Beyond* (Oxford: Oxford University Press, 2000). Recent edited collections addressing the topic include S. Benhabib (ed.), *Democracy and Difference: Contesting the Boundaries of the Political* (Princeton NJ: Princeton University Press, 1996); J. Bohman and W. Rehg (eds), *Deliberative Democracy: Essays on Reason and Politics* (Cambridge MA: MIT Press, 1997); J. Elster (ed.), *Deliberative Democracy* (Cambridge: Cambridge University Press, 1998).

2 This brief definition conceals some ambiguities over how deliberation is supposed to lead to decisions that command widespread if not universal consent. I return to these later in the chapter.

3 Among those who implicitly or explicitly criticize deliberative democracy from a realist perspective are G. Sartori, *The Theory of Democracy Revisited* (Chatham NJ: Chatham House, 1987); A. Przeworski, *Democracy and the Market* (Cambridge: Cambridge University Press, 1991); D. Zolo, *Democracy and Complexity: A Realist Approach* (University Park PA: Pennsylvania State University Press, 1992).

4 See W. H. Riker, *Liberalism against Populism* (San Francisco: Freeman, 1982); J. Coleman and J. Ferejohn, 'Democracy and social choice', *Ethics*, 97 (1986), pp. 6–25; J. Knight and J. Johnson, 'Aggregation and deliberation: on the possibility of democratic legitimacy', *Political Theory*, 22 (1994), pp. 277–96; D. Van Mill, 'The possibility of rational outcomes from democratic discourse and procedures', *Journal of Politics*, 58 (1996), pp. 734–52.

5 I have responded to the social choice critique in 'Deliberative democracy and social choice', *Political Studies*, 40 (1992), special issue *Prospects for Democracy*, pp. 54–67, reprinted in D. Miller, *Citizenship and National Identity* (Cambridge: Polity Press, 2000). See also J. Johnson, 'Arguing for deliberation: some skeptical considerations', in Elster, *Deliberative Democracy*, and J. Dryzek and C. List, 'Deliberative Democracy and Social Choice Theory: a Reconciliation', MS (1998).

6 L. Sanders, 'Against deliberation', *Political Theory*, 25 (1997), pp. 347–76; I. M. Young, 'Communication and the other: beyond deliberative democracy', in Benhabib, *Democracy and Difference*; I. M. Young, 'Difference as a resource for democratic communication', in Bohman and Rehg, *Deliberative Democracy*; I. M. Young, 'Inclusive Political Communication: Greeting, Rhetoric and Storytelling in the Context of Political Argument', paper presented to annual meeting of the American Political Science Association, Boston MA, September 1998.

7 Vigorous arguments for and against can be found, respectively, in I. M Young, *Justice and the Politics of Difference* (Princeton NJ: Princeton University Press, 1990), chapter 6, and C. Ward, 'The limits of "liberal republicanism": why group-based remedies and republican citizenship don't mix', *Columbia Law Review*, 91 (1991), pp. 581–607. For more nuanced discussions see C. Sunstein, 'Beyond the republican revival', *Yale Law Journal*, 97 (1988), pp. 1539–89; W. Kymlicka, *Multicultural Citizenship* (Oxford: Clarendon Press, 1995), chapter 7, and, especially, A. Phillips, *The Politics of Presence* (Oxford: Clarendon Press, 1995).

8 Sanders, 'Against deliberation' pp. 363–66.

9 *Ibid.*, p. 366.

10 R. Hastie, S. D. Penrod and N. Pennington, *Inside the Jury* (Cambridge MA: Harvard University Press, 1983), chapter 8. Verdict-driven juries are those which take an early ballot to reveal the level of support for each possible verdict: jurors then tend to act as advocates of one or other position, giving arguments that support that verdict. Evidence-driven juries try to form an agreed interpretation of the evidence presented to them, without individual members committing themselves to any particular verdict, and ballots are taken only late in the proceedings (or sometimes not until the very end, to confirm a consensus).

11 See N. Marsden, 'Gender dynamics and jury deliberation', *Yale Law Journal*, 96 (1987), pp. 593–612.

12 Young, 'Communication and the other', p. 123.

13 See A. Coote and J. Lenaghan, *Citizens' Juries: Theory into Practice* (London: IPPR, 1997); G. Smith and C. Wales, 'Citizens' juries and deliberative democracy', *Political Studies*, 48 (2000), pp. 51–65.

14 Young, 'Communication and the other', p. 123

15 *Ibid.*, p. 124.

16 Sanders, 'Against deliberation', p. 370.

17 See especially Young, 'Inclusive Political Communication', and Sanders, 'Against deliberation'.

18 That deliberation and bargaining are mutually exclusive is standardly assumed in most discussions of deliberative democracy. See, for instance, J. Elster, 'The market and the forum: three varieties of political theory', in J. Elster and A. Aanund (eds), *The Foundations of Social Choice Theory* (Cambridge: Cambridge University Press, 1986). In his later work Habermas, by contrast, makes room for bargaining within a more pluralist account of deliberation. He is careful to insist, however, that the bargaining has to be regulated to ensure fairness between the parties – each must have 'an equal opportunity to influence one another during the actual bargaining, so that all the affected interests can come into play and have equal chances of prevailing' (J. Habermas, *Between Facts and Norms: Contributions to a Discourse Theory of Law and Democracy*, Cambridge: Polity Press, 1996, pp. 166–7). Whether 'bargaining' that is so constrained can properly be described as bargaining is moot. The general point is that deliberative theorists must be selective about what they will count as deliberation if the process is going to yield outcomes that meet the relevant ethical standards.

19 See J. Rawls, *Political Liberalism* (New York: Columbia University Press, 1993), lecture VI; J. Rawls, 'The idea of public reason revisited', *University of Chicago Law Review*, 64 (1997), pp. 765–807; J. Cohen, 'Deliberation and democratic legitimacy', in A. Hamlin and P. Pettit (eds), *The Good Polity* (Oxford: Blackwell, 1989), reprinted in Bohman and Rehg (eds), *Deliberative Democracy*; J. Cohen, 'Pluralism and proceduralism', *Chicago-Kent Law Review*, 69 (1994), pp. 589–618; J. Cohen, 'Procedure and substance in deliberative democracy', in Benhabib, *Democracy and Difference*, and in Bohman and Rehg, *Deliberative Democracy*; J. Cohen, 'Democracy and liberty' in Elster, *Deliberative Democracy*.

20 Cohen, 'Procedure and substance in deliberative democracy', in Benhabib, *Democracy and Difference*, p. 100.

21 I have developed this point with respect to environmental goods in D. Miller, 'Social justice and environmental goods', in A. Dobson (ed.), *Fairness and Futurity: Essays on Environmental Sustainability and Social Justice* (Oxford: Oxford University Press, 1999).

22 Gutmann and Thompson, *Democracy and Disagreement*, chapter 2.

23 For instance, in the case of abortion they suggest that the state might introduce a

scheme whereby those who favoured the state funding of abortion could indicate their consent to be taxed for the purpose while those who objected could exempt themselves from paying the tax.

24 This conclusion needs qualification in one respect: certain reasons are ruled out by the requirements of deliberation themselves. Among such excluded reasons are those that challenge the equality of members of the deliberating body, e.g. racist arguments whose import is that some people should be deprived of equal rights of citizenship by virtue of their race, and those that involve the threat of violence or other forms of coercion. Where such reasons are presented, deliberation in the form of a free and open discussion among equals cannot proceed. In contrast, reasons that invoke personal ideals and values that others may not share need not be excluded. All that deliberation requires is willingness to shift ground in the event that reasons of this kind turn out not to be persuasive.

25 This assumes, of course, that the deliberating body is an on-going institution with a stable membership. Although this is not a necessary condition for successful deliberation – juries, including citizens' juries, provide a counter-example – I believe that, particularly where participants are being asked to make personal sacrifices for the sake of reaching agreement, it is strongly conducive to it. See further my argument in 'Bounded citizenship' in K. Hutchings and R. Dannreuther (eds), *Cosmopolitan Citizenship* (London: Macmillan, 1999), reprinted in Miller, *Citizenship and National Identity*, about the link between responsible citizenship and continuity in the decision-making body.

26 This moral requirement applies only on condition that others reciprocate, by themselves seeking agreement on terms that respect *us* and *our* convictions. This means in particular that disadvantaged groups are not required to show respect for the reasons advanced by members of advantaged groups unless they are reasonably confident that the latter will reciprocate and not simply rely on their superior bargaining power to win the day. I am grateful to Amy Gutmann for insisting on this point.

27 For a good example of how emotional speech and rational speech can work together to promote deliberation see the discussion of Carol Moseley Braun's opposition to the patenting of the Confederate flag in Gutmann and Thompson, *Democracy and Disagreement*, pp. 135–7.

28 Sanders, 'Against deliberation', p. 362.

29 On an alternative reading of her claim, Sanders may be saying that a decision does not qualify as democratic unless it addresses the demands of marginalized groups. But this requires us to apply a substantive criterion of justice to the outcome and to count as democratic only those decisions that meet the criterion, no matter what procedure has been followed. There are familiar problems with this move. Even if we think that deliberative democracy is the political decision procedure *most likely to* lead to just outcomes, it is a mistake to link the two conceptually in this way.

30 S. Benhabib, 'Toward a deliberative model of democratic legitimacy', in Benhabib, *Democracy and Difference*. I am not proposing a blanket ban on the use of rhetoric in democratic debate, which in any case would be impossible to enforce. Rhetoric which reaches across group boundaries to highlight shared aims and values undoubtedly plays a positive role. I am drawing attention, rather, to speech that uses rhetorical devices to promote causes favoured by particular groups, which invites counter-rhetoric from the opposition. It seems odd that an author such as Young who denounces the forms of argument found today in parliamentary debates and adversarial court proceedings should go on to defend the use of rhetoric by disadvantaged groups, which encourages precisely the confrontational style she elsewhere deplores.

31 In addition, one should take note of John Dryzek's observation that each of the

alternative forms of communication favoured by Young can have a coercive character: modes of greeting can serve to exclude or even intimidate outsiders; rhetoric can be used to discredit certain speakers; storytelling can be constrained by norms of what constitutes a 'correct' story line within a particular group. See Dryzek, *Deliberative Democracy and Beyond*, chapter 3.

32 Young, 'Communication and the other', p. 132.

33 Young, 'Inclusive Political Communication', p. 36.

34 Cf. Gutmann and Thompson, *Democracy and Disagreement*, p. 137.

35 Young, 'Difference as a resource for democratic communication', pp. 403–4.

36 I do not mean to give the impression that this is an easy question to resolve. The difficulties are well explained in G. Marshall, A. Swift and S. Roberts, *Against the Odds? Social Class and Social Justice in Industrial Societies* (Oxford: Clarendon Press, 1997).

37 Young, 'Difference as a resource for democratic communication', p. 402.

38 I draw here on two unpublished papers by Yuen J. Huo: 'Boundary Effects in Judgements of the Deservingness of Justice: Conflict, Identification and Values' and 'Justice and Exclusion: Exploring the Boundaries of our Moral Community'. Some of the relevant evidence is reported in Y. J. Huo, 'Defining moral communities: normative and functional bases of the allocation of social goods', submitted for publication to the *Journal of Experimental Social Psychology*.

39 See T. R. Tyler, R. J. Boeckmann, H. J. Smith and Y. J. Huo, *Social Justice in a Diverse Society* (Boulder CO: Westview Press, 1997), chapter 10.

40 D. Miller, *On Nationality* (Oxford: Clarendon Press, 1995), chapter 4; D. Miller, 'Group identities, national identities and democratic politics', in J. Horton and S. Mendus (eds), *Toleration, Identity and Difference* (London: Macmillan, 1999), reprinted in Miller, *Citizenship and National Identity*.

41 This brings to mind the famous passage from *The Merchant of Venice* in which Shylock protests against the calumnies he has suffered at the hands (especially) of Antonio by invoking the common humanity of Jews and Christians: 'Hath not a Jew eyes? Hath not a Jew hands, organs, dimensions, senses, affections, passions? Fed with the same food, hurt with the same weapons, subject to the same diseases, healed by the same means, warmed and cooled by the same winter and summer, as a Christian is? If you prick us, do we not bleed? If you tickle us, do we not laugh? If you poison us, do we not die?' (Act 3, scene 1). Shylock goes on to couple this with a threat of revenge, but up to this point the passage says, 'How can it be fair for injustices to be heaped upon the head of one who shares so much with you?' This is the most emotionally and morally powerful appeal that a member of an oppressed minority can make, and Shakespeare as usual gives it perfect expression.

42 Sanders, 'Against deliberation', p. 372.

43 *Ibid.*, p. 372

Index